AMERICANS ABROAD

AMERICANS ABROAD

Two Centuries of European Travel

Foster Rhea Dulles

The University of Michigan Press Ann Arbor

112536

Acknowledgment is made to the following for material for the illustrations:
For the old train from *Thirteen Views of the Dublin and Kingstown Railway* (Dublin, 1834), for the railway station from Thomas Roscoe's *The London and Birmingham Railway* (London, n.d.), for the Grand Saloon from *All About the Great Eastern* (London, n.d.), and for a photograph of a print of the "Great Eastern"—the Transportation Library of the University of Michigan;

For photographs of the Franklin passport and the newspaper clipping—from the originals in the William L. Clements Library of the University of Michigan;

For photographs of the American Express offices in Nice and Paris—the American Express Company;

For photograph of a plane window—Air France

For the photograph of the American Embassy in London by Baltazar Korah—the U.S. Department of State;

For photographs of Herman Melville, F. Scott Fitzgerald, Gertrude Stein, and Ernest Hemingway—Wide World Photos, Inc.;

For photographs of Henry James and Mark Twain—Underwood and Underwood.

Designed by Quentin Fiore

Preface

This book is an exploration of American travel abroad. It begins with some account of the little colonies in Paris and London at the close of the eighteenth century and carries the story through to the annual invasion of Europe by the tourist hordes of the mid-twentieth century. It describes such travel as it has gone through the amazing transformation from sailing packet and stagecoach, to the jet plane and chartered autobus. It also tells something of the impressions and reactions of these travelers under the changing circumstances in the historic relationship between Europe and America.

My major interest has been the everyday tourists happily vacationing overseas. Where I have dwelt upon the artists and writers living for a time abroad, the members of society who have down through the years made occasion to cross the Atlantic, and the students in European universities, it is primarily in their parallel role as sightseers. They have reflected the more general experiences of their traveling countrymen. The activities of diplomats and the expanding role of businessmen have been touched upon only lightly. I have stressed the social implications of travel rather than political or economic history.

The diaries and letters, the journals and travel books, through which so many Americans have recorded their overseas experience, weave a fascinating tapestry of European travel. They have provided the basic source material for this book throughout (the more representative writings are listed in the Bibliographical Notes), and I have quoted from them freely for contemporary descriptions of the European scene and of changing modes of travel.

I am greatly indebted to a number of friends who have assisted me along the way, but would especially single out my daughters for their interest and encouragement: Mary Rhea Waller, Sara Dulles Taylor, Connie Dulles Weems, and Lynn Dulles. The book could not possibly have been written except for the patient and unfailing editorial assistance of my wife, Marion Dulles.

Contents

Americans have a special call to travel. It is the peculiar privilege of their birth in the New World, that the Old World is left them to visit.

NORTH AMERICAN REVIEW, 1856

I. THE LURE OF EUROPE

> Sitting, as it were, in the gateway between the Old World and the New, where the steamers and packets landed the great part of our wandering countrymen, and received them again when their wanderings were done, I saw that no people on earth have such vagabond habits as ours.... It seemed to me that nothing was more common for a young American than deliberately to spend all his resources in an aesthetic peregrination about Europe, returning with pockets nearly empty to begin the world in earnest.

SO WROTE Nathaniel Hawthorne more than a century ago when he was serving as American consul at Liverpool in the 1850's. American travel abroad had long since had its pioneer beginnings; it was to become increasingly popular in future years. Even in the midnineteenth century it was estimated that possibly as many as 30,000 Americans went abroad every year, and while some of them had business or other special purposes in mind, the new transatlantic steamers of that day had opened the floodgates of tourism. Such travel was still largely restricted to the well-to-do. "All the world (our world) is going to Europe," wrote Philip Hone, the rich merchant and onetime mayor of New York, but the ever-increasing number of Americans sailing overseas appeared to bear out fully Hawthorne's comment on his countrymen's instinctive wanderlust.

Born of a restlessness, a sense of adventure, an insatiable curiosity that has been repeatedly noted as peculiarly characteristic of Americans, this wanderlust was perhaps a part of their Anglo-Saxon heritage and at the same time a product of their environment. It was only natural that having crossed the ocean to seek out the New World, they should be drawn back to revisit the Old.

Europe has always exerted an almost irresistible attraction. For some transatlantic travelers it remained the "old home" to which they were bound by invisible ties, a world familiar through personal associations; for others it had the fascination of the unknown, a strange and almost mysterious continent—the source of their civilization. Whatever the reason, Europe has been a lodestone drawing back across the Atlantic barrier, first a thin trickle of expectant visitors and ultimately an engulfing flood.

At the close of the eighteenth century, a flamboyant nationalism militated for a time against foreign travel. In declaring its independence the United States had rejected all Europe—its politics, institutions and outworn feudalism, its entire civilization. The young new republic sought to deny its own heritage:

Why should our thoughts to distant countries roam
When each refinement may be found at home?

Thus, in his immensely popular play *The Contrast,* first staged in New York in 1787, Royall Tyler implied that to go abroad was somehow to betray the American spirit.

So too Noah Webster, whose spelling books and dictionary were in themselves a declaration of cultural independence, frowned on overseas travel. It might have been encouraged before the Revolution, he wrote in the *American Magazine,* but now it should "be discountenanced, if not prohibited." For those who felt compelled to travel, he advised a change in their itinerary from Europe to their own country.

In this early period the idea was also widely prevalent—as it would continue to be in some quarters down through the years—that Americans crossing the Atlantic somehow risked moral infection in exposing themselves to the profligacy and vice of the Old World. They were better advised to stay at home and preserve the innocence inherent in the American character. Thomas Jefferson, for all his own deep appreciation of European art and culture, held this fearful view so far as young people were concerned. "It appears to me," he wrote a friend in 1785, ". . . . . that an American, coming to Europe for his education, loses in his knowledge, in his morals, in his health, in his habits, and in his happiness." Jefferson felt that the tender flower of republican virtue could be successfully nurtured only in its own carefully tilled garden.

These views did not long prevail, however. As soon as Europe was opened up to travel at the close of the Napoleonic wars, an annual transatlantic migration got under way. Moreover these visitors in the early years of the nineteenth century set patterns that have remained remarkably unchanged through the years. The literary pilgrims who first rushed abroad foreshadowed a constant stream of later writers, and so too a handful of painters showed the way to what were in time to become the thriving American art colonies in Rome, Florence, and Paris. The aspiring members of society who as early as the 1820's wished "to seek the acquaintance of distinguished and above all titled people" were to have countless successors following their ambitious path. The students who first sought out European universities set a precedent which a century later would lead to an academic flood. And finally, the few tourists with no objective other than that of sightseeing and enjoying themselves were the pioneers of today's jet-borne multitudes.

Europe has always represented limitless opportunity for all the special joys of sightseeing—unfamiliar scenery, new cities, strange customs; castles, palaces, cathedrals and museums. It has represented in its long historic past an antiquity that has always had an immense appeal to the American imagination, and as a great storehouse of art for which the United States even today has no real equivalent, it has had a further charm. Indeed a century ago, before the establishment of their own galleries, museums, and opera houses, a European visit was the only way—Royall Tyler to the contrary notwithstanding—in which Americans could see very much in the way of painting and sculpture, the drama and opera. "It is for want of self-culture," Emerson once wrote, "that the superstition of traveling, whose idols are Italy, England, Egypt, retains its fascination for all educated Americans."

The trip abroad has also represented since the start of overseas travel a good deal more than this search for culture or the experience of seeing at firsthand the historic monuments of the Old World. Many a transatlantic journey has been undertaken for rest or recuperation from illness. Throughout the nineteenth century, the long, leisurely sea-voyage, the change of climate, the waters at the continental spas, were considered more conducive to good health than any possible vacation in the United States. Nor is it

3

necessary to wait until the 1920's, when Europe was so often described as "a tumultuous playground," to discover Americans enjoying Europe as a carefree vacation, an escape from the restraints of a country dominated by Victorian conventions. The opportunity to experience a "larger liberty" has repeatedly drawn Americans abroad. Europe has stood for diversity as contrasted with conformity, play as contrasted with work, pleasure as contrasted with duty.

The conditions and circumstances of travel have obviously been subject to continual change. New means of transportation, both for the Atlantic passage and overland on the continent, have replaced old-fashioned ways; pre-arranged package tours have come to offer a substitute for the independent exploration of an earlier day. Popular itineraries, however, have remained very much the same for a hundred and fifty years. Guidebooks early established the major objectives of the Grand Tour, itself the heritage of aristocratic English travel in the eighteenth century, and even today only the enterprising few very often depart from its prescribed routes. The capitals of western Europe, the mountains of Switzerland, the English lake country, the Italian hill towns, the watering places of Germany and the beaches of France, attracted the majority of visitors in the nineteenth century as they do in the twentieth.

What has happened most importantly in the general picture of travel, is the steadily increasing number of Americans visiting Europe and the progressive democratization of such overseas journeying. Today's tourists embrace an extensive cross-section of the people as a whole and a European trip has attained a significant place in the wide spectrum of popular recreation.

The position or status of Americans abroad has always occasioned many complexities. Sensing the greater sophistication of Europe, such temporary exiles from everything that was familiar to them were particularly hard put in the nineteenth century to maintain the natural self-confidence that was their American heritage. Their attitude almost invariably revealed that basic ambivalence, characteristic of the general viewpoint of Americans, wherein a sometimes reluctant appreciation of the Old World's highly developed artistic culture was combined with a deep and abiding scorn for its outmoded political system—monarchy, aristocracy, and privilege. The problems of adjustment were further compounded for those who wished to be accepted in European society by the difficulty of reconciling their fascination for aristocracy with their republican principles.

In the years before the Civil War—a period of intense chauvinism and contemptuous scorn of Europe—many travelers found themselves almost lost in seeking some accommodation to a society into which they knew they did not really fit. They remained convinced of their own superiority but did not quite know how to establish it. "An American leaves his country," wrote Alexis de Tocqueville, as keen an observer of Americans abroad as of Americans at home, "with a heart swollen with pride; on arriving in Europe, he at once finds that we are not as engrossed by the United States and the great people who inhabit them as he had supposed; and this begins to annoy him." His patriotic vanity disturbed by this unexpected loss of status during the transatlantic voyage, the American's almost invariable recourse was "to invidious comparisons and lofty boasts."

Among the common run of tourists, this instinctive impulse to refuse to be impressed by Europe and to brag of America would seem to have generally prevailed until almost the middle of the twentieth century. Critical comments on this inveterate boastfulness run through the entire literature of travel. The challenge to their own self-confidence in being confronted by an older, more polished civilization than their own, has until very recent times placed traveling Americans on the defensive, led them to seek reassurance in noisy braggadocio.

If this attitude has been made a recurrent charge, tourists have also been assailed on other counts. Their ignorance, their insensitivity, and their lack of manners have been repeatedly singled out by critics. Such derogatory comments attained something of a climax with Henry James. Deeply interested in the more subtle aspects of the relationship between aristocratic Europeans and socially acceptable Americans, he had little patience with the average tourist, dismissing the whole tribe as "vulgar, vulgar, vulgar."

In considering the extent to which the majority of travelers reflected the sometimes contradictory point of view of most Americans toward Europe, the question immediately arises as to how

5

much their experiences abroad may have affected preconceived opinions. A consensus seems to be that many of them might as well have stayed at home. Their writings suggest that they found in all too many instances exactly what they were seeking, and returned with all their prejudices happily confirmed. Others unquestionably shed much of their insularity. Deeply impressed by what they had seen and learned, they thereupon exercised no little influence in helping to deflate the blown-up and over-assertive patriotism of their stay-at-home countrymen.

It was only through travel, we find a contributor to the *North American Review* advising as early as 1819, that Americans could ever get to know the virtues of Europeans as individuals. And such an experience, he continued, quickly enabled one "to perceive the absurdity of that spirit of bitterness, too often displayed by turns in this country against the different portions of the European world." The impact of changing events was of course far more important in altering the onetime popular image of the Old World as effete and decadent, oppressed by the tyranny of kings. Nevertheless the reports of returning travelers had their part in gradually correcting such exaggerations, enabling Americans to view Europe more reasonably and with greater understanding and sympathy.

By the early 1900's, perceptive visitors could not fail to realize that Europe had not only transformed many of its old ways, but in some respects was significantly ahead of the United States in social progress. If there had always been admirers of its artistic and literary achievements, the Old World in this period was commanding increasing respect for its widespread political and economic reforms.

The years between wars then found Americans again becoming highly critical ("What an overestimated place Europe is!" Scott Fitzgerald wrote during his first visit in 1921), and the rise of fascism soon revived the democratic contempt once directed against kings. While many travelers were perhaps almost completely oblivious of what was happening, others became convinced, as one observer phrased it, that Europe was experiencing "the rapid shrinkage of querulous decrepitude." Whether or not this was an accurate description, the reports of returning tourists in

6

the 1930's on conditions in Italy and Germany greatly influenced American attitudes.

Whatever the travelers' shifting and sometimes contradictory views on Europe, whether in the nineteenth or early twentieth century, one thread of consistency may be discovered in almost all their writings. This was the belief that the European experience helped them better to understand and appreciate their own country. In the nineteenth century particularly, they came home with a new awareness of the benefits of their own more open society after having observed the ponderous weight of the relics of feudalism throughout the Old World. Even those who most appreciated the antiquity and the art of Europe appeared to have been convinced in those days that the political liberties American society offered outweighed its cultural deficiencies. "I had no idea until I came here," the great preacher Phillips Brooks once wrote, "what a tremendous American I was."

This patriotic reaction generally persisted until well into the twentieth century. Always there have been a few exceptions. But for the most part the experience of European travel has served not only to break down the provincialism of the American abroad, but to bring into ever sharper relief his basic feeling for his own country.

The Second World War has brought about immense and fundamental changes in the whole picture of overseas travel and also in the attitudes of traveling Americans. Primarily as a consequence of the threat of international communism and possible aggression by Soviet Russia, there has been deeply impressed upon every visitor to Europe a new conception of what had been traditionally called the Old World. In the troubled circumstances of the midtwentieth century, it has been borne home that what western Europe and America have in common in their basic beliefs and way of life, is far more important than such differences as may still be found in their separate cultures.

II. EIGHTEENTH CENTURY

ABIGAIL ADAMS, the perceptive, spirited wife of John Adams, arrived in London in July 1784. She was on her way to join her husband who had served as one of the commissioners to conclude the peace in which Great Britain recognized the independence of the United States, and who was soon to become the first American minister at the Court of St. James's. "I hardly know how to think myself out of my own country," Mrs. Adams wrote her sister, "I see so many Americans about me."

Her statement was perhaps something of an exaggeration. Nevertheless in the early years of the new republic, there were more Americans abroad than might have been expected. In England a number of them were of course of the Tory persuasion, and most notably among the others were a group of distinguished painters. On the continent, there were not only official envoys and "the militia diplomats" who had scoured all Europe seeking aid for the American cause, but earlier visitors who had stayed on after the outbreak of war and also a few new arrivals. So the patterns of Americans abroad began to take shape; these late eighteenth-century travelers included the vanguard of the future tourists.

During the Revolution the foremost American in Europe was Benjamin Franklin. He had long since been a world figure and as the first American minister to France from 1778 to 1784, he completely bewitched Parisian society. Deliberately dressing in rustic apparel and, as he proudly wrote, "with grey hair appearing under a Martin fur cap among the powder'd heads of Europe," he was equally at home in aristocratic salon or popular café. The shops were so full of his portraits, carved on medallions and snuff

8

boxes, that his face became as well known "as that of the moon."

Around him gathered a strange and interesting group of his countrymen. Some of them were on official missions; others engaged on their own account in securing supplies for the continental army. There was a considerable trade developing between France and the newly formed United States, and in Paris and also in the seaport of Nantes, the little American colonies flourished. One traveler reported in 1779 seeing in nearby Angers "several gentlemen from Boston, acquiring the French language, and moving in the best circles." Franklin's first diplomatic confreres were Silas Deane, commissioned by the Continental Congress to seek the aid of France even before the former's own appointment, and Arthur Lee, another congressional appointee authorized to negotiate for recognition of the United States at other continental capitals. Somewhat later, and more importantly, Franklin was joined on the peace commission by such able envoys of the new republic as John Jay and John Adams.

Deane was a strange, enigmatic figure, so fearful of British spies during his operations in Paris that he adopted the name of Jones and wrote all his letters in invisible ink. He was highly successful in obtaining military supplies for his country, but after being accused of juggling his accounts, he was called home. The charges against him were never clearly proved but Congress dismissed him and he then returned to Europe, an embittered expatriate, living in Ghent and as hostile to the patriotic cause as he had once been warm in its support.

Lee, a jealous, quarrelsome irascible Virginian, traveled all about Europe in his private coach but was completely ignored by the Prussian court and refused entrée on a projected mission to Madrid. It was he who first brought charges against Deane, and his suspicious nature turned him also against Franklin, telling his brother that he was convinced "that the old doctor is concerned in the plunder." Congress soon recalled Lee, as well as Deane, on the grounds that such petty quarreling was "highly prejudicial to the honor and interests of the United States."

Among the so-called militia diplomats were also William Lee, a brother of the distrustful Arthur, who was equally unsuccessful in trying to win recognition from the Austrian emperor Joseph II and from Frederick the Great of Prussia; Ralph Izard, a hot-tempered South Carolinian living in Paris who never reached the post to which he was assigned as envoy to the Grand Duchy of Tuscany, and Francis Dana of Massachusetts, who made his way to St. Petersburg (a fourteen-year-old John Quincy Adams was his secretary) only to spend weary month after weary month waiting for an audience with the Empress Catherine which never materialized. Futile though these men were as diplomats, they at least traveled all over the continent.

They were happier in this aspect of their European stay than another envoy who was later to serve on the peace commission. Henry Laurens, one-time President of the Continental Congress, set out as special commissioner for Holland in 1780 but the ship on which he was sailing was captured by a British war vessel. Laurens threw his official papers overboard but they were "hooked up" out of the sea and on discovering their contents, the British declared war on Holland and imprisoned Laurens in the Tower at London until the end of the war.

Thomas Paine, who had fired American patriotism with his flaming pamphlet *Common Sense*, was a visitor to France in 1781 as member of a purchasing mission. He soon returned to the United States to work—of all things—on the invention of an iron bridge, but was again in Paris in 1792. After becoming a French citizen and winning election to the National Convention, he fell out with the Jacobins and narrowly escaped the guillotine. A less well known but also dramatic figure was Louis Littlepage, a young American who for a time served with John Jay on his mission to Madrid, broke away to come to Paris in 1783, and then wandered off to Poland. There he became chamberlain to King Stanislaus and for the next fifteen years played a mysterious role—diplomat and soldier of fortune—in the political intrigues of eastern Europe.

The man who became Franklin's trusted secretary during these days has an even more surprising story. Dr. Edward Bancroft, born in Westfield, Massachusetts, had been doctor, writer, and inventor before undertaking his secretarial duties in Paris. He served faithfully and well, and after peace had been concluded, went to England where he discovered a new dye for treating textiles, wrote a novel assailing Christianity, and died peacefully in 1821. Something like a century later it was revealed that he had been a British spy. For years while in the employ of the Americans he had been corresponding regularly with the authorities in London, secreting his letters in the hole of a tree in the garden of the Tuileries where they were duly picked up and forwarded to England by his Majesty's minister in Paris.*

Another particular friend of Franklin's—by her account if not his—was Patience Lovell Wright. New Jersey born, this unusual woman had lived for a time in London before the war and made a conspicuous place for herself as a modeller of wax figures, becoming, it was said, a friend at court. Highly eccentric, forceful, and outspoken, she took it upon herself to supply Franklin with confidential news about affairs in England and on at least one occasion (rather against his advice) reported to him in person in Paris. One contemporary account describes her as "a tall, and athletic figure; walked with a firm, bold step, and erect as an Indian. ... Her sharp glance was appalling; it had almost the wildness of a maniac." In spite of such rather unprepossessing characteristics, a contemporary wrote that Mrs. Wright was not only a good friend of Franklin but was "visited and caressed by all the respectable Americans in Paris."

Among these visitors to Europe in revolutionary days was one American who may be singled out as the first tourist—even though the word itself ("one who makes a tour, esp. for pleasure") did not come into currency until about 1800. Elkanah Watson, a native of Plymouth, Massachusetts, arrived in Paris in 1779 bearing dispatches from the Continental Congress for Franklin and a commission from John Brown of Providence, Rhode Island (one of the founders of Brown University), for the procurement of army supplies. Although he was to set up a mercantile business of his own at Nantes, his major interest in Europe would clearly appear to have been travel for its own sake, and remaining abroad five years, this enterprising, enthusiastic young man (just twenty years old when his adventures began) toured some 2000 miles through France, the Austrian Netherlands, Holland, and England. He was constantly absorbed, as he wrote in the journal later incorporated in his *Memoirs,* "by the novelties around me: new faces—new objects—strange customs and language."

* In his recent *The Craft of Intelligence* (New York, 1963), Allen Dulles suggests that Bancroft was one of the first "double agents" in our history.

Watson crossed the Atlantic on the little 70-ton packet "Mercury," narrowly escaping capture at sea by a British frigate before landing at the port of St. Martin, near La Rochelle. The passage had taken twenty-nine days but like many transatlantic voyagers, he could hardly adjust himself to the fact that within what seemed to him so short a time, he found himself standing on a quay in France. "What a transition," he noted in his journal. But Watson lost no time in continuing his journey, and having secured a private carriage hurried on to Paris. He was entranced by everything he saw: the beauty and luxuriance of the French countryside; the flourishing towns and cities over whose cobbled streets his carriage rattled so swiftly; the Roman towers, Gothic cathedrals and imposing chateaux seen in the distance. Everything "conspired to give animation and interest" to the unfamiliar scene.

As he approached Paris, his excitement mounted. Bowling along the broad avenue from Versailles, a lively postillion (with cocked hat, powdered and perfumed queue, heavy boots) whipping up the horses, his carriage fought its way through growing crowds to the city barrier. The route then led through the Place Louis XV (soon to become the Place de la Concorde), past the gardens of the Tuileries and the somber gray walls of the Louvre, and across the Pont Neuf to the Seine's Left Bank. Finally it drew up at its passenger's prospective lodgings—the Hotel d'York on the Rue Jacob in the Faubourg Saint Germain. A plaque still marks the ancient building as the place where four years after Watson's arrival the British and American peace commissioners signed the treaty that established the independence of the United States.

After "shaking off the dust of travel," as he wrote, Watson promptly sought out Dr. Franklin, who greeted him cordially and asked him at once to take his letters, addressed by Congress to Louis XVI, back to Versailles. There Count Vergennes received the young American with the utmost civility and had his secretary show him about the palace and gardens where he caught a glimpse of Louis XVI and Marie Antoinette— the latter "an elegant person, a fine figure, an imposing aspect."

Having completed his official mission, Watson was in the next few days to take up sightseeing with untiring zest. He went to the Louvre and was deeply gratified to find a portrait of Franklin hanging in its art gallery, wandered through the Tuileries gardens which he discovered to be a delightful and popular resort for all Paris, and going to Notre Dame—"an object of strong interest" —climbed its tower to get a better view of the city. He was greatly impressed by the "Hospital des Invalides," considering it the noblest monument of the reign of Louis XIV, and praised the Luxembourg as one of the most gorgeous and magnificent palaces in all Paris. He drove through the Bois de Boulogne, made excursions to St. Germain and St. Cloud, and promenaded on the boulevards. Everything pleased this young man. "Constantly bewildered in astonishment and admiration," he was carried away by the gayety and abandon which characterized "the giddy population of Paris."

At the same time Watson was a New Englander. Having the conscience of his puritan forebears, he could hardly approve the way in which the Parisians gave over Sunday to recreation and amusement, with cafés crowded and people singing and dancing. He was scandalized by the gambling and vice encouraged at the Palais Royal, and bluntly characterized that popular resort as "a mass of moral corruption." He was troubled by some of the plays he saw and confessed that after learning French, "the gross double entendre and shameful indecencies which characterized their performances . . . . shocked my American modesty." But like so many later travelers whose enjoyment of Parisian life was perhaps sharpened by the twinges of a puritan conscience, Watson soon became philosophic over whatever differences he found in the moral standards of French and Americans. "Custom," he wrote after commenting on the theater, ". . . disguises and tolerates all things."

During this and later visits to Paris, Watson often saw the venerable Franklin, finding that great man's manners "so pleasant and fascinating that one felt at ease and unrestrained in his presence"; and he several times called on John Adams who soberly advised him never to dance with the ladies, play cards, or go to the theater. He should devote himself to business and study, Adams said, rather than "dissipation and pleasure." Watson also met Dr. Bancroft, describing him as an "ardent Whig," Louis Littlepage, "esteemed a prodigy of genius and acquirements," and Thomas Paine—"coarse and uncouth in his manners, loathsome in his appearance, and a disgusting egotist." One day at the Hotel d'York, he heard a powerful female voice cry out from an upper story: "Who are you? An American, I hope! ... Wait a minute, I am coming down!" It was the formidable Patience Lovell Wright.

Watson's first trip beyond the confines of France (after deciding to stay abroad and setting up his mercantile house at Nantes), took him in the autumn of 1781 to Ostend, Bruges, Ghent and Brussels. What fascinated him most were the luxuriously outfitted barges—floating hotels carrying a hundred or more passengers—which were drawn leisurely by a pair of horses along canals elevated several feet above the surrounding countryside. He found this an "exceedingly amusing and agreeable" mode of travel and was so intrigued that after his return to America he became a zealous promoter of canals, one time urging upon George Washington the development of "lock navigation" from the Hudson to Lake Ontario. With such experiences his tour through Belgium was a great success, and it came to something of a climax on his return to Paris in mid-November. He found the entire city ablaze with illuminations celebrating the news of American victories in the war and the surrender of Cornwallis at Yorktown.

After some further time at Nantes engaged in his business affairs, Watson decided to visit England. It took a great deal of finagling to get the necessary passports and papers, but Franklin rather reluctantly helped him and he was further fortunate in being entrusted with official dispatches by Benjamin Vaughan, the emissary of Lord Shelburne in opening negotiations with the American peace commissioners. Thus armed, Watson crossed the Channel and landed on British soil in September 1782. "This was the land of our rancorous foe," he wrote dramatically in his journal; "still it was the land of our forefathers."

Once again Watson was the zealous and indefatigable sightseer in "exploring the spectacles of London." He greatly admired St. Paul's, visited the House of Commons, and drove out to Windsor and Richmond. Entertained by a friend at "one of the sumptuous seats" near Blackheath, he was impressed by the splendor and magnificence of English country life but rather appalled by the distant, cold, forbidding air of British women as compared with the airy and animated carriage, the grace and elegance, of those of France. A provincial tour took him to the Midland manufacturing towns, but its high point was Stratford-on-Avon. "Stimulated by an ardent and deeply excited enthusiasm," he wrote in good tourist fashion, "I abandoned my friend at the Inn, and hastily ran to contemplate the object of my anxious inquiries— a little, old and dilapidated building—the birthplace of Shakespeare."

A quite different experience awaited him on a visit to Bath where he enjoyed himself amid its "gay and dissipated circles" and wonderingly inspected its famous baths. From the pump room, as he described the scene, one could look down upon the great open pool where bathers of both sexes ("equipped in proper dresses") nonchalantly walked about in water up to their necks. They were generally hidden by clouds of steam but with every puff of wind presented "a most singular and ludicrous spectacle; old and young, matrons and maidens, beaus and priests, all promiscuously wading and splashing in the bath, a band of music the while playing some solemn march or exhilarating dance."

Back in London—on December 5, 1782—Watson had the unique experience of attending the session of Parliament at which George III announced his decision to recognize the independence of the United States. Furthermore he met Shelburne, Pitt, Burke, Fox, and Sheridan on the floor of the House of Commons. "Mingling thus by a happy concurrence of events with the great luminaries of England," this fortunate young man confided to his journal, "I felt that I was occupying exalted and privileged ground."

Another memorable tour took him to Holland in the spring of 1784. Visiting Rotterdam his heart bounded with joy once again to see "our glorious stripes" streaming from among the shipping in its crowded harbor. The Hague exceeded all his "most ardent imaginings" with its art galleries—"eminently interesting and demanded the closest examination"—and various museums. In Amsterdam he was shocked by the "spill houses"—legalized brothels —which he visited (under the guidance of a police official) and found "too loathsome and abhorrent to be endured." He had a happier time once again taking a canal boat, and observing the Hollanders in their homes and gardens, confessed that he "almost envied them the calm and delightful repose of their country life."

Watson finally returned to America in 1784. He was vigorously to promote his ideas on canals, and later win an enduring fame as the founder of the Berkshire Agricultural Society and originator of country fairs.

The same year that Watson returned to the United States, Jefferson arrived in Paris to join the mission that was to negotiate peace with Great Britain, and a year later he succeeded Franklin as minister at the court of Louis XVI. The center for Americans in Paris was now transferred from Franklin's comfortable home at Passy to Jefferson's house, the Hôtel de Langeac, on the corner of the Champs-Elyseés and the Rue Neuve de Berry. "He lives well," one visitor wrote. "Keeps a good table and excellent wine, which he distributes freely, and by his hospitality to his countrymen here possesses very much their good will."

The whole Adams family, "very cleverly situated" in a large house in Auteuil before John Adams went on to London, were close friends of Jefferson, and in his more immediate entourage were an interesting group of young men. David Humphreys, a Yale graduate, a poet, a soldier who had become "the belov'd of Washington," was secretary of the mission. He was very patriotic, somewhat pompous; "a stout warlike looking gentleman," as Mrs. Adams later recalled. He continued in the diplomatic service as minister to Spain and Algiers, and when about to return to the United States in 1802, had a herd of merino sheep driven across Spain and Portugal and then conveyed by sloop to his home in Derby, Connecticut. Jefferson's private secretary and a great favorite with him was William Short, a young man "modest and soft in his manners" who had been one of the founders of the Phi Beta Kappa Society at William and Mary College. He was to become very much at home in Paris, appointed chargé when Jefferson returned to become his country's first Secretary of State in 1789.

Among the unofficial visitors to Paris in these days, notable particularly for the manner of his arrival, was John Jeffries, a Harvard-educated man, wartime loyalist and surgeon with the British army. He appeared in January 1785, having crossed the British Channel as a passenger on the pioneering balloon flight of Jean Pierre Blanchard. Ignoring his loyalist record, the Americans in the French capital entertained him royally. He records one dinner given by Franklin (who had not yet left for home) which included John Adams, "his lady and daughter, all of whom were very civil to me," Edward Bancroft, Colonel Humphreys, and "the celebrated and brave commodore Paul Jones."

This was not the first time John Paul Jones had been in Paris. He was there originally in 1780, after the famous battle of the "Bonhomme Richard" and the "Serapis," and somewhat ironically in view of the latter's surreptitious activities, had been a guest of Bancroft's. Paris society dined and feted the doughty commodore, who was more than ready to make the most of "the pleasure which Paris affourds," and Louis XVI presented him with a gold-hilted sword. On the occasion of the dinner for Jeffries he was once more living in Paris, seeking to collect prize money for the ships he had captured during the war, and then after an ill-starred interlude in the service of the Russian navy under the Empress Catherine, he was once again to return to the French capital. John Paul Jones's last years were an unhappy anticlimax to his stirring deeds during the revolution, for he died in Paris almost completely neglected by both the French and his countrymen.

One of his companions for a time, hatching up an ambitious but never realized scheme for fur trading on the Northwest Coast, was the enterprising John Ledyard of Connecticut. This famed traveler, whose goals reached far beyond the tourist routes of western Europe, could never remain long in one place. Encouraged by Jefferson, of whom he saw a great deal while in Paris, he set out to cross Russia and then make his way to the Oregon country by sailing across the north Pacific. An irate Empress Catherine had Ledyard arrested some two hundred miles short of Kamchatka and transported back to Poland across the vast wastes of Siberia in a closed carriage.

Joel Barlow, the Hartford Wit and author of *The Vision of Columbus*, came to Paris in the late 1780's in a somewhat new capacity for Americans abroad. A highly agreeable, good-looking, socially inclined young man (his puritan orthodoxy was said to have "dropped from him like a mantle" on his introduction to Parisian society), he was trying to sell shares in the Scioto Company, a speculative land company with extensive holdings in Ohio. He stayed on in Paris during the French Revolution, and joining forces with Thomas Paine, became a vigorous adherent of the republicans. He wrote a vitriolic pamphlet, *Advice to the Privi-*

leged Orders, in support of their cause and in 1790 drew up in behalf of the American colony in Paris a letter of congratulations to the National Assembly. For all this strenuous activity there were apparently moments when Barlow was homesick, for it was during this stay in France (he was later to return as American minister) that he wrote his best-known poem, "Hasty Pudding," with its nostalgic memories of New England's corn-meal mush.

Another land speculator—and future minister—in the American colony was Gouverneur Morris, who had been a member of the Constitutional Convention. His wealth, his affability, and his excellent knowledge of French soon won him a very special place in Parisian society. Stamping about on his wooden leg, gay and cynical, he was as Franklin had been—though never as greatly respected—very much at home in drawing room and salon. "He hath the art of winning the good graces of the ladies," a contemporary commented; "he is a very devil in political gallantry, notwith-standing his wooden leg."

As early as 1787 two elegant young men from wealthy and distinguished families arrived with no other purpose than embarking on the traditional Grand Tour. They were Thomas Lee Shippen of Philadelphia and John Rutledge, Jr., of Charleston. Jefferson generously advised them on the best inns, the best *valets de place* (or local guides), and the best wines to be found in the cities they planned to visit. As pioneer of another type, there also appeared "a Mr. Langbourne of Virginia" who had the novel idea of traveling the continent on foot.

Finally, among many others, there were Mr. and Mrs. William Bingham of Philadelphia, forerunners of those wealthy and socially ambitious Americans who were drawn abroad by the sophisticated pleasures of European society. The Binghams lived most luxuriously. They drove about Paris in an elaborate coach drawn by four horses and attended by three liveried servants, and the aspiring Mrs. Bingham managed to be presented at the court of Louis XVI, and, on a visit to London, at that of George III. She was a high-spirited girl in her early twenties who won the universal praise of her fellow Americans. The rather more sedate Mrs. Adams, who knew Mrs. Bingham both in Paris and London, lamented that too much frivolity and dissipation had given her an unfortunate thirst for the luxuries of European life, but nonetheless greatly admired her youth and beauty. The young John Quincy Adams stated succinctly and without equivocation that she was "the finest woman I ever saw," and Thomas Jefferson appears to have been equally impressed by "the fine figure and beautiful person" of this first American star in the bright constellation of European society. On returning to her native Philadelphia, Mrs. Bingham became an acknowledged leader of fashion, occasionally startling that conservative city by serving very special French dishes at her elegant dinner parties.

The American colony across the Channel was quite different. John Adams did not take up his London post until 1785 (finding the atmosphere somewhat chilly for a time) but the countrymen whom his wife had noted on her first visit were supplemented by new arrivals. The American painters were still most prominent. "In England at present," Franklin had noted two years earlier, "the best Historical Painter, West, the best Portrait Painter, Copley, and the best Landscape Painter, Taylor . . . are all Americans." It was London, and not Paris, that provided a first example of that strong attraction which ever since the close of the eighteenth century has drawn so many American artists to study and live in the Old World.

Benjamin West was the recognized dean of this art colony. He had visited Italy in the 1760's, pioneering where so many of his fellow-American artists were later to follow, and on coming to England had settled down and become not only Historical Painter at the court of George III, but a close personal friend of that unfortunate monarch. Yet in spite of his official position, West never lost his sympathies for his own country and openly supported its cause during the Revolution. He cordially welcomed all Americans visiting London and his studio remained a center not only for artists but for other travelers from the United States until his death in 1820.

As an almost equally distinguished member of the group, John Singleton Copley was at the very peak of his fame in the 1780's. His major portraits were those of British statesmen, most notably "The Death of Lord Chatham," but he was also to paint many of the important Americans in London, including John Adams, John Quincy Adams, and also Elkanah Watson. Like

West he had toured the continent before settling in England and would not return to the United States.

Gilbert Stuart was also in England during these days. A one-time student of West, he had become a highly fashionable portrait painter, and the most glamorous figures of the British aristocracy crowded his studio. He himself moved in the topmost reaches of society, entertaining lavishly with a French chef and a band of Italian musicians. After twelve successful years in London and a briefer stay in Ireland, he returned to his native land in 1792 with the ambitious plan, in which he so notably succeeded, of making "a plurality" of portraits of George Washington.

During the war itself, John Trumbull joined this artist colony and Robert Fulton arrived in 1786. The former had served for a time with the revolutionary forces as an aide to Washington, but feeling unequal to such "elegant duties," had taken the surprising step, even while hostilities continued, of making his way to London to study painting under West. At the instigation of British loyalists he was arrested on suspicion of treason and ordered out of the country. He returned, however, with the conclusion of peace, living for six years intermittently in London and Paris where he painted his great historical canvasses of the American Revolution.

Fulton on his arrival soon became one of West's outstanding pupils, and then moving to Paris in 1796 had a great success in painting panoramas. His inventive curiosity, however, had from the first overshadowed his interest in painting and even while in London he became engaged in the experiments with which his name is so much more closely associated—a machine for dredging canals, a submarine, and a steamboat. Seven years after settling in Paris, Fulton made a successful trial run with his steamboat, and enlisting the support of Robert Livingston, who was at the time minister to France, he was able to return to America to develop his invention further. He was dramatically successful, and in 1807 the "Clermont" made her epochal run up the Hudson River.

A number of other well-known artists studied in England at a time when the Napoleonic wars largely cut off travel on the continent, staying on even during the hostilities with the United States in 1812. It was not for another decade that Rome and Florence began to eclipse London as centers for American painters

20

and sculptors. The influence of West, Copley, and Stuart reached well over into the new century.

Among these later artists in England were Rembrandt Peale, a son of the Philadelphia painter Charles Willson Peale; Washington Allston, one of the most imaginative of early American landscapists, and Samuel F. B. Morse, better known as the inventor of the telegraph. Writing half a century later, Charles Leslie, a close friend of both Allston and Morse, has left a lively and engaging account of their gay London life. Many of them also traveled and studied on the continent, especially in Paris, but London was their first love. Leslie described the picnic excursions of these youthful, aspiring painters to Richmond and Greenwich, their theater parties (agreeing that Mrs. Siddons was "the greatest actress that ever trod the stage"), and their sumptuous dinners at the York Chop House.

Abigail Adams knew the American painters living in London in the 1780's as well as her compatriots in the circle revolving about Jefferson in Paris. Outspoken and amusing, she wrote to her sisters and nieces an inimitable series of letters during these years that provide a vivid account of early Americans abroad.

She had made the voyage to Europe on the ship "Alert," carrying a dozen or so passengers and a cargo of oil and potash. Crowded and dirty, the little vessel was so mercilessly tossed about by the heavy seas that her harassed passengers could scarcely crawl to the cold, damp deck for an occasional breath of fresh air. The tiny stateroom assigned to Mrs. Adams opened directly on the general cabin, where the entire ship's company spent the daytime hours and the men slept at night. The door had to be kept open for ventilation. "We have curtains, it is true," Mrs. Adams wrote, "and we only in part undress, about as much as the Yankee bundlers .... but what should I have thought on shore, to have laid myself down in common with half a dozen gentlemen?" She was happy to add that the deportment of the gentlemen was "agreeable to the strictest delicacy, both in word and action."

Once ashore she traveled to London by postchaise with her daughter Abby, marveling at a countryside that appeared to be cultivated like a garden and greatly appreciating the excellent roads and the comfortable inns. However, on stopping at Canterbury, she was not at all impressed: "The old Gothic cathedrals, which are all of stone, very heavy, with but few windows, look more like jails for criminals, than places designed for the Worship of the Deity." Passing through Rochester and Chatham, across the waste of Blackheath where highwaymen were almost commonplace (a postchaise just ahead of theirs had been held up), they finally reached the "great monstrous" city of London. Mrs. Adams and her daughter found lodgings at Osbourne's New Family Hotel, and it was here that her many American callers made her feel almost as if she was in her own country.

She went herself not only to the studios of West and Copley, but also to that of Mrs. Wright where her reception once again suggests the eccentric character of this most unusual American abroad:

> Upon my entrance, (my name being sent up), she ran to the door and caught me by the hand; 'Why is it and in truth Mrs. Adams? and that your daughter? Why you dear soul you, how young you look. Well, I am glad to see you. All of you Americans? Well, I must kiss you all.' Having passed the ceremony upon me and Abby, she runs to the gentlemen. 'I make no distinction,' says she, and gave them a hearty buss; from which we all would rather have been excused, for her appearance is quite slattern.

Mrs. Adams' husband and son soon arrived, and the whole family was shortly off for Paris and the lively social life of the French capital. The first impressions of Mrs. Adams were far from favorable. Paris was "a horrid dirty city"; for the most part the streets were narrow, the shops and houses "inelegant," and the churches cold, damp, and forbidding. The famous city struck this loyal New Englander (except for a few public buildings) as much inferior to Boston.

She looked rather askance, as had Elkanah Watson, at many aspects of Parisian life, but to her own wondering dismay came to be very fond of the theater and the ballet. She wrote her sister of what must have been a rather confusing experience for a settled matron of Quincy, Massachusetts, and the wife of staid John Adams:

22

The first dance which I saw upon the stage shocked me; the dresses and the beauty of the performers were enchanting; but, no sooner did the dance commence, than I felt my delicacy wounded, and I was ashamed to be seen to look at them. Girls, clothed in the thinnest silk and gauze, with their petticoats short, springing two feet from the floor, poising themselves in the air, with their feet flying, and as perfectly showing their garters and drawers as though no petticoats had been worn, was a sight altogether new to me.

And then asking her sister whether she should speak the truth, she went on to make the self-conscious admission:

repeatedly seeing these dances has worn off that disgust which I at first felt, and . . . . I see them now with pleasure.

In many other ways Mrs. Adams gradually came to like Paris, especially admiring the civility and politeness of the people, the easy deportment and musical voices of the women. She describes amusingly in letters home her encounters with French society, the manners and customs of the court, and the current fashions. It was with some regret that she left France in the spring of 1785 and took up in London the more formal life she was called upon to play there as the wife of the American minister.

Nevertheless England soon became "the country of my greatest partiality," as she wrote her sister, and once again her witty letters bring to life scene after scene in London. She was presented at court, where George III decorously saluted her left cheek; attended any number of fashionable routs at which whist and cribbage were followed by tea, coffee, and lemonade; visited the art galleries and museums; went often to the theater; and faithfully attended Sunday services at St. Paul's and Westminster Abbey. There were also excursions to Windsor and Blenheim, which charmed her with their lovely gardens; a trip to Oxford whose colleges she found very interesting; and a more extended tour with a considerable party of Americans which took her among other places to Bath and Southampton.

She found the former resort, where the American visitors would appear to have been quite occupied with "three balls, two concerts, one play, and two private parties, besides dining and breakfasting abroad," to be something quite different from anything she had known at home—"one constant scene of dissipation and gambling." Southampton interested her particularly because of the sea bathing, a practice apparently quite unknown at this time in New England. She decided to try it for herself. "You have a woman for a guide," she wrote, "a small dressing-room to yourself, an oilcloth cap, a flannel gown, and socks for the feet." It all seemed eminently proper and she quite enjoyed herself.

Mrs. Adams stayed some three years in London (with one further continental visit to Holland), and in spite of the nostalgic tone of many of her letters, enjoyed her life there a great deal. But as time drew on she was more than ready to return home and in 1788 wrote her good friend Thomas Jefferson ("one of the choice ones of the earth") in happy anticipation of her approaching departure. "Retiring to our little farm, feeding my poultry and improving my garden," she said, "has more charms for my fancy, than residing at the Court of St. James's where I seldom meet with characters as inoffensive as my hens and chickens, or minds so well improved as my garden."

The Americans visiting Europe in these years, as may be seen from their diaries and journals, had much in common with their countless successors. They felt the almost irresistible lure of the Old World, and yet were strongly repelled by monarchial rule and the harsh oppression of the common people. They were fully convinced that in contrast to the inherent virtues of their own republican society, there was something corrupt and decadent in that of aristocratic Europe. Reflecting the strong nationalistic tides sweeping over their own country, their experience abroad served to deepen their convictions of the New World's superiority over the Old World.

In one letter to her sister, half-mocking though its tone may be, Abigail Adams expressed what Americans so generally felt:

> Do you know that European birds have not half the melody of ours? Nor is their fruit half so sweet, nor their flowers half so fragrant, nor their manners half so pure, nor their people half so virtuous?

And another time after describing to one of her nieces the wretchedness and misery she had so often encountered in Europe, she commented more seriously on how much better off America was in every way: "Let it excite us to thankfulness, my dear girl, that our lines have fallen to us in a happier land, a land of virtue and liberty."

Elkanah Watson on his return home said that he wished the farmers of America could witness the suffering and poverty he had seen in Europe, overwhelmed as the people were, even in England, by taxes, tithes, and rents. "They would kiss the soil of America," he exclaimed, "and call it blessed, and raise their hearts in pious gratitude to the Giver of all good."

III. A FIRST INVASION

THE LONG years which found Europe convulsed by the wars growing out of the French Revolution and the immense ambitions of Napoleon largely cut off further American travel abroad until about 1815. It then started up with a vigor that it would never again lose except during those later periods of European strife in the twentieth century. The number of those able to take the time for the long ocean voyage and any sort of stay in Europe, and who could afford the relatively high costs of such travel, inevitably remained very small indeed by modern standards. It is nonetheless amazing to discover how many Americans did visit Europe during the first half of the nineteenth century and how widely they traveled. Many of them made long visits, stretching to several years; others had to be content with what Edward Everett Hale would describe in his *Ninety Days' Worth of Europe* as "a happy little dash."

A regularly scheduled transatlantic service was first made available in 1818 when the popular Black Ball Line began to operate between New York and Liverpool, soon putting its sailings on a fortnightly basis. Its lead was followed within a few years by four rival companies, strenuously competing for a steadily growing number of potential passengers: the Red Star Line, the Swallow Tail Line, the Dramatic Line (its ships were named "Shakespeare," "Sheridan," "Garrick," and "Siddons") and the French Line, sailing to Le Havre.

The ships of these various companies—little sailing packets of no more than 300 or 400 tons burden—carried twelve to fourteen cabin passengers, making the eastward crossing in about three weeks and the westward run in an average five, which might in winter stretch to as many as seven. The usual one-way passenger

26

rate was $140, including mattresses, bedding, wines and all other stores. The Dramatic Line charged only $120 but this did not include beverages, not apparently because of any feeling about temperance but because "many a bottle of good wine is wasted by passengers, when the article is so included."

The packets had a main cabin, about forty by fourteen feet, with a long dining table down the center and upholstered benches along the walls; off this saloon opened seven low-ceilinged little staterooms with double bunks. Some of the ships provided a small library and what the advertisements called "a bathing room." The latter was no more than a secluded part of the deck where an obliging seaman might occasionally be prevailed upon to dash a few buckets of cold salt water over the hardy bather. It was an invariable practice to pen a cow somewhere on the deck to provide fresh milk, while the longboats would be made over into quarters for a sheep, pigs, and chickens.

If accommodations were very confined and rather on the primitive side, the packets were tough little ships, manned by comparably tough crews, and were amazingly seaworthy. In the period stretching from 1815 to 1848, only three out of some 150 were lost at sea. Prospective voyagers were not deterred by the possible dangers of shipwreck. Anywhere from two to eight thousand—the number varying according to economic and other conditions—took off every year between the 1820's and the 1850's.

These travelers fell into a number of special categories. There were first the businessmen. Among them in early nineteenth century days were cotton factors, like John Allan, the foster father of Edgar Allan Poe, who lived in England; and importers such as Allan Melville, father of Herman Melville, who periodically visited France to buy fabrics, gloves, and perfume. The great Boston merchant Thomas Handasyd Perkins (he had been in Paris during the revolution and watched with horror the guillotining of Robespierre) repeatedly visited Europe, and the business affairs of James Wadsworth of Geneseo, New York, founder of a famous family, often took him to Paris in search of foreign investors for his various enterprises. Among many bankers were Joshua Bates, born in Weymouth, Massachusetts, who settled in London as early as 1816 as representative of the shipping interests of William Gray of Boston, then becoming a partner in Baring Brothers, fiscal agent for the United States; and somewhat later George Peabody, who was to take Junius Spencer Morgan into partnership in his firm dealing with American securities, progenitor of the great banking house of J. P. Morgan and Company. In midcentury Peabody, an urbane, kindly, generous bachelor, had won a unique position for himself as an American ambassador of goodwill, and every Fourth of July gave an imposing banquet to which all American visitors in London were invited.

Apart from those whose professional or business interests took them abroad, the wealthy members of society's more exclusive circles along the Atlantic seaboard probably accounted for the largest number of Americans visiting Europe. William Tudor, founder of the *North American Review* and a European traveler himself, was to boast in 1820 that there was a large group of both sexes in his native Boston who had not only seen London and Paris, but also Rome and Naples. A few years later Francis Lieber, the German-American editor of the *Encyclopedia Americana*, expressed his amazement that ladies of fashion in New York thought no more of a trip to Paris than those of London. Society already had an international flavor; the ambitious had discovered the prestige of having been in Europe. The course set by the William Binghams in the 1780's was being followed forty years later by the elite of Boston and New York, Baltimore and Philadelphia.

During this same period a quite different category of traveling Americans—initiating what was to become a popular practice—were clergymen whose congregations had given them a European trip to restore uncertain health or wearied spirits. Many of them wrote back pastoral letters instructively describing, usually with grave reflections on their low moral tone, the customs and manners of the Old World. William Ellery Channing, the famous Unitarian preacher, was among such travelers; and another was Bishop Philander Chase of Ohio, who had a special purpose for his trip in raising funds for Kenyon College.

The Reverend John A. Clark of St. Andrew's Church in Philadelphia, who went abroad in 1840, suggests the vogue for ministerial travel when he speaks of finding aboard his ship a "pleasant, sober, clerical group." He raised a delicate question, however, in his rambling and discursive *Glimpses of the Old World*. Clark was afraid that many of the clergymen whom he met in Europe

28

had left their charges "under the pretext of enfeebled health" and actually had no more reason for going abroad than "a desire to enjoy the pleasures" of their trip.

Two rather more unusual traveling clergymen in midcentury were John Overton Choules, a New Englander who took with him on his trip a party of young boys whose experiences were described in *Young Americans Abroad; or a Vacation in Europe*, and Jacob Abbott, who was engaged in gathering material for such widely known children's books as *Rollo on the Atlantic, Rollo in England, Rollo in Paris* ... No writings were more indicative of the mounting popular interest in foreign lands and the culture-conscious attitude of so many transatlantic voyagers. Little Rollo not only saw all the galleries and museums in the European capitals, but he also visited cotton and silk mills, iron foundries, and factories. When on one occasion he gave signs of becoming somewhat bored by such strenuous sightseeing, his inestimable mentor, Mr. George, called him gently to account: "We are traveling for improvement not play.... So we must do our duty."

The university students (somewhat older than Little Rollo), who have always made up such a considerable portion of Americans going abroad, began to cross the Atlantic even before Waterloo. If foreign study had been discouraged in the nationalistic fervor of the 1780's, as a consequence of both the popular conviction that each refinement could be found at home and the moral risks of exposure to the depravity of the Old World, such an attitude changed as Americans began to realize, however reluctantly, that decadent though its society might be, Europe still had something to offer the intellectual world. A contributor to the *North American Review* in 1819 even went so far as to suggest that its allurements to vice were no more to be dreaded than those which might tempt unwary youths who stayed at home.

Among the student pioneers ready to brave the dangers of moral temptation in seeking out the sources of foreign culture, were a distinguished group, coming largely from the strongly cultural environment of Boston. It included George Ticknor, who was to become the great Harvard professor of modern languages; Edward Everett, the future scholar, orator, and diplomat who would share the platform with Lincoln at Gettysburg; Joseph Green Cogswell, founder of the modern library system; and the historian George Bancroft. The German universities drew these young men in the first instance, but they toured all Europe with immense enthusiasm.

Another group of travelers who helped to develop the cultural ties between the Old World and the New were various professional scholars. Noah Webster, who had doubted in the 1780's that Europe had much to offer traveling Americans, visited England to work on his great dictionary; and Jared Sparks labored among British documents gathering material for his biographies of revolutionary heroes. Among many others on the continent were Richard Henry Wilde, a congressman from Georgia and author of "My Life Is Like a Summer Rose," who studied in the archives of the Medicis in Florence, and John Izard Middleton, the first of American archaeologists, engaged in excavating among the ruins of Italy. A quite different student of European culture was Zachariah Allen who wrote *The Practical Tourist*, not a guidebook but an account of the effects of machinery on the general state of society in England, France, and Belgium. John James Audubon was abroad in the 1820's seeking subscriptions for *Birds of the United States*. He was known in London as "the American woodsman" and had his portrait painted in wolfskin coat and hunting dress.

The most conspicuous if not the most numerous of American travelers, however, were the literary pilgrims, and it is from their diaries, journals, and travel books that the most illuminating picture of Americans abroad may be drawn. Through their writing they portrayed the scene, outlined the tours, and reflected the experiences of more ordinary tourists, and they also greatly influenced contemporary attitudes toward Europe.

"Authorship and traveling are all the fashion," the *Quarterly Review* commented in 1829, and the record bears this statement out. Every important American writer of the first half of the nineteenth century lived or traveled abroad except Thoreau and Poe. Scores of lesser literary lights also crossed the Atlantic and every one of them, it would appear, presented his impressions of Europe to an avid public in letters, journal, or diary. In time these travel accounts became something of a drug on the market. "I am sick of descriptive letters and will have no more of them," Horace Greeley, editor of the *New York Tribune*, irritably told a prospective contributor in 1846. Five years later, however, his own letters, to be published in book form as *Glances from Europe*, were appearing as a special *Tribune* feature.

The spirit in which these travelers sought out Europe was nostalgic and sentimental. Theirs was a romantic return to the past, a devoted search for the wellsprings of their own culture. They viewed with enthusiasm the sites and scenes that they associated through history or literature with their European heritage. "Everything we saw," William Cullen Bryant was to write of his first trip abroad in 1834, "spoke of the past, of an antiquity without limit." This sense of history, marking such a contrast with their own country which seemed to have no history, made a great impact on all visitors to the Old World, and most tourists were also wonderfully impressed with the overtones of a sophisticated, cultured society which again seemed to contrast so sharply with everything America represented.

Longfellow reflected the spirit in which a whole generation of travelers sought out Europe in the introduction to his *Outre-Mer*, sketches of his own experiences in the 1820's:

> To my youthful imagination the Old World was a kind of Holy Land, lying afar off beyond the blue horizon of the ocean; and when its shores first rose on my sight, looming through the hazy atmosphere of the sea, my heart swelled with the deep emotion of the pilgrim, when he sees afar off the spire which arises above the shrine of his devotion.

Washington Irving was one of the first well-known Americans to go abroad after the Napoleonic wars. He had made an even earlier trip when he was sent to Europe by his brothers in 1804 for his health, a carefree, handsome young man wandering casually about the continent in spite of its wartime restrictions. He returned to England on the eve of Waterloo, ostensibly to engage in the family business, but actually to travel, and then turned more seriously to writing.

His descriptive accounts of English backgrounds and English life are found in *The Sketch-Book* and *Bracebridge Hall*, and his further European stories in *Tales of a Traveler* and *The Alhambra*. They could hardly have been more romantic and sentimental, but they were very popular, no less in England than in the United

States. It was the Europe he depicted, especially his vision of the "Old Home," that helped to create in the American mind an appealing counter-image to that of a Europe oppressed by its kings and aristocracy, with a downtrodden peasantry and harshly treated workers. Countless tourists were to approach Europe—as did Longfellow in 1826—with a thrilling sense of anticipation largely inspired by Irving's books.

His own European life, from 1815 to 1832, was a great success. He traveled everywhere, taking walking trips through England and Scotland, coursing over the continent in his private carriage; and he lived not only in London, but in Paris, Dresden and Vienna, Salzburg and Prague. After publication of *The Sketch-Book* he became "the most fashionable fellow in London," welcomed in the great country homes of the English gentry and knowing everybody in society. His personal charm, his pleasantly harsh voice and winning smile, enabled him to ingratiate himself with brilliant success into the goodwill of literary and social England.

His life on the continent was no less glamorous. In Dresden he became a familiar figure in the little court of Frederick Augustus, taking part in court theatricals and on occasion hunting wild boar with the friendly king; in Paris he was very much the man of fashion, with his claret-colored coat, light waistcoat, and tight, flesh-colored silk stockings; in fact he went out in society so much that his writings grievously suffered. He had good friends among other Americans in Paris, including Samuel Griswold Goodrich, the author of children's books under the name of "Peter Parley"; and John Howard Payne, who had fled London from his creditors but would win enduring fame when he wrote for his opera *Clari, or the Maid of Milan,* the nostalgic "Home, Sweet Home." The final stages of Irving's European experiences were his years in Spain, a new world of poetry and romance, which are best remembered from his story of the Alhambra.

More the ordinary tourist and less the literary lion was a young Virginian, William C. Preston, who in 1817 was Irving's companion on a walking tour in Scotland. The great fame of Sir Walter Scott made a trip to Edinburgh and the Trossachs one of the first objectives of most American visitors in Europe up until the Civil War. Preston was later to recall in his *Reminiscences,* published after a memorable career as senator from his adopted state of South Carolina, how fortunate he had felt to make this tour with Irving. The two worshipful young men took *The Lady of the Lake* as their guidebook, visiting every scene it portrayed— Loch Lomond, Loch Katrine, Ben Nevis, and "huge Benvenue."

Going on to the continent, Preston stayed for a time in Paris, where he both enjoyed his sightseeing and saw many other Americans, and then with a party of friends took off in a private coach-and-four for Italy. This was traveling in style, and it was maintained when they reached Rome during Holy Week. Finding everything very crowded, they took over an unfurnished palace, rented the necessary furniture and other equipment, and hired a platoon of servants. Preston enjoyed Rome but was deeply offended by what he considered the superstitious aspects of its Catholicism; indeed, his "bosom was filled with sorrow, disgust, and horror."

As good tourists, a trip to Naples and ascent of Vesuvius were very much in order, and Preston took an obvious delight in describing the experiences of the one woman in the party on this formidable expedition. The climb had to be made by donkey-back but since this modest lady "revolted with horror from the idea of riding man fashion," she was carried to the edge of the lava bed in a chair somehow strapped to the donkey's back. She managed the last part of the trip to the crater's edge successfully on foot, but on her downward passage suffered something close to disaster—at least to her dignity:

> She came plunging along knee deep in pumice, having lost her shoes, and torn her stockings, her dress in the most tumultuous disarray, her bonnet hanging on her back, her frigette flying at random, the sweat streaming down her face, mixed with ashes, sulphur and rouge.

Preston continued his Italian tour with visits to Florence and Venice. He appears to have liked Florence chiefly because it had fewer priests, beggars, and prostitutes than any other Italian town; and commented on Venice that it *"looked* and I thought felt damp." He then started back to Paris across the Alps, lamenting as would so many Americans in later years that it was "with a sad and sorrowful feeling that one quits Italy."

33

George Ticknor has left the most interesting account of the experiences of that first group of American students to attend German universities, thereby setting a precedent that was to have the most far-reaching consequences for American scholarship. He was a golden youth: twenty-three years old, handsome and vivacious, completely self-assured; and happily blessed with intellectual genius, important letters of introduction, and plenty of money. Sailing for Europe with Edward Everett in the spring of 1815, he was to study at Göttingen until the end of 1816 and then travel— sometimes with Everett or Joseph Green Cogswell—through Germany, France, Italy, and Spain. Ticknor saw everything and met everyone. All doors were open to this talented young man who quickly discovered, at least in his case, that Americans in Europe "are now treated with the most distinguished kindness and courtesy."

Upon his arrival in London, Ticknor almost immediately called upon Lord Byron and was with him when news was received of Waterloo. "I'm d...d sorry for it," Ticknor reported the poet as saying. An easy friendship sprang up between the two men and it was to be typical of Ticknor's social success wherever he went. The Boston visitor, either on this occasion or on a later visit to England, met Wordsworth and Southey, Charles Lamb, Sydney Smith, and William Hazlitt, and visiting Scott at Abbotsford, enjoyed long walks and talks with his friendly host.

Ticknor's first stay in England was very short, however, and going on to Germany he was soon deeply absorbed in his studies at Göttingen—German, Greek, and natural history. Both he and Everett maintained a very strict schedule of work, but they also set aside time to participate in the life of the students, took up fencing in approved German style, and made a number of vacation walking tours. On one of them they called upon Goethe at Weimar and were received "without ceremony, but with care and elegance." They found the great German poet's person imposing and his manners simple, but "his whole countenance is old."

In the spring of 1817—he had now been in Europe two years —Ticknor was in Paris, plunged in a lively social life that fills his letters and journal. He knew Lafayette, now living in retirement but as always hospitable to Americans; met Baron von Humboldt, who read to him from the account he was then writing of his travels in South America; and had long talks with Talleyrand about the French minister's early days in America. Ticknor also dined frequently at the home of Madame de Staël, who told him that such young Americans as himself were the advance guard of the human race—"vous êtes l'avenir du monde!" On one occasion, to his great delight, he met Madame Récamier, but sadly admitted that for all her vivacity, "the lustre of that beauty which filled Europe with its fame is certainly faded."

Ticknor next went with friends to Switzerland and then by way of the Simplon Pass—"a most astonishing proof of the powers of man"—to Milan, Florence, Venice, and Rome. He considered the latter "worth all the cities in the world," enjoying immensely both its grandeur and its society. Attending the fashionable Italian *conversaziones,* he met all the local celebrities, as he had in Paris, and became especially intimate with the family of Lucien Bonaparte. Cogswell had joined him in Rome and the two young Americans had a private audience with the Pope, who told them, as Ticknor recorded in his journal, that he was convinced that "the time would soon come when we [America] should be able to dictate to the Old World."

Spain afforded even more unusual experiences. The roads were still abominable in that poverty-stricken country and the cart in which Ticknor rode from the French border to Madrid, reading Don Quixote aloud to his traveling companions, could make no more than about twenty miles a day. The taverns were miserable hovels, where everyone slept uncomfortably on the stone floor, and the available food was not only very poor but often insufficient. "And yet," Ticknor wrote home, after vividly describing all the hardships of the journey for his Boston friends, "will you believe me when I add to all this that I never made a gayer journey?"

Madrid delighted him. He was immensely impressed by Spanish painting, enjoyed walking the streets and stopping for an ice in one or another of the city's many coffee houses, and again was entertained in the highest social circles. He went to the bull fights, but Ticknor was no Hemingway. "The horrid sights I witnessed," he wrote of the *toros,* "completely unmanned me, and the first time I was carried out by one of the guards, and the second I was barely able to get out alone."

His Spanish tour also took him to Cordova, Granada, and

Seville, and he was almost as much overwhelmed by the beauty and the romance of these picturesque cities as Irving. Going on to Lisbon he traveled in the company of a band of smugglers, as the best possible protection against the roving robbers with which Spain and Portugal were infested at this time, and for eight days journeyed happily with these "high-spirited, high-minded fellows." They were armed with guns, pistols, swords, and dirks, but proceeding by muleback during the day and sleeping at night around the camp fire, the little party had no misadventures. Commenting on this phase of his travels, Ticknor wrote that "Spain and the Spanish people amuse me more than anything I have met in Europe."

After another visit in Paris with more "ultra society," Ticknor was back again in London early in 1819 and ready to return home. He had been nearly four years in Europe, learning its languages, studying its cultures, absorbing everything. As he prepared to board the New York packet (one of his fellow passengers was William Preston, whom he described as "an admirable fellow, of splendid talent"), this still young man was probably better informed upon the Old World, and more steeped in its culture, than any American of his day.

Jefferson was prepared to offer him upon his return a professorship—"Ideology, Ethics, Belles-Letters, and the Fine Arts"—at the new University of Virginia. Ticknor was destined, however, for Harvard and its specially created chair of modern languages.

Longfellow, visiting Europe a decade after these first post-Napoleonic travelers, was at once a literary pilgrim in the fashion of Washington Irving and a student in Germany in the tradition of George Ticknor. The different aspects of his stay abroad from 1826 to 1829 are contrasted in *Outre-Mer*, a travel book in the same genre as Irving's *Sketch-Book*, and the realistic, down-to-earth letters he wrote family and friends. *Outre-Mer* gives a picturesque, sentimental, literary view of his travels, sometimes touched with romantic melancholy, as he walked through France, smoked his pipe in Flemish inns, mused among the classic scenes of Italy, listened to the gay playing of guitars in Spain, and trimmed his midnight lamp in a German university town. He was constantly being overcome by an "exquisite beauty baffling the

36

power of language" and taking trips "written in my memory with a sunbeam." His letters, however, are full of pointed comments; sharp, satirical touches, and sometimes barbed criticisms of the countries and cities which he saw before settling down for his studies.

Longfellow was only nineteen when he landed at Havre on June 16, 1826. His first impression of the foreign scene did not reflect those romantic emotions that he summoned up in the introduction of *Outre-Mer*. "I was irresistibly seized," he wrote home in describing his first reactions to what he considered the odd customs of the French, "with diverse fits of laughter." And while he outgrew such uncontrolled amusement, he never really liked France. Paris seemed to him a dark and gloomy city, streaked and defaced with smoke and dust, its streets deep in mud, and the "noise and stench enough to drive a man mad." Actually Longfellow was working hard, struggling with French and attending lectures; a very serious young man who dutifully reassured his father that he could avoid vice quite as well in Paris as anywhere else. He did not try to keep a journal during this part of his trip, he wrote home, because "of the little interest I attach to anything in Paris, and a thorough disgust for French manners and customs."

Spain was something else again. It exercised its enchantment on Longfellow, whose natural good spirits immediately returned when he left France, as it had on Irving and Ticknor. The country itself had "a cold, inhospitable, uncultivated look," but he was to find Madrid and the cities of the south infinitely fascinating. He was carried away by the Alhambra, an experience to which "romance could add nothing, and which poetry itself could not beautify."

On the first stage of his journey to Madrid he traveled by diligence, but noted upon leaving Bayonne a local custom that he wished he had followed. It was travel on horseback with a dark-eyed Basque girl for guide and companion sitting with one on the same horse. "I wished myself out of the diligence," Longfellow wrote, "a thousand times." In southern Spain conditions were more hazardous, Longfellow confessing that he started his tour with "fear and trembling" because the country was still reputedly overrun by robbers. He did not meet any and the danger would appear to have given a special zest to his travels.

37

Longfellow was in Spain for eight delightful months and then went on to Italy. His reactions to the latter country were decidedly mixed. There was much that he enjoyed—the great monuments of Rome, the lovely sunshine that he found in Naples, the delights of Venice which he considered the most beautiful city he had ever seen. But he completely failed to experience "the romantic feeling which everybody else has, or pretends to have." He was perhaps still under the spell of Spain, looking for something he had found there but could not discover in Italy. A note of mockery sometimes creeps into his letters anticipatory of Mark Twain a half century later. "Can you believe," he wrote his mother while in Florence, "that the Arno. . . . is a stream of muddy water, almost entirely dry in summer?"

The close of this year of travel finally found Longfellow, after passing through Trieste, Prague, and Dresden, enrolled at Göttingen, where he presented letters of introduction from Ticknor and Bancroft. He undertook some further vacation trips in Holland and Flanders, was for a time in England, but the rest of the time during the first of what was to prove his many trips to Europe was largely taken up by his studies. He sailed for home in June 1829.

Another traveler in Europe, arriving just after Longfellow concluded his first visit, typified a quite different approach to Europe from that of the romantic pilgrims. This was Emma Willard, the strong-willed, serious-minded, rather imposing founder of the Troy Female Seminary, an outstanding leader in the cause of women's education and the author of "Rocked in the Cradle of the Deep." She embarked on her trip in 1830, accompanied by her son and several friends, for the sake of her health, but she soon proved to be an indefatigable sightseer. Her letters and journal not only give a vivid account of what she did, but also reflect her sometimes stern judgment on the European scene.

Her impressions of Paris, the first major stop on her continental journey, alternated between a moderate enthusiasm and the disapproval born of the puritanical prejudices that she shared with so many American travelers. Immediately upon her arrival she sent a long letter back to her "dear pupils" at the Troy Female Seminary in which she most interestingly described a first walk that took her past the Louvre, across the Pont des Arts, along the quays on the Seine's Left Bank, back across the Pont Royal, and through the Place de la Concorde to the garden of the Tuileries. She spoke of the busy traffic, the cheerful crowds of people, the general air of gaiety that seemed to characterize Paris. But there had to be a moral for the young girls to whom she was writing. "Give me for real, enduring happiness," she added to her letter, "the faces of the throng, who issue from the door of a New-England church, rather than those of the crowds I meet in the Tuileries."

Her social life in Paris owed a great deal to Lafayette, an old friend whom she had met at Troy when he was visiting the United States on his triumphal tour in 1824–25. She went frequently to the soirées that he continued to hold, and under his auspices attended a royal ball given in the salons of the Palais Royal and was presented at court.

"How could I then have believed," Mrs. Willard wrote in a letter recalling her childhood in a little Connecticut village, "that a time would come, when I should enter the court of France alone, pass through long rooms, guarded by files of soldiers, officers, and royal attendants. . . ." She had indeed come a long way. Even in comparison with social life in Troy, the society of the French court must have represented something of a change.

Yet Mrs. Willard could never escape her conscience. "Amidst all the gaiety which I describe," she wrote her sister as her visit in Paris drew to an end, "I often bear an aching heart. . . . This is not the kind of life to make me happy; rather give me back my cares and toils, with the consciousness of living to a good and useful purpose; give me back too a society, whose conversation shall lead my mind to better things, than the toys of this world."

When soon afterward she bore her aching heart to London, she discovered more serious things to do and would appear to have enjoyed conversations that may have led her mind to better things. For in addition to her assiduous sightseeing in London and a tour that took her through a great part of England and Scotland, she managed to visit a great many girls' schools and meet a number of the leading English reformers. Still, she was not always pleased. On one occasion when a very genteel English headmistress admitted that if she had private means, she would not be teaching, Mrs. Willard promptly took occasion to lecture her severely: "God has not placed us in this world to be idle or useless."

Mrs. Willard liked England, appreciating its familiar atmosphere and the boon of a common language, but she was highly critical of the attitude of many of the people she met. She felt that contempt was being constantly thrown upon her country and upon her sex. As an American and a woman, she wrote, she could never be happy in English society.

Throughout her travels she continued to remember her pupils (inserting in her letters little notes of advice: "Exercise, and do not bend over tables when you write. . . . Be obedient"), and as the close of the school year approached, she hurried home as she had promised to be back for the examinations in June.

The most important literary figure abroad in this period (after Washington Irving) was James Fenimore Cooper. He first arrived in Europe in 1826, at the very peak of his fame as the author of *The Last of the Mohicans*, and was to remain some seven years with his wife and daughters. For the greater part of the time he lived in Paris, but there were also visits (traveling rather elegantly with two private carriages, a cook, and a valet) to Italy, Switzerland, and Germany, together with a stay in England. He was writing assiduously (one of the books of this period was as distant from the European background as *The Prairie*), and each of his novels was promptly translated into half a dozen languages. No American author was ever more popular in Europe.

"Here I am in Paris," we find him commenting soon after his arrival, "half pleased, half vexed, getting reconciled to a strange country made up of dirt and gilding, good cheer and *soupe maigre*, bed bugs and laces." A picture of his daily life is given in an account of how he persuaded his good friend Samuel F. B. Morse, even though the latter was already greatly interested in his "talking spark," to paint the interior of the Louvre. Cooper would spend the morning reading and writing, and then rush off to the Louvre where, perching on a chair, he would tell Morse just what he should do. "Damn it—if I had been a painter," the novelist wrote, "what a picture I should have painted." Another time he told of how he "strolled in the gardens, visited the churches, loitered on the quays," while in the evenings there were dinners, theater parties, and fashionable soirées.

Cooper entertained his fellow countrymen in Paris with the utmost hospitality, giving great breakfast parties at which he served home-cooked buckwheat cakes. He became a good friend of Lafayette, and together with other Americans attended his family's evening parties and occasionally visited his country home at La Grange. Cooper was the center of a coterie that reminds one of that half a century earlier gathered about Jefferson. "There are few pleasanter circles," one visitor of these days wrote, "than that of the Americans in Paris."

The experiences of these travelers in the 1820's and 1830's, whether writers, students, or more casual tourists, varied a great deal, but they set a common example for the future as far as their itineraries were concerned and their choice of the places Americans going abroad should see. Generally speaking, however, they were a more selective group than their successors. They had both money and leisure; they had a cultured and sophisticated background; and they had the connections that won them an entrée into European society. But while such advantages enabled them to enjoy "the intoxicating whirl" of the social life of London and Paris, Rome and Madrid, far beyond the hopes or expectations of average Americans, they were still tourists and sightseers.

They continued to view Europe, for the most part, through the rather rose-tinted spectacles bequeathed them by Irving. Some among them were deeply affected—as the eighteenth-century travelers had been—by the unhappy evidence of surviving feudalistic restraints on freedom. But the Old World more often symbolized not tyranny and injustice, but art, music, and literature. Against the background of the leveling influences of Jacksonian democracy, with its lack of concern for things of the spirit, Europe appeared bright and glowing in comparison with what so many of these travelers considered the flat dullness of the American scene.

Cooper was to point up the ambivalence in the attitude of so many of these travelers more than any other writer of his day. Staunchly patriotic, fully committed to American ideals of freedom and republicanism, he knew full well, as one of his friends wrote, "the hollowness of all the despotic systems of Europe." At the same time, he deeply appreciated its cultural and intellectual climate, and the values of an aristocratic order in comparison with what he found on his return home to be a pushing, unmannered, materialistic society. He tried to make such distinctions in some of his books, notably *Home as Found*, but many of his countrymen, in the self-conscious and boastful nationalism of that day, felt only that he was glorifying Europe and vilifying his own country.

Whatever influence the travelers' tales may or may not have had in this respect, they served greatly to increase popular interest in the Old World. They further whetted the American appetite for foreign adventure. Moreover, as the 1830's came to an end, the opportunities for such an experience were suddenly—and dramatically—expanded. The introduction of transatlantic steamers gave a spur to European travel that almost overnight increased some sixfold the number of Americans annually going abroad.

IV. TRANSATLANTIC PASSAGE

ON APRIL 23, 1838, a bright spring day, New York's waterfront was crowded with "myriads of persons" who had gathered to see the thrilling finish of the race between the two pioneer steamships to cross the Atlantic. The first to arrive was the 700-ton "Sirius" which had taken just eighteen days to make her epochal voyage; twelve hours later the "Great Western," nearly twice her size, steamed into port, smoke billowing in great clouds from her single funnel, only fifteen days out of Bristol. The city went wild. Throngs of excited visitors boarded the two vessels and the newspapers were filled with glowing accounts of what this miraculous conquest of the Atlantic by steam meant for the future.

Philip Hone noted the advent of the transatlantic steamship in his famous diary:

> Everybody is so enamored of it that for a while it will supersede the New York packets—the noblest vessels that ever floated in the merchant service. Our countrymen, 'studious of change and pleased with novelty,' will rush forward to visit the shores of Europe instead of resorting to Virginia or Saratoga Springs; and steamers will continue to be the fashion until some more dashing adventurer of the go-ahead tribe shall demonstrate the practicality of balloon navigation, and gratify their impatience on a voyage *over*, and not *upon*, the blue waters in two days instead of as many weeks.

There was greater validity to this prediction than the rather skeptical Hone realized, and events were immediately to confirm the forward rush to visit Europe by means of the new vessels. Both the "Sirius" and the "Great Western" were to obtain easily a full complement of passengers for their return trip, and their successful voyages promptly inspired a fierce rivalry between newly formed American and British steamship companies in this promising field of ocean transportation. By 1850 two major lines, the Cunard Company and the American-owned Collins Line, were operating little fleets of fast-sailing "liners" on a regular weekly service between New York and Liverpool. The Inman Line had also introduced a number of relatively fast and comfortable ships on this same run, and other services were available to French and German ports. In such circumstances the number of transatlantic passengers increased in midcentury from perhaps 5000 a year to anywhere from 25,000 to 30,000.

Among the most enthusiastic of New Yorkers to hail the new era inaugurated by the "Sirius" and the "Great Western," was James Gordon Bennett, the jaunty and irrepressible editor of the New York *Herald*. After attending a gala reception aboard the "Sirius," he recorded his conviction that by linking the New World and the Old so closely, the steamship would end all petty jealousies between nations and foster a mutual love and respect among peoples everywhere. It would also serve to inspire, Bennett continued in his rhapsodic prose, "a generous emulation in the onward march of mind, genius, enterprise and energy towards the perfectability of man."

His vision of the future may have appeared, even in 1838, to have been somewhat extravagant, but his interest in the conquests of steam was not merely rhetorical. He promptly engaged passage on the "Sirius" as a special ambassador of goodwill to Europe, commenting without undue modesty that he did not suppose any person would doubt his capacity to fill this important role.

There was once again great excitement when the "Sirius" (she was followed six days later by the "Great Western") took her departure. From his vantage point on the deck of the outgoing steamer, Bennett described the crowds massed on the waterfront— "the flags—the ladies—the music—the smiles—the shouts—the bonnets—the petticoats—the pretty faces—the white handkerchiefs." In a final message to the *Herald* sent ashore by the pilot, he did not touch upon the glories of steam navigation nor upon the dawn of the new era in commercial expansion and world fellowship. It was a very brief message indeed:

44

The steamships that made up the fleets so soon put into operation by the Cunard Company and the Collins Line (continuing to carry sail to supplement their power-driven paddle wheels) made the transatlantic passage in about the same time as had the "Sirius" and the "Great Western"; that is, from fifteen to eighteen days. This was a good deal faster than anything the regular sailing packets could ever anticipate. It did not equal the amazing runs of the magnificent clipper ships of this same era, crossing the Atlantic under their great clouds of billowing canvas in twelve and thirteen days, but they were cargo ships rather than passenger vessels. And even the clippers' records were soon to fall as new steamers began to report passages of nine and ten days—half the *average* time of the regular sailing ships.

While the greater speed of the steamships had to be acknowledged, grave doubts were felt as to their safety. It remained to be seen whether they could outride heavy storms, and even more important, how they could cope with the new hazards of possible boiler explosions and uncontrollable fires. Time was to demonstrate the general dependability of steamships (the Cunard Company was not to lose a single passenger or piece of mail until the sinking of the "Lusitania" in 1915!), but the misfortunes of some of the steamship lines in the 1840's and 1850's provided considerable substance for popular anxiety.

The "President," an ambitious 2386-ton ship built by the British and American Steam Navigation Company which had sponsored the voyage of the "Sirius," was lost at sea with all hands only a year after her launching in 1840. She was last seen by a Black Baller in a heavy sea between Nantucket and the Banks, "pitching and laboring tremendously." Six years later the little "Sirius" herself, which had been taken off the Atlantic run, struck a reef on the Irish coast and went down with nineteen lives lost; and soon afterwards two ships of the Inman Line, the "City of Glasgow" and the "City of Philadelphia," were total losses. The former disappeared without trace on an Atlantic crossing, and the latter was wrecked off Cape Hatteras on her maiden voyage. The two greatest sea tragedies of midcentury, however, were suffered by the Collins Line which in its emphasis upon speed, as contrasted with the more cautious operations of the Cunard Line, ran grave risks. The "Arctic" collided with a small French steamer in 1854 and sank with the loss of 322 lives, including the wife, son, and daughter of the line's owner. Two years later the "Pacific," another fast ship, was lost at sea without any survivors under circumstances never fully known, but suggesting that she must have hit an iceberg.

"What becomes of the whole theory of progress," asked the New York *Tribune* as news of these disasters at sea and other travel accidents piled up, "when men approaching or leaving, or resting in this metropolitan City of the United States, have little more security than among the nomadic tribes of the desert? Is this an exaggeration? Look at our steamers—look at our railroads —look at our streets.... May we not accept the old average of uncertainties and vibrate between crib and coffin with a less menacing swing in life's pendulum?"

If risk for a time warred with speed in the development of the steamship, there was never any question of the greater convenience and comfort of the new means of crossing the Atlantic. Far roomier and more luxurious passenger accommodations combined with the shorter length of the crossing to give an entirely new character to the ocean voyage. While the steamships long retained many of the characteristics of the sailing packets they were replacing, they gradually began to take on more and more the features of "floating hotels." The Collins Line was proudly advertising in the 1850's that the transatlantic voyage was no longer an ordeal, but a pleasant two weeks' excursion.

So far as costs were concerned, the first steamships charged rates that were about the equivalent of those of the sailing packets. The owners of the "Sirius" advertised cabin fare for her return voyage to England at $140 including wine, while the "Great Western" charged $145. Something over a decade later the fare for the new Collins ships was $150. The rates were usually somewhat higher for the westward crossing, and with increasing competition there began to be much more variation, but it was not until the advent of the first screw-propelled steamships in the late 1850's that fares appreciably declined.

These were still cabin or first-class fares, but some steamships also began to offer, at considerably lower rates, second-class accommodations that were reasonably comfortable, or at least much more so than the old steerage. The differentiation in the fares aboard such ships might range from $160 first-class to $80 for the second cabin.

The most popular ships for Americans in midcentury were the four new vessels of the Collins Line: the "Atlantic," the fastest ship afloat; her companion ship the "Baltic" which was later to carry supplies for the relief of Fort Sumter; and the two ill-fated vessels which were lost at sea—the "Arctic" and the "Pacific." Skepticism was widespread for a time as to the ability of these new liners to compete successfully with the Cunarders. Their splendid performance, however, soon led even the British to hail them as "the finest vessels in the world," ships representing to a wonderful degree "the absolute poetry of motion." Their acknowledged superiority to the Cunarders provoked *Punch* to satirical verse:

> *A steamer of the Collins Line*
> *A Yankee Doodle notion*
> *Has also quickest cut the brine*
> *Across the Atlantic Ocean*
>
> *And British agents, no way slow*
> *Her merits to discover,*
> *Have been and bought her—just to tow*
> *The Cunard packets over!*

The Collins liners were wooden ships of around 3000 tons burden, with an over-all length averaging 300 feet and a 45-foot beam; their paddle wheels were 36 feet high and driven by engines of an indicated 2000 horse power. They had two masts, a rather short, dumpy funnel, and their sides were painted black with a single dark red line. Each ship could accommodate from 160 to 220 passengers and carried a crew of about 150, including 30 to 40 servants. The two main saloons were 67 feet by 20 feet (nearly three times the size of the old sailing packets' single cabin), and while the staterooms were still very small by modern standards,

47

they were a great improvement over those of earlier ships. Passengers who had not crossed the Atlantic before often complained that they were no more than close, low-ceilinged closets; more experienced travelers spoke of them as relatively light and airy. The ships were steamheated, lighted by lamps, and had a system of bells for summoning the stewards.

The principal saloon in each ship, elaborately furnished with exotic woodwork, rich carpets, upholstered sofas and chairs, and marble-topped tables, had a general air of elegance, enhanced by a multitude of mirrors and gilt chandeliers, that might have put the most fashionable hotels to shame. Not as ornate as the lounge but still very tastefully decorated, was the dining saloon, with racks suspended over the tables to hold glasses. An added facility to meet the complaints of lady passengers was a smoking room amply equipped with the most handsome spittoons.

The passengers aboard the Collins liners appear to have been generally enthusiastic. They were immensely impressed by their furnishings—"very elegant—rich enough for a nobleman's villa," wrote the eminent Yale scientist, Benjamin Silliman, sailing on the "Baltic" in 1851; and John Overton Choules, aboard the "Arctic" with his party of boys in 1855, described her as of "vast size and splendid accommodations." There was general agreement (before two of them were lost at sea!) that these ships were "the safest and most commodious sea-boats in the world."

The transatlantic voyagers also thoroughly approved the elegant meals, with their wide variety of dishes, finding them quite as well prepared as at the best hotels. It was no longer necessary to pen livestock on deck or keep chickens in the lifeboats; fresh meat was packed in ice. One traveler (his views have been echoed down the years) noted that "the table is only too rich and abundant." The busy schedule of frequent meals and snacks was already a tradition: breakfast from eight-thirty until ten, lunch at twelve, dinner at four, tea and coffee at seven, with the steward always available to dispense his plentiful supplies of soda water, cider, ale, wine, and stronger drinks.

Occasionally accounts of this phase of shipboard life recall memories of the old days of packet ships, for not all the new steamers were as modern and well-equipped as the Collins liners.

Harriet Beecher Stowe, crossing in 1853 for what was to prove a great triumphal tour of Europe (she had published *Uncle Tom's Cabin* the year before) described in her *Sunny Memories of Foreign Lands* a very melancholy, sad-eyed cook whom she watched at his tasks from a sheltered spot in the lee of the smoke stack. "Now I see him resignedly stuffing a turkey," she wrote, "now compounding a sauce, or mournfully making little ripples in the crust of a tart; but all is done under an evident sense that it is of no use trying." The consequences of these sad labors, however, did not belie the general consensus that shipboard meals were usually very good—"mighty rounds of beef, vast saddles of mutton, and the whole tribe of meats in general, come on in a superior style." Mrs. Stowe complained only of the coffee.

Bathing facilities remained very primitive on most midcentury steamers and as in the days of sail, a sequestered spot on the upper deck generally constituted the "bathing room." Even as late as 1870 one Cunarder, the "Tarifa," had no baths and only two toilets. Moreover, when her passengers complained on their arrival at Liverpool of a number of other minor inconveniences, including the lack of any table napkins in the dining saloon, they got little satisfaction. They were told by the line's officials, one of them later recalled, that "going to sea is a hardship, that the Cunard Company did not undertake to make anything else out of it, and that if people wanted to wipe their mouths at a ship's table, they could use their pocket handkerchiefs." The Cunard Line undoubtedly felt that its outstanding record for safety compensated for any possible lack of comfort aboard its ships.

The most important innovation in steamship construction in midcentury was the introduction of screw-propelled and iron-built vessels. Nevertheless, style and comfort still made the greatest appeal to passengers. In 1858 the North German Lloyd launched what it described as the luxury liner "Bremen." She was a 2674-ton ship carrying her passengers in three classes—first class, 60, second class, 110, and steerage 400. In addition to many other novelties, her sponsors proudly advertised two bathrooms!

Thirteen years later, in 1871, still more modern advances were initiated when the White Star Line's crack 3708-ton "Oceanic" entered the transatlantic service. She was not only screw-propelled and iron-built, but from the passengers' point of view had an even greater advantage over all her rivals in that the dining saloon and first-class cabins had been moved from the stern to the middle of the ship. Among her other more distinctive features were an especially elegant main lounge with two coal-burning fireplaces, marble mantels, and a Broadwood piano; individual chairs in the dining saloon in place of the usual long benches; a ladies' boudoir and a bridal suite; and fresh and salt running water in the staterooms.

One other very special ship of these years was the gigantic "Great Eastern," which was built in England and made her maiden voyage in 1860. Her 19,000 tons and nearly 700-foot length made her more than twice the size of any other steamship of that day, and indeed her tonnage would not be equaled for another forty years. But this first leviathan proved to be an unhappy liability for her over-optimistic owners. Although she could carry 4000 passengers, it never proved possible to attract more than a fraction of this impressive total. On her first voyage she carried only forty-six. They had a marvelous time playing skittles on her long decks, wandering about her immense public rooms, and listening to the ship's orchestra. But while the "Great Eastern" created a sensation on her arrival in New York, being visited by nearly 150,000 people at fifty cents a head, no more than sixty-eight passengers were aboard on her return voyage to England.

One suggestion for the use of this gigantic ship was to sail her to Portland, Maine, and while she remained at anchor in that city, to allow her passengers to make excursions in the United States and Canada. "What in the name of Malthus and Cotton Mather," the *Scientific American* commented on this scheme, "would she do there? Why, in two trips to Europe, if her passenger lists were full, she would take away the whole population of that enterprising city, leaving its streets as deserted as Pompeii."

The "Great Eastern" was obviously much too large for the times and could not be operated profitably. She was soon diverted from the transatlantic passenger service (although on one occasion she was specially chartered to take tourists to a Paris exposition), and performed the most useful function of her erratic career in laying the transatlantic cable in 1865. Her ultimate fate was to be permanently docked as a popular amusement hall.

The patterns of shipboard life aboard such successful ships as the Collins liners and the Cunarders were beginning by the 1850's to fall into increasingly familiar grooves. While the deck space aboard a paddle-wheel steamer remained somewhat limited, it was much more extensive than on any sailing packet. There was plenty of room for deck chairs (which at this period the passengers themselves provided), and for the usual shipboard occupations of sitting in the sun, reading, talking, knitting. Many diarists nostalgically described the long, lazy hours of doing nothing whatsoever as the ship ploughed steadily ahead, its great paddle wheels churning the endless sea. Those who wanted exercise could even then try the deck sports which have become such an integral part of shipboard life—"shovel-board," quoits, and various other games. One amusement, long since given up, was helping the officers sort whatever mail the ship might be carrying.

Apart from the customary card playing or chess, evenings aboard ship offered auctions on the day's run, occasional dancing, the ship's concert when money would be raised for indigent seamen, and the captain's dinner, with its toasts in the champagne generously provided by the steward at the ship's expense. There was also in the midnineteenth century, as in later years, the smoking room crowd, closely attached to the wine and spirits that so effectively helped its members combat the voyage's monotony.

Crossing one time on the "Great Western," that same Reverend John A. Clark who found among his fellow passengers "a pleasant, sober, clerical group," was quite shocked at some aspects of shipboard life. Going on deck one evening when the sea was particularly smooth, he discovered "a gay company, full of wild merriment, tracking the mazes of the dance." It did not seem quite proper. "Above us the vaulted sky, and beneath the calm, unruffled ocean," Clark wrote to his congregation. "The ocean and the sky so calm, so sweet, so beautiful, seemed written all over with the goodness and glory of God. But alas, God seemed not to be in the thoughts of that gay company."

And even more alarming was what might go on in the grand saloon whose two long tables, running from one end of the room to the other, were crowded with tumblers and wine glasses. "You could not but groan in spirit," Clark lamented, "to see the oceans of Sherry, Champagne, and Hock—of Port, Madeira and Claret—

51

of ale, porter, brandy, whiskey, and gin—that are swallowed down."
And another time he even more grimly described the nightly scene
—"drinking, swearing, card-playing, loud laughing, cracking of
jokes, and sharp disputing . . ."

Another picture of shipboard life (among many other less
puritanic records than those of the traveling clergymen) may be
found in the letters and reminiscences of Julia Ward Howe, the
future champion of women's rights, who crossed the Atlantic in
1843 aboard a small Cunarder as the young bride of Samuel Gridley Howe. Described at the time as "a pretty bluestocking" who
dreamed in Italian and quoted French verse, Mrs. Howe was gay
and high-spirited, sometimes to the distress of her eighteen years
older and far more serious-minded husband. "I was grieved to see,"
we find her writing her sister on one occasion, "how much he
seemed pained at my frivolity." But there was no quenching what
she later recalled as "the mischief of which I was then full to over-
flowing."

There was aboard their ship another newly married couple,
Mr. and Mrs. Horace Mann, of educational fame, and also Jacob
Abbott, of the *Rollo* books. This little group became close friends,
but while Mrs. Howe enjoyed their company, she also went her
own way. She loved to walk the decks by herself—"tumbling all
over the ship, singing at the top of my voice," as she wrote her
sister; and somewhat to the distress of her companions, she was
enthusiastic over the captain's dinner, with its free serving of
champagne and all the customary toasts. This occasion indeed inspired her to stage a mock celebration in the ladies' cabin where
comparable toasts—but this time the beverage was tea—were
drunk in honor of the ship's cow, and of a bewildered stewardess
for whom the future author of "The Battle Hymn of the Republic" composed some appropriate verses:

> *God save our Mrs. Bean,*
> *Best woman ever seen*
> *God save Mrs. Bean*
> *God bless her gown and cap*
> *Four guineas in her lap,*
> *Keep her from all mishap*
> *God save Mrs. Bean!*

There was another side to shipboard life, however—somewhat less enjoyable. Far from having done away with seasickness, the steamships' paddle wheels often made the motion of the ship, even in moderate weather, more violent than that of sailing ships. A horrible roll sometimes served to lift one of the great wheels completely out of the water. Moreover, the ship's engines added a new ingredient to the various smells afflicting all vessels, contributing still further to the ocean travelers' woes.

The author of *Uncle Tom's Cabin* soon discovered on her voyage that "ship life is not at all fragrant":

> Particularly on a steamer there is a most mournful combination of grease, steam, onions, and dinners in general, either past, present, or to come, which floating invisibly in the atmosphere strongly predispose to that disgust of existence .... which makes every heaving billow, every white-capped wave, the ship, the people, the sight, taste, sound and smell of everything a matter of inexpressible loathing!

Mrs. Howe also fell victim to the usual malaise, but fighting it valiantly with brandy and water, recovered sooner than her companions and took occasion to describe graphically the ladies' cabin whose still grievously distressed inmates were mournfully calling upon the stewardess for aid and succor. It was "strewn with sick ladies and grannies of both sexes," Mrs. Howe wrote, "and .... ever resounds with cries of Mrs. Bean! Mrs. Bean! soda water! Mrs. Bean soup! Mrs. Bean gruel with brandy in it! Mrs. Bean hold my head! Mrs. Bean wag my chaws!"

Even Ralph Waldo Emerson, a frequent transatlantic voyager, once admitted that he had been an unhappy victim of seasickness and spent hours of "meditations in the berth." But like most passengers he eventually recovered, and walking vigorously about the deck, found his appetite wholly restored. "What is a passenger?" he wrote. "He is a much enduring man who bends under the load of his leisure. He fawns upon the captain, reveres the mate, but his eye follows the steward."

Whether the voyage was smooth and uneventful, or rough and storm-tossed, there was never any question of the delight with which land was first sighted. Fifteen days or more in what were at best very closely confined quarters gave a tremendous zest to the idea of finally getting ashore and feeling firm land underfoot. The sea breezes could never make a steamer completely fragrant, nor could there be any real escape from the queasy roll induced by paddle wheels. Moreover, for most of the voyagers in midcentury, the Europe toward which they were heading was a wholly new and exciting experience. Their sense of personal discovery as land loomed over the eastern horizon had a tremendous imaginative impact.

"None but those who have experienced it," Irving had written in his *Sketch-Book*, "can form an idea of the delicious throng of sensations which rush into an American's bosom when he first comes in sight of Europe.... It is the land of promise, teeming with everything of which his childhood has heard, or on which his studious years have pondered."

V. THE WAYS OF CONTINENTAL TRAVEL

"Nothing but the consideration that we were traveling for pleasure," Mrs. Stowe noted on one occasion during her continental tour, "could for a moment have reconciled us to such inconveniences."

Once the transatlantic voyagers had disembarked, these inconveniences were indeed ever-present as compared with the luxurious ease of modern travel: slow, crowded coaches and diligences; hotels and inns that all too often were barren of any real comfort, sometimes dirty and ill-kept; and maddening delays and vexations upon crossing the seemingly innumerable national frontiers at a time when Europe was composed of so many petty states. Yet the eager and curious visitors from the United States dauntlessly made their way across the continent with unflagging energy and stoical determination.

Neither travel agencies nor guided tours were yet available to smooth the tourist's path. Thomas Cook was actually on the eve of his memorable career for it was in the 1850's that he started managing local excursions in England and became so imbued with the tourist spirit, as he later wrote, that "I began to contemplate foreign trips." In the meantime, however, Americans unfamiliar with the customs and languages of Europe (as they almost all were) often employed couriers, who made all their travel arrangements, or, if they could not afford such an expense, relied on the local *valets de place*. Neither arrangement was very satisfactory, as sadly related in many journals. Sharp and frequent are the complaints against the shortcomings of all types of European guides. One irate traveler dismissed the whole system of couriers as "this essential humbug."

55

A number of guidebooks had already been published. The most universally used was "Murray's infallible hand-book," first published in England in 1836. A few years later the even more famous Baedekers (although not printed in English until 1861) began to appear with all their wealth of meticulously detailed information. A pioneering American guide was a little volume brought out in 1838 by George P. Putnam—*The Tourist in Europe*. Although it purported to be no more than a personal record of the author's own trip abroad ("let me remind you again, my dear ———, that these rough words are not intended to edify any one but yourself"), it described tours, methods of transportation, and places to stay, together with practical advice on passports, visas, and customs regulations.

The Tourist in Europe suggested—and other travel accounts emphasized even more strongly—that crossing national frontiers demanded infinite patience. The red tape was seemingly endless, passport and visa regulations were being constantly changed without notice, and the American accustomed to the unrestricted travel in his own country felt himself, in the phrase of one discouraged tourist, to be in "a vast prison" from which there was no escape. "Of all the rascally systems ever devised for the plunder, discomfort and annoyance of travelers," exploded J. Ross Browne, writing of his experiences in *An American Family in Germany*, "the most essentially rascally is the passport system of Continental Europe."

The frustrating inconvenience of customs inspections, especially when all the baggage had to be awkwardly unloaded and then loaded again on stage coach or diligence, is vividly described in the lively articles with which N. Parker Willis, journalist and poet, first delighted the readers of the *New York Mirror* and then published in book form as *Pencillings by the Way*. In recounting his experiences in crossing the frontier between Switzerland and France, he wrote:

> Four trunks, carpet-bags, hat-boxes, dressing cases, and *portfeuilles* were . . . . dismounted and critically examined —every dress and article unfolded; shirts, cravats, unmentionables and all, and searched through by two ruffians, whose fingers were no improvement upon the labors of the

washerwoman. . . . We were then requested to unbutton our coats, and begging pardon for the liberty, these curious gentlemen thrust their hands into our pockets, felt in our bosoms, pantaloons, and shoes, examined our hats, and even eyed our 'pet curls' very earnestly, in the expectation of finding us crammed with Geneva jewelry.

In making their European tours before the advent of railways, the more wealthy Americans might, in the tradition of eighteenth-century travel, have their own private coaches. Most of them, however, were dependent upon public means of conveyance, and this of course meant the stage coach in England, and on the continent the more awkward and cumbersome diligence.

Americans delighted in the English stage coach. This stylish vehicle, so familiar through prints and literary description, apparently lived up to all expectations. Travelers vied in their glowing praise of its clean lines and polished woodwork; the beautifully groomed horses; the dignified coachman in drab breeches, white-topped boots, and silk hat seated magisterially on the box; the smartly dressed guard with his bugle; and the always polite and courteous postboys.

On the continent, however, coaching was a different matter altogether. The French diligence appears to have been the most complicated vehicle ever devised for the transportation of man. Every traveler, with varying degrees of awe or consternation, wrote that it could not possibly be described—and then tried his very best to do so.

The diligence was a huge, unwieldy contraption weighing from five to six tons with as many as five separate compartments: the *coupe*, with three places, in the front section; the *interieur*, or major compartment, with six places; the *rotonde*, also with six places, in the rear; a *banquette* just behind the coachman's seat, usually with accommodations for three, and finally a large area on top for the baggage. Looking somewhat like three coaches built on the base of a single carriage with a cabriolet on top of it all, according to one traveler's description, this appalling vehicle could thus carry up to eighteen passengers, together with a great mountain of trunks, suitcases, and carry-alls. It was usually drawn by six horses, roughly tied together rather than carefully harnessed, and driven by a haughty *conducteur,* with one or sometimes two ragged postillions riding the off animals.

It took considerable skill to handle a diligence, but accidents appear to have been rare and passengers complained rather of the dull monotony of driving "on, on, on, day and night, night and day." For while there were frequent halts to change horses, the diligence made no leisurely stops for the convenience of passengers, whether for meals or sleeping. Moreover, it was almost invariably crowded ("twelve persons packed into a box not large enough for a cow," one unhappy victim recorded); the seats were hard and uncomfortable, and the windows in every compartment were always kept tightly shut.

William Preston was one American who in spite of all its short-comings nevertheless preferred travel by diligence to travel by coach. The English passengers aboard the latter, he commented, were "quiet, clean and glum, each sitting bolt upright with an umbrella standing between his legs," whereas on a French diligence there was "much drinking of wine, eating of cake . . . infinite fun and laughter."

Another diligence enthusiast in later years was the Reverend Charles Beecher, who accompanied his sister, Mrs. Stowe, in 1853:

> I had the idea that a diligence was a rickety, slow-moving, antedeluvian nondescript, toiling patiently along over impassable roads at a snail's pace. Judge of my astonishment at finding it a full-blooded, vigorous monster, of unscrupulous railway momentum and imperturbable equipoise of mind. Down the macadamized slopes we thundered at a prodigious pace; up the hills we trotted with six horses, three abreast; madly through the little towns we burst, like a whirlwind, crashing across the pebbled streets, and out upon the broad, smooth road again.

As the reference to railway momentum suggests, a wholly new means of transportation was by this time beginning to encroach on the preserves of stage coach and diligence, and was soon to replace them altogether just as the transatlantic steamships were taking the place of the old sailing packets. On his tour in 1851, Benjamin Silliman had the unique experience of making a trip between Paris and Dijon in which railroad and diligence were neatly combined.

58

The passengers first rode from hotel to railway station in a diligence. From a platform at the station, their vehicle was then lifted from its wheels by a hoisting machine (which Silliman describes as rather like the old-fashioned hay scales in New England), and transferred with its entire load of passengers and baggage intact to a railway truck. The entire party then proceeded comfortably in this *railway-diligence* until some five hours later they reached the end of the railroad line. The body of the diligence was then taken off the railway truck and replaced on carriage wheels. New horses were harnessed, the driver cracked his whip, and the diligence was off. They now drove merrily the rest of the day and through the following night, reaching Dijon—213 miles from Paris—at five in the morning, some twenty hours after they had first taken off. Silliman (he was seventy-two at the time) greatly enjoyed this novel trip and further reported—an indication of the indestructibility of this generation of tourists—that after a quick breakfast and the very briefest rest, "we were soon in condition to be active again."

The first railroad line in Europe, linking Manchester and Liverpool, was built in 1830; shortly afterwards Paris and Versailles were joined by rail, and Germany soon built its pioneer line between Nuremberg and Furth. The further development of railroads was relatively slow, however. Not until the mid-1840's was England, and then somewhat later the continent, swept by the "railway mania" which was gradually to revolutionize European travel as it was simultaneously beginning to transform that in the United States.

The reports of the first passengers on the European railroads varied considerably. One of them who rode on England's original line between London and Manchester spoke of the fearfully rapid motion, fields, houses, and trees rushing by, and confessed that the delight which such a scene might have inspired was dimmed by "the feeling of danger which came over us, as we shot, by the power of steam along these high embankments." Another, more sophisticated, tourist considered railway travel unprofitable and stupid in comparison with the more leisurely coaching. By mid-century, however, railroad service had so improved that Americans generally were praising the European trains—their speed and convenience, the efficiency of operation, and their comfortable coaches. An enthusiast of such travel wrote glowingly of going from Paris to Geneva "by the pleasantest of cars, over the smoothest of rails," and was then even more thrilled by the railroads in Germany where one would "roll on at a most agreeable pace from one handsome station house to another."

Italy was very slow in building railroads and in the pre-railway days it had its own system of transportation somewhat different from that of either England or France. It was customary for the traveler of means to conclude a special contract for a *vettura*, or privately-owned carriage, whereby the owner-driver assumed all the responsibilities, including expenses on route, for getting the contracting party from one city to another. One American describes a journey between Rome and Florence in such a *vettura*, drawn by six horses, that took five days.

If there continued to be variations in the methods of transportation, even greater differences existed in respect to the available hotel accommodations in England and on the continent. Again the Americans were more favorably disposed toward England. There was not only the immense advantage of a common language, but on every count travel seemed easier and more comfortable. This was not so much because of the hotels in the major cities, those in London for example perhaps being no better than those in Paris, but because of the country inns whose pleasant atmosphere appealed greatly to all transatlantic visitors.

They often described the English inns, indeed, in almost ecstatic terms—the homelike dining and reading room, with its blazing coal fire, damask curtains, and Turkey red carpet; the clean and comfortable bedrooms, and the air of cheerful and friendly hospitality which pervaded the entire establishment. Americans in these midnineteenth-century years were also impressed by the courteous service of the attendants and the alacrity with which the waiter, summoned by bell rope, sought to satisfy the traveler's every want. Quite often the more democratic-minded described the English servants as too obsequious, but this would not appear to have affected a grateful acceptance of their service.

Opinions on the food served at either hotels or inns in England were not always so favorable. One traveler arriving at Dover after a continental tour was grievously disappointed to be faced with "a leathery beef-steak burned and half cold—three small potatoes, and as many green beans as could have been taken up in a single table-spoon. The desert to this was a very sour plum-tart, hardly eatable." But another lauded the "comfortable suppers" at another inn—sole and cutlets, beefsteak and potatoes, sherry and port served at candle-lit tables before an open fire. A third happily recalled a typical lunch with "a cold round of beef, juicy and tender; ham, perfectly cured, delicious bread and butter, or, indeed, what you will, and all so neatly served."

Across the Channel there could be no assurance of comfortable accommodations except in the major cities. Paris had a number of hotels which were beginning to adapt themselves to the somewhat peculiar habits of English and American travelers. The Hotel Choiseul on the Rue St. Honoré and the Hotel Meurice on the Rue de Rivoli were especially popular, and by midcentury the number of Americans they had entertained was legion. On the other hand, the provincial inns in France were generally condemned as unfit for anyone. Since the diligences traveled by night as well as by day, sharply reducing the demand for overnight lodgings as compared to conditions in rural England, little effort appears to have been made to please travelers. Americans who happened to stop in villages or small towns frequently expressed their astonishment that, for all the boasted refinements of France, the inns along even well-traveled roads should remain in what they described as "semi-barbarous conditions."

French food was another matter altogether. Almost all the diarists seemed by their comments more than ready to accept the dictum of one of them that "no cookery could ever equal that of France." There was glowing appreciation of the lavish *table d'hôte* dinners served at the hotels, and even greater praise for the epicurean meals of such already famous Paris restaurants as Vevour, the Café de Paris, the Café Anglais, and the Trois Frères Provenceaux. ("My verdict is for Vevour," James Russell Lowell stated flatly.) Americans also liked the more modest *déjeuners à la fourchette*, with their chops, omelets, potatoes and wine, and some among them, though by no means all, were happy with the *petits déjeuners*, enjoying the delicious *café au lait* and *petits pains* served with neatly stamped pats of fresh butter. The New Englanders faced with a meal once described by Emerson as consisting of no more than "a certain number of mouthfuls," were apt to recall nostalgically the more ample breakfasts with which they were accustomed to start the day. It should be noted, however, that for all his want of enthusiasm over the *petit déjeuner*, Emerson not only enjoyed French food but found one aspect of dining that especially delighted him. "What a luxury it is," he wrote, "to have a cheap wine for the national beverage."

Italy perhaps offered the poorest travel accommodations in all Europe. The major cities had seemingly impressive hotels, one-time palaces with great high-ceilinged rooms embellished with carved woodwork, gilt ornamentation, heavy tapestries, and innumerable paintings and mirrors. However, they hardly lived up to the promise of such grandeur. The rooms were not noted for cleanliness, the service was poor or nonexistent, and the food apparently left a great deal to be desired. And whatever might be said about the city hotels, the inns in the smaller towns and villages were execrable. Horace Greeley once wrote that between Civita Vecchia and Rome there was not a single tavern that would be considered tolerable even in the least civilized parts of Arkansas and Texas.

The greatest annoyance, in the hotels quite as much as the inns, was the prevalence of fleas and bedbugs. Every traveler complained of what appears to have been an invariable, inescapable, and acutely distressing feature of Italian hotel life. "Of the Perugian beds," wrote one long-suffering tourist, "I may say that if they are gloomy, it is not for want of life."

The countries of northern Europe, not surprisingly, had a far better reputation for the comfort and cleanliness of their hotels and inns, and almost every visitor also noted their friendly, welcoming atmosphere. It was already agreed that in such matters Switzerland was without a peer. Its hotel-keepers catered especially to English and American tourists, providing many services not to be found in other countries. One happy visitor, for example, noted that Switzerland was the only place outside America where one could get cream with one's coffee.

The author of an anonymous travel book of the 1850's— *Doré, by a Stroller*—gives an intriguing picture of the daily scene at a Swiss resort hotel with the carriages and omnibuses arriving and departing, the *garçons* strapping and unstrapping the baggage, and the general hum of activity among the tourists, mountain climbers, and other guests of all nationalities. "The English noises prevail," he wrote; "in fact a Swiss hotel in midsummer is either English—or Bedlam." He was critical of inns that tried—unsuccessfully—to ape the big city hotels, but he found those that preserved their simplicity, completely delightful.

Except at some of the larger hotels and popular tourist resorts, language of course was always a major problem. Moreover, it appears that the promise of "English spoken" was not always an unmixed blessing even in these very early days of foreign travel. "The *maitre d'hotel* here spoke English," one tourist noted in his diary, "and we were very much cheated, two facts which are said to be concomitant." The increasing number of both American and English tourists nevertheless encouraged more and more English-speaking among those catering to their needs. By the late 1850's an American was said to be able to travel from London to Vienna and find his language spoken everywhere.

The minor difficulties and petty tribulations singled out in diary and journal during these days have a most familiar ring. The American tourists were continually annoyed by the ubiquitous and insistent guides who hung about every museum, cathedral, and public monument. They were plagued by swarms of beggars, especially in Italy, who followed them wherever they went. They felt frustrated and victimized by the incessant demands upon their purse for tips and gratuities.

Quite naturally—then as now—they often missed things to which they were accustomed at home and found it difficult to adjust themselves to foreign ways. The hotels did not have bathrooms (though this was often true in America as well as Europe); the general lack of soap was underscored by a midcentury comment that the Hotel Meurice in Paris was the only place on the continent where it was available; and a most common complaint is suggested by a discouraged journal entry—in the 1840's—noting that the American fondness for ice water seemed to be "rather mal-apropos in Europe." Some years later Phillips Brooks was more explicit. "The worst thing to me about this traveling," he wrote disconsolately from Bonn on October 2, 1865, "is that you can't drink water. . . . I would give a dollar for a pitcher of ice water tonight."

There were frequent laments in proverbial tourist style about expenses—the high charges for meals and accommodations, the seemingly exorbitant fees for guides, the extortions of coachmen and omnibus drivers, and the general propensity of all those dealing with tourists—especially American tourists—to consider them legitimate prey. But continental travel was not actually as costly —on a relative basis—as the expenses of the transatlantic voyage.

An inclusive figure for a seven months trip given in *The Tourist in Europe* was $821, but a more intriguing approach to the question of midcentury travel costs is found in *Rollo in Paris*. Mr. George, talking with young Rollo, rebukes his charge for wanting to go fishing in the Seine. Such an idea is preposterous, Mr. George says indignantly, for every hour spent in Europe is costing Rollo a dollar. He then explains this very carefully. The round-trip transatlantic fare is $300 and other expenses for a hundred days' tour approximate $500—an over-all average of $8 a day for the time actually spent abroad. Since only eight hours are available each day "for going about and seeing what is to be seen," Mr. George continues, there can hardly be any justification for wasting any one of these dollar-hours in such a frivolous pursuit as fishing. A crestfallen Rollo could not but agree.

It was possible to make a less expensive trip. The second-class accommodations on the newer steamships were reasonably comfortable (although there was nothing like tourist class), and some savings could always be made in continental travel. But it was difficult for the ordinary tourist to cut his expenses very much, and he did not have the opportunities to economize that were to develop in later years. One adventurous young man, forerunner of the countless students who have in more recent years gone abroad on a shoestring, was Bayard Taylor, the future poet and diplomat. In 1844 he took what passed for second-class on a sailing packet, being required to provide his own bedding and food, and then walked through Europe "with knapsack and staff." He had almost no money and relied entirely upon commissions that he hoped to receive from letters sent back to the *United States Gazette* and the *Saturday Evening Post*. Traveling for the most part on foot, he stayed at the cheapest inns and limited all his other expenses to the barest minimum. "You may live on a crust of bread for a day," he wrote dramatically, "but lower than four cents for a bed you cannot go."

At the close of nearly two years wandering, a tour that took him through Germany, Italy, Switzerland, France, and England, with long stays in such cities as London, Paris, Frankfurt, and Florence, Taylor reported that his total expenses for the entire venture, including steamship passage, had been about $500. But his ability to make the usual cost of a few months tour cover two years of foreign residence had little relevancy for the average traveler. It was a journalistic stunt.

One further aspect of travel in the midnineteenth century comes as something of a surprise. In spite of their relatively small number—a handful in comparison with the hordes a hundred years later—Americans going abroad were already finding Europe crowded with fellow tourists. Contemporary articles warned that it was hard to escape being submerged in a tourist flood! One writer gave the explicit advice to anyone who really wanted to see Europe: "find out where your countrymen resort and do not go there."

Moreover, these travelers were taking on what has always been the lamentable coloration of tourists as seen by other tourists. There is hardly a diary or journal in which a somewhat smug writer does not scornfully criticize his compatriots for the way they are acting. In apparent confidence that his own behavior is above reproach, he finds that of everyone else thoroughly objectionable.

A few observers were even more critical of the tourists of other countries. One characterized the English swarming over the continent as "generally vulgar people." Another felt they were "the most disagreeable" of the tourist tribe. A third blamed them for introducing "expensive and corrupting" habits which were spoiling travel for everyone else. Americans generally, however, bore down hardest on their fellow countrymen.

They frowned upon the careless, ignorant, hurried manner of their sightseeing, the childish bragging of how much they had been able to do in a single day. Longfellow once wrote of having encountered a tourist for whom a Roman aqueduct, a Gothic cathedral, two or three churches, an ancient ruin or so, were "only a breakfast." They poked fun at the self-conscious Yankee who always sought to adapt himself to the fashions of whatever country he was visiting: "in Vienna he will wear a beard,—in France, a mustache,—in Spain, a cloak,—and in England a white cravat." They could at times be even more sarcastic or derogatory. The fastidious Charles Sumner, touring Europe in the 1830's as a very elegant young man, snobbishly wrote of his countrymen's "dirty shirts—their nasal conversations—their want of manner either of the scholar or the man of the world."

This was also the period when the most common criticism— of tourist by tourist—was leveled against the boastful spirit which led the American overseas to be forever declaring how far superior everything in his own country was to what he was seeing in Europe. A contributor to the *North American Review* wrote indignantly of those Americans who declared to anyone who would listen to them that the Rhine was no more than a brook compared to the Hudson, the Alps could not hold a candle to Niagara Falls, and that neither London nor Paris could offer anything comparable to New York's Fifth Avenue, Central Park, or Stewart's Department Store. "This is not an exaggeration," he commented irately. "Every educated American has been made to blush by this gasconade of his countrymen, if he is not driven to avoid them as he would the pestilence."

If such diatribes seem hard to understand at a time when American travelers were still largely restricted to the more cultivated and well-to-do classes, Alexis de Tocqueville's comment on the discomfiture of these very people on finding themselves not as greatly appreciated in Europe as they had expected may well be the explanation. They were not immune to the popular view at home that in comparison with the Universal Yankee Nation, Europe was but a patch on the earth's surface. They were driven somehow to reassure themselves of the greatness of a country which the Europeans so often seemed to disdain.

Margaret Fuller, writing of her European experiences during the 1840's in *At Home and Abroad*, carefully analyzed her traveling compatriots. She singled out "the servile American" who came to Europe to spend his money, seek social acclaim, and ape the Old World aristocracy; the "conceited American" who had no

knowledge of Europe whatsoever, ignorant, critical and boastful—
"the booby truant"; and finally "the thinking American" who was
honestly seeking out whatever was interesting and worthwhile,
neither cringing to aristocracy nor bragging about America.

There was astute observation—not only for the midnineteenth century but for other periods—in her comments. But whatever else may be said of American travelers in Europe in these
years, it may perhaps be safely assumed that each of them was
fully convinced as to where he stood in any such tourist classifica-
tion. He belonged to that more select group whose members were
with intelligence and perception making the most of their opportunities better to understand the Old World.

VI. THE GRAND TOUR

THE OUTLINES of the Grand Tour were well defined before the middle of the nineteenth century. There was first England, so often approached with what one traveler described as "a kind of thrill and pulsation of kindred." Then Paris. It was Thomas Gold Appleton, a wealthy, debonair Bostonian, who originated in the 1850's the phrase that Oscar Wilde was later to borrow: "Good Americans when they die go to Paris." And finally (apart from briefer ventures to Switzerland, Germany, and the Low Countries) the romantic glamor of Italy with its "remote, dreamlike, Arcadian charm." These were the phrases of the literary pilgrims, but they nevertheless reflected what would appear to have been the general tourist attitude toward the Old World. "The image of Italy," wrote George Hillard, a popular essayist, "dwells in our hearts like that of a woman we have loved."

As Americans rode for the first time from Liverpool to London through "the cultivated loveliness" of the English countryside, they found everything that Washington Irving had promised them —the accumulated treasures of age, the ruined castle and falling tower, the quaint peculiarities of ancient and local customs. They were intrigued no less by the picturesque villages, with their neatly thatched cottages than by the great country places whose houses might be distantly glimpsed through gateways in the ivy-covered walls that enclosed their wooded parks and shaded lawns. Journals and diaries reflected a joyous appreciation of these novel scenes— "impressed by vivid admiration on the living tablets of the mind" —that differed so greatly from those of the sparsely settled and wilder countryside of America.

London fascinated the tourists with its well-paved streets,

68

crowded with hansom cabs and omnibuses; the buildings superior even to those of New York; the elegant shops along Bond Street; and the wealth of restaurants, taverns, and coffee houses. They went to the Tower, the Houses of Parliament, the British Museum, the National Gallery, and Madame Tussaud's—"a charming cockney sight." They may have been hurried, but they were thorough. "We climbed towers, we descended into crypts," wrote one indefatigable sightseer; "we examined tombstones, we gazed upon mummies." Rare indeed was such an outburst as that which Caroline Kirkland, a popular Western writer describing her trip abroad in 1849, once allowed herself:

> We have walked through the British Museum with how little satisfaction! If one had the courage to omit such things, and come home with the honest confession that one had not seen them, how much fruitless labor would be spared.

The museum and the galleries still had no counterpart in American cities, however, and London could also offer theater which far outshone that of New York. In these midcentury years Charles Macready was the leading Shakespearean star; there were also Charles Kemble (and his daughter Fanny); Ellen Tree and Charles Keen; the ballet at Sadler's Wells; Fanny Essler and the great Taglioni among the dancers; and the incomparable Jenny Lind who in 1850 was to achieve an even greater triumph in the United States under the astute management of P. T. Barnum. Some among the Americans had never before seen a theatrical performance, restrained by the puritan inhibitions which were so easily shed in Europe.

It was perhaps Fanny Essler and Taglioni who evoked the most enthusiasm. There was the reputed exchange on the former's dancing between Emerson and Margaret Fuller:

> Margaret, this is poetry.
> Waldo, this is religion.

As for Taglioni, one rapt observer reported that she swam "in your eye like a curl of smoke." Another wrote that "her grace is God's beautiful gift," only to add: "But could not this grace be equally demonstrated with a skirt a few inches longer and rather less transparent?"

One performance none of the transatlantic visitors had ever witnessed was Queen Victoria making a royal progress through London streets, her coach glittering with gold, the horses splendidly caparisoned, outriders decked in showy livery and cocked hats. Americans might be highly scornful of kings and princes, but they could hardly identify England's queen, who in spite of all the trappings of royalty seemed to be such a comfortable, ordinary little woman, with tyranny and despotism. Certainly the opportunity to see so famous a personage was one which even the stoutest republican had no intention of missing.

The summer of 1851 provided a further attraction, drawing more tourists to London than ever before. England staged that year the "Great Exhibition" at the Crystal Palace—forerunner of so many international expositions—to celebrate the felicities the country was enjoying under Victoria's happy and benign rule. The Crystal Palace itself, arising from Hyde Park "like an exhalation, a magical illusion of the senses," was one of the wonders of the nineteenth century world. Horace Greeley and his rival editor of the *New York Times*, Henry Raymond, were alike in hailing its magnificence, the one characterizing it as "a fairy wonder," and the other declaring it surpassed "in elegance and splendor" anything of which he had ever dreamed. Even more ecstatic was the description given by Cleveland Coxe, one of the traveling clergymen:

> The crystal roof showered a soft daylight over the immense interior; the trees and curious plants gave it a cheerful and varied beauty; the eye bewildered itself in a maze of striking objects of luxury and taste; musical instruments, constantly playing, bewitched the ear, their tones blending from various distances and directions, in a kind of harmonious discord; fountains were gurgling and scattering their spray, like diamonds and pearls, and the rank and pride of England mixed with the auxiliar representatives of foreign states. . . .

For the American visitor there was nevertheless one most unhappy feature about the Crystal Palace. The exhibits from the United States showed up very badly—the object of "persistent and unsparing disparagement" in the British press—and were a source of self-conscious embarrassment. For while there were a great many of them (the United States standing fifth among the participating nations in the actual number of its offerings), they were entirely utilitarian. Ploughs and reaping machines, agricultural products, model railways, dental instruments, Indian rubber goods .... but little to suggest any interest in the arts and crafts which might disabuse Europeans of their firm conviction that the United States represented a wholly materialistic society, with no appreciation of the finer things of life.

Yet there was one exception to any such generalization on the character of the American exhibits. The Vermont-born Hiram Powers' "Greek Slave," an impressive statue which in later years was to be reproduced in countless little sugar-white alabaster models that adorned drawing-rooms throughout the land, created a sensation. There were those who on viewing the nude figure objected that "the subject is a sensual one, and does not appeal to any lofty sentiment," but the "Greek Slave" was nevertheless singled out in the very capital of Queen Victoria as the most admired of all the works of art at the Great Exhibition.

One further triumph was won by the United States this same summer which greatly encouraged the crestfallen American visitors so upset by the London newspapers' criticism of their country. The yacht "America" handsomely won the first international cup race.

While every tourist visited the Crystal Palace, the more favored among them had the privilege of entrée into the social and literary world of London. English society cordially welcomed those who bore letters of introduction from earlier visitors, and continued to entertain them with the distinguished kindness toward Americans that Ticknor had noted in the immediate aftermath of the Napoleonic wars. These midcentury years would appear to have seen closer associations among members of the English and American social worlds, and also between literary figures from the two sides of the Atlantic, than would be the case in any other later period.

When Charles Sumner, still a young, unknown lawyer, reached London on his European tour, he presented several letters from prominent Bostonians who had been there before him. He was at once given guest cards to four clubs, invited to a number of country houses for weekend visits, and given the opportunity to spend a day at Windsor Castle. A strikingly handsome young man, with a warmth and friendliness that hardly foreshadowed the harsh, intractable statesman of later years, Sumner found himself to his delighted surprise enjoying what he described as "the life of life."

So too Daniel Webster was most cordially received a few years later, meeting Palmerston and Disraeli, Dickens and Thackeray, and also Carlyle. The latter was not as impressed as Webster liked to imagine, and in a letter to Emerson somewhat sardonically described "that amorphous, crag-like face" and said he found his American visitor very dignified and a little pompous. The Queen received Webster at court where he appeared in all the formality of small clothes and a lace-ruffled shirt.

Emerson met everyone, including not only the English writers but the Duke of Wellington and the Prince of Wales. Margaret Fuller and Harriet Beecher Stowe found all doors open. The Samuel Gridley Howes appear to have made an unusual splash in both the literary and fashionable world. "None of our country-men since I have been here," wrote Edward Everett, serving as American minister at the Court of St. James's during their visit in 1843, "have excited greater interest,—received more attention,—or left a better impression than the Howes."

Mrs. Howe's letters are a catalogue of distinguished names: the Earl of Carlisle and the Marquis of Lansdowne ("a devilish good fellow! ho! ho!"), the Duchesses of Gloucester and Suther-land; and also Thackeray, Dickens, and Wordsworth ("a crabbed old sinner, who gave us a very indifferent muffin"). She and her husband attended fashionable breakfast parties, formal routs where servants with powdered heads served the refreshments, and a grand ball at Almack's. Mrs. Howe was greatly impressed with London and "the clever people collected there."

Once they had encompassed the sights of London and the fortunate few had experienced their fling in society, the American travelers ventured forth to other parts of England. They usually went to Canterbury, where a more romantic generation than that of Abigail Adams found much to admire in its cathedral; drove to Stratford-on-Avon which by midcentury had become "hackneyed ground" with a Shakespeare Club busily engaged in renovating the poet's house; and visited Cambridge or Oxford where a number of American students—long before the days of Rhodes Scholarships—were always enrolled. Farther afield, they appeared to have enjoyed especially the Lake Country where Wordsworth still lived in his "florid, fair old age."

A few tourists went to Ireland; almost all of them to Scotland. Sir Walter Scott had died in 1832, but his immense popularity in the United States continued to make the Trossachs, the ruins of Melrose Abbey, and Abbotsford as great attractions as anything in all the British Isles. It was reported in 1846 that five hundred Americans had that summer inscribed their names on the porter's book at Abbotsford. The tough, realistic New York state political leader Thurlow Weed stated some years after his visit that he would have gone to Europe just to see that one place.

A few Americans discovered that there were poverty and suffering in the British Isles, and the more sensitive occasionally described in their diaries the squalid slums of London and the wage slavery of colliery and mill in the midland industrial towns. Hawthorne believed that there was more hardship than in America behind the pleasant façade where the English upper classes lived their "beautiful lives," and that in the light of the increasing gap between rich and poor, "the gentlemen of England will be compelled to face this question." Margaret Fuller could never forget the beggars of Liverpool, the shabby and coarse mill girls in the streets of textile towns, the flamboyant gin palaces of London. "The homes of England!" she exclaimed. "Their sweetness is melting into fable."

For the most part, however, Americans in England found what they had come to see in the cultured atmosphere of Europe. The Old Home came alive for them in the sentimental and nostalgic mood that the literary pilgrims had created on their first return. They may not all have agreed with Emerson that England was "the best of actual nations," but they were generally admiring as their visits drew to an end and they braved the awful hazards of the English Channel on their way to Paris.

"You come in at a South-Bostonian sort of place," wrote one visitor, quite naturally a New Englander, on first arriving at the French capital. His somewhat provincial comment, however, by no means reflected the excitement and enthusiasm with which most

Americans recorded their first view of Paris. They found it unlike anything they had ever experienced—beautiful, colorful, lively. It was the "longed-for Paris, gay Paris," one of them wrote in typical exuberance, "*la belle ville*, enchanting city."

There was certainly nothing in Boston, New York, or Philadelphia that could rival the "gay, beautiful, bustling boulevards." The overseas visitors in midnineteenth century were generally entranced, as their accounts make abundantly clear, by the crush of coaches, cabriolets, fiacres, and great lumbering omnibuses making the "Tous les Boulevards" circuit; the throngs of strolling pedestrians, and the popular cafés with their little marble-topped tables encroaching ever farther on the crowded sidewalks. They wrote happily of "tasting ice-cream" on some sunlit terrace and watching "the vivid, almost weird, life of the Parisian streets." There were jugglers and fiddlers, men with monkeys and vendors of toothpicks, colorfully garbed Turks selling oriental rugs, ragged beggars and (a more typically nineteenth-century touch) well-dressed dandies with curling whiskers and round straw hats. Other visitors noted the flower stalls at almost every corner; the little *boutiques* along the Boulevard des Italiens displaying everything from walking sticks to goldfish; the *vingt-cinq-sous* stores where it was said anything could be bought for a quarter of a franc— except a wife and firewood. Those who wandered to the other side of the Seine invariably noted the book stalls along the quays.

Again, as in London, there were certain sights that had to be seen. The gardens of the Tuileries remained a center for family recreation, the children sailing toy boats on the park's many ponds, driving little goat-drawn carts, watching Punch and Judy shows, and clambering on the "hobby-horses flying about on whirligigs." At the Hôtel des Invalides, veterans of Napoleon's armies could be seen taking their leisure, wrinkled old men basking in the sun as they relived their memories of Austerlitz and Marengo. After visiting such pleasant outdoor places, the tourists conscientiously went through museums and churches (still finding Notre Dame "dark and gloomy"), and they almost invariably spent some time going through the cemetery of Père-LaChaise. Among other places outside of Paris, they drove to Versailles, but while most of them admired the palace and its gardens, others were highly critical. One visitor found the "spurting monsters" of its fountains "a disgust-

74

ing and outrageous perversion"; another saw in the whole scene no more than "a striking monument to the selfish profligacy of king-craft."

The Louvre had an immense appeal for those culture-starved Americans who had never before had the opportunity to see great painting and sculpture. They filled their letters and diaries with descriptive accounts, not failing to assume the air of expert connoisseurs. Some among them found their Victorian susceptibilities outraged by the prevalance of nudes (one straitlaced matron reporting that she had not even looked at the sculpture: "I should be ashamed to say I had"), but they were more generally excited by a wealth of art beyond anything they had ever imagined. The immense canvasses of Rubens—"great, joyous, full-souled, all powerful Rubens," as Mrs. Stowe enthusiastically exclaimed—appear to have been the most popular paintings, and there is hardly a travel book which does not single them out.

Little Rollo, as Jacob Abbott described his sightseeing in Paris, visited the Louvre. "Were the pictures pretty?" asked his young cousin when he returned to the hotel. "Not very," answered Rollo. "At least I did not think so; but Uncle George told me it was a famous gallery."

The women—and a surprising number of them recorded their travels—invariably went shopping, finding the stores along the Rue de Rivoli, the Rue St. Honoré and the Rue de la Paix "abundantly supplied with the most elegant articles." Indeed, in some cases they would appear to have spent quite as much time at shops and dressmakers as in pursuit of culture. There was also much dining out. Caroline Kirkland, traveling with three other women, was at first worried about the propriety of going to such places without a male escort. "One feels at first as if it were a transgression," she wrote, "but after a while this subsides into a feeling of agreeable abandon, unalloyed by any sense of naughtiness, and a dinner at a restaurant becomes one of the natural events of a Paris day."

The free and unrestrained atmosphere of Paris—"a place of the largest liberty that is, I suppose, in the civilized world," wrote Emerson—affected the American travelers' attitude toward other aspects of Parisian life. Many of them were shocked, as Abigail Adams and Elkanah Watson had been, by the casual disregard of

75

the Sabbath. But except for the more serious-minded clergymen (one reported going in despair to spend the day meditating among the tombs at Père-LaChaise), they soon became adjusted to it. They enjoyed the *cafés chantants* and occasionally even went to the races at the Champs de Mars. "Having been accustomed to the Puritan Sunday of restraint," Elizabeth Cady Stanton, the future feminist, wrote disarmingly in her reminiscences, "I found that day gay and charming."

The most popular resort for those who wanted to see Paris night life—it would appear to have been something of a nineteenth-century tourist trap—was the Jardin Mabille, on the Champs Elysées. Charles Beecher was among those who visited it, and its dancers rather intrigued this venturesome clergyman. "Round and round, in a vortex of life, beauty and brilliancy they go in a whirlwind of delight," he wrote. "Eyes sparkling, cheeks flushing, and gauzy draperies floating by; while the crowd outside gather in a ring and watch the giddy revel." Although he saw no gesture of impropriety or immorality, Beecher nonetheless felt obliged to warn that "dancing along the path to ruin, with flowers and music" could be quite as disastrous as attending more blatant haunts of vice.

Although they might condone—or at least come to accept without too great a sense of outrage—the Parisian Sabbath and even the Jardin Mabille, Americans generally were scandalized by the popular masked balls (they hinted only vaguely of what they feared might take place) and by the current mania for gambling. They continued to describe the Palais Royal as probably the most corrupt spot on the face of the earth, and severely censured the notorious Frascatti's whose four gambling salons were crowded every night with both men and women. The Reverend John A. Clark, who had been so concerned over shipboard drinking and dancing, expostulated angrily over "those dreadful gambling houses—those fearful haunts of profligacy—those hells." But far more worldly travelers also condemned such phases of Parisian night life. After giving a vivid account of his own tour of a number of questionable resorts, the debonair Nathaniel Willis warned of the temptations to which they subjected the unwary: "I am not very particular, I think, but I would as soon expose a child to the plague as give either son or daughter free rein for a year in Paris."

Apart from more casual visitors during those days in the 1830's when James Fenimore Cooper was giving his buckwheat-cake breakfast parties, the Americans residing in Paris added up to no more than a few dozen. Their number gradually increased, and among them were several expatriates who stood out for their sharply individualistic traits. Colonel Herman Thorn, a onetime purser in the United States navy, leased the Hotel Monaco (once the residence of Talleyrand) and lived there *en prince,* with his private chapel and chaplain; the eminent surgeon Dr. Valentine Mott developed a practice that included many of the continent's crowned heads; and somewhat later Thomas W. Evans, a dentist, became a good friend of Louis Napoleon, amassing a fortune from real estate which he bought up on advance information given him of Baron Haussman's building plans.

By midcentury there was an American chapel in Paris, an American tailor, an English newspaper—*Galignani's Messenger,* precursor of the Paris *Herald,* which James Gordon Bennett, Jr., was to found in 1887—and a restaurant where one could get pumpkin pie. When in 1855 France staged an international exposition to rival the Crystal Palace, commissioners were appointed from many of the American states (although there was no representative from the federal government), and among other distinguished visitors was former President Van Buren. A few years later Charles Sumner was again living in Paris, seeking to recover from the injuries he had suffered after being brutally caned on the Senate floor by Preston Brooks. Raymond of the *New York Times* spoke of his apartment on the Rue de la Paix as a meeting place where he saw Theodore Parker; Hamilton Fish, the future Secretary of State; John Bigelow of the *Evening Post,* and any number of other prominent fellow countrymen.

A number of Americans were excited eye-witnesses of the revolution of 1848 and Louis Napoleon's coup d'état three years later. Their sympathies were overwhelmingly with the republicans, and at the time of the overthrow of Louis Philippe they drew up an address of congratulations for the new Provisional Government. Samuel G. Goodrich, after describing in his *Recollections* his own ventures abroad as the rioting French mobs tore up paving stones, cut down trees, overturned omnibuses to throw up barricades, recalled the presentation of this document:

> All things being duly prepared, the Americans, about two hundred and fifty in number, marched in procession to the Hôtel de Ville, the striped bunting and the tricolor waving together in harmony over our heads. The citizens of Paris looked upon us with welcome, and frequently the cry arose —"Vive la Republique Americaine!"

The later turn of events that found Louis Napoleon assuming supreme power and establishing the Second Empire was a bitter disillusionment for those democratic-minded Americans who had seen the revolution of 1848 as the dawn of a new era of republicanism throughout Europe. William Cullen Bryant heard the new Emperor make the fateful announcement that sealed his coup d'état. "From the crowd which stood around me," he reported, "not a single cry was heard." He could not believe that the French people would long accept the Empire. But Louis Napoleon consolidated his regime and a Paris made all the more glamorous by the presence of the bright, glittering court over which he presided with his beautiful empress was soon attracting visitors as never before. Moreover, the city was being rebuilt in greater splendor: the broad, sweeping avenues laid out by Baron Haussman, the great new opera house, additional bridges over the Seine. Paris was more cosmopolitan and dazzling than it had ever been; it seemed to exist only for pageantry, gaiety, and amusement.

The Second Empire was to last through the 1860's. Among the many tourists during these years was a youthful Henry Cabot Lodge, touring Europe in 1866 with his family and a private tutor. In his *Early Memories* he vividly recalled the great parades when the Emperor reviewed his troops marching down the Champs Elysées, the gay life centering about the cafés and other places of amusement, the fashionably dressed men and women that every evening thronged the gas-lighted boulevards. "The whole pageant of life just then," Lodge remembered, "was very brilliant and very imposing too." And an even younger visitor was the future novelist Edith Wharton, who as the daughter of a wealthy, traveled family spent much of her childhood in Europe. Writing many years later in *A Backward Glance*, she described as one of her keenest memories of those days a beautiful lady driving beneath the flowering horse-chestnut trees in an open carriage flanked by outriders —"flounces of feuille-morte taffetas billowing about her, and on her rich auburn hair a tiny black lace bonnet with a tea rose over one ear." But within a year, Mrs. Wharton continued, the Empress Eugenie and everything she represented "had vanished in a crimson hurricane."

It was a hurricane—the bloody days of France's defeat by Germany and the brief rule of the Commune—which swept over Paris with devastating consequences. The Tuileries were destroyed, the towering column of the Place Vendôme torn down, the Hôtel de Ville burned to the ground, the boulevards torn up for barricades, the Bois de Boulogne left a treeless plain. The city, one visitor reported, looked like the scene of a "savage, barbarian massacre."

Of course Paris rose again, rose to attract even more tourists and visitors from across the Atlantic. It once more became "the wonder-full Paris" that Americans had considered it to be since the eighteenth century.

From Paris the tourists usually proceeded to Italy. It was quite customary, after first visiting perhaps Chartres and Rouen, to take a river steamer from Chalon-sur-Saône to Lyons and on down the Rhone to Marseilles, and then continue by diligence or private coach along the Grande Corniche to Genoa. Or one could strike off from Lyons and drive by diligence (there were still no trains here) through Chambéry and across rugged mountain passes to Turin.

The diaries of the travelers who followed the former course single out Avignon with its papal palace and "the beautiful ruin" of its famous bridge; the great Roman amphitheater at Arles which in midcentury was still choked with twelve feet of rubbish while some two thousand people lived in its stone vaults and arched passageways; and finally Nice, already a popular resort where visitors of every nationality crowded the boulevards and promenades of "the new town." What every traveler found most exciting, however, was the magnificent drive along the Grande Corniche. Among so many others Benjamin Silliman made this breathtaking trip ("a dizzy business from beginning to end") with a party of

eight in their own landau driven by four horses. His account re-
calls the continual excitement of the road, seemingly suspended
in midair between the mountains and the sea, and he concluded
emphatically that the Grande Corniche was "one of the wonders
of the world."

From Genoa—or from Turin—all roads led to Rome, and
the imperial city evoked an enthusiasm in some cases even greater
than Paris aroused. It was "the city of all cities," "the city of the
soul," "a world of astonishment." The layer beneath layer of history, the crumbling monuments of the ancient world, the number
of churches, the great collections of art—Americans were both
awed and enraptured by all this glory and grandeur. "This dream
of my boyhood," wrote an ecstatic Bayard Taylor, "—giant, god-
like, fallen Rome—is around me, and I revel in a glow of anticipation and exciting thought."

One and all among the visitors tell of going to the Vatican
("a wilderness of marble"), seeing the Sistine Chapel, joining
with the great Sunday throng for a service at St. Peter's, wandering through the Coliseum by moonlight, driving out to see the
fountains and gardens of the Villa Borghese. "The Capitol, the
Forum, St. Peter's, the Coliseum," Taylor further rhapsodized,
"—what few hours ramble ever took in places so hallowed by
poetry, history and art?"

A number of Americans had audiences with the Pope but
most of them, vigorous Protestants and strong republicans, re-
sented the Catholic Church for what they regarded as its degrad-
ing superstitions in matters of religious faith and tyrannical exercise of political power. From this point of view, there was much
about Rome that seemed to them cruelly oppressive, and they
were persuaded to condemn out of hand "the imbecility of the
papal government."

Florence stood out conspicuously as it always had as a mecca
for tourists but visitors in the midnineteenth century differed a
great deal in their first impressions. One contemporary account
speaks of "this most beautiful city"; another states that "a dingier
town is nowhere to be seen." It had perhaps already been over-
romanticized through all its artistic and literary associations, too
much glorified in guidebook and travel story. The more sentimental were disillusioned to find a newly opened railroad, gas lighting

in the streets, and the storied Arno "very muddy and yellow."
Yet for the most part its visitors grew to appreciate more and more
all that Florence represented as the very embodiment of the
Renaissance.

For untutored, untaught Americans, the wealth of painting
and statuary in the Uffizi and Pitti Palace—"those immortal
creations of the old masters—those poems written in marble and
on canvas"—was even more dazzling than the masterpieces they
might already have seen in other churches, palaces and museums.
Some few of them confessed to what Hawthorne once called
"that icy demon of weariness who haunts great picture galleries,"
but letters and diaries were much more likely to be full of the
wonder of it all. The visitors to Florence also admired the Duomo,
where in these days the Grand Duke of Tuscany presided over
the religious ceremonies held every Sunday and church holiday;
eagerly bought souvenirs at the little shops lining the Ponte Vec-
chio; stopped for tea or ices in the elegant surroundings of the
Café Doney; and drove out to see the villas and gardens in the
surrounding countryside.

"Venice! Queen of the Adriatic! .... How can I ever forget thee," a rapt Horace Greeley wrote home to the readers of the
New York Tribune, and many other visitors expatiated on the
charms of this city which they tended to find "all romance from
beginning to end." Siena did not prove to be so popular in these
years, one visitor writing that at the most it was worth no more
than an hour or two, but Padua attracted many Americans, one
of them noting as early as 1832 that he found the names of fifty
of his countrymen inscribed on the visitors' book—"such a wandering nation we are." Its great cathedral gave Milan a special
appeal. Stopping there in the early 1840's with a party of young
girls, Catherine Sedgwick, the popular author of Hope Leslie,
noted a propensity of Italian men that has not passed unobserved
by later visitors. On walking through the market place the idlers
"collected about us," Miss Sedgwick wrote in her Letters from
Abroad to Kindred at Home, "and stared so unmercifully at the
girls they clung to me, and I felt, for the first time in my life,
rather Duenna-ish, and glad enough to get back to the hotel."

A resort more popular in midcentury than in later years was
the little hill town of Lucca, some sixty miles north of Florence,

where many tourists sought relief from the oppressive heat of the Italian summer. It was very fashionable with members of the Italian nobility, who had their private lodgings in the surrounding hills, and the casino, where once a week the Duke of Lucca gave a public ball with music and dancing, was the center of a gay social life. Nathaniel Willis, enjoying Lucca very much, characterized it as the Saratoga of Italy and "quite a little paradise."

Hawthorne once described Italy as "a sort of poetic and fairy precinct," and such it was for most of its American visitors. Those among them who looked beneath the surface, however, could not help being appalled by the utterly wretched circumstances that marked the life of the peasants in their "picturesque" and "quaint" villages. In addition to the ubiquitous beggars ("vexing as moschetoes in a walk in the woods" was one apt description), there was the evidence on every hand of a people "not merely enslaved but debased" by a measure of political tyranny found nowhere else in western Europe.

Margaret Fuller was one American who became deeply involved in the uprisings of 1848 when the Italian people fruitlessly tried to throw off the yoke of both their own and Austrian tyrants. She had been enamored of Italy on her arrival in 1847, and for her Rome was beyond description, the owls hooting in the Coliseum by moonlight, as she once wrote, speaking "more to the purpose than I ever heard any other voice upon the subject." But the suppression of liberty haunted her, and when the revolutionary spirit spread through Italy, she threw herself wholeheartedly into the cause of the *Risorgimento*.

She had married an Italian, the handsome, dashing Marquis Ossoli, and while he was fighting with the Civic Guards, she stayed on in Rome during the city's fateful seige by the French troops summoned to the aid of the Pope. On June 10, 1849, she wrote Emerson of her experiences in helping to nurse the wounded, but even as she composed her letter ("amid the rounds of cannonade—a terrible battle"), she realized the Roman Republic was lost. "I know not, dear friend," she said, "whether I shall ever get home across that great ocean, but here in Rome I shall no longer wish to live. O Rome, *my* country! could I imagine that the triumph of what I hold dear was to heap such desolation on thy head!" Forced to flee the Papal States, she set out with her husband and child to return to America, but the ship on which they sailed from Leghorn was wrecked off Fire Island and the little family were among those drowned.

In her love for Italy, her deep sense of injustice at the oppression of the people, and her warm support for the republican cause that had so dismally failed, Margaret Fuller reflected the views of most of her countrymen. But what most appealed to them as they saw Rome, Florence, and Venice, the little medieval hill towns, was a sense of the past. Italy more than any other country in Europe brought out all the sharp contrasts between the Old World and the New.

After Italy there were for most American tourists a brief stay in Switzerland, sometimes a tour in Germany or at least a boat trip down the Rhine, and then some final, hurried sightseeing in Holland and Belgium before recrossing the Channel and sailing for home.

Their journals repeatedly describe the hazardous carriage trip over the St. Gothard Pass (the road linking Milan and Lucerne was built in the 1830's) and the dazzling mountain scenery. Geneva, with Lake Leman sparkling in the sunshine, was a favorite resort. Here one could take a little lake steamer to visit the Castle of Chillon and explore the shops of Geneva's already "far famed jewelers." Some tourists made the arduous climb by muleback to the *hospice* of St. Bernard. When Mrs. Stowe undertook this venture she was greatly disappointed, after having struggled so bravely through the deep snow, to find the little porch of the hospice "crowded with gentlemen smoking cigars, and gazing on our approach just as any set of loafers do from the porch of a fashionable hotel." Zermatt—soon to become "a considerable resort"—was occasionally visited, and the trip to Chamonix was also popular, the ascent to the Mer de Glace having to be made by muleback in these days before the cog railway was built.

The visits to Germany—except on the part of students— were more rare and only a few Americans got as far as Berlin. Those that did so found the Prussian capital a rather somber city. Even though they might admire Unter den Linden, the Thiergarten, and the ornate palaces of Charlottenburg, they were oppressed by the autocratic rule of Frederick William IV. William

Wetmore Story, the Boston sculptor, was one American who lived for a time in Berlin. "Something it has," he wrote home with that inevitable tendency of Bostonians to compare any city with their native town, "that makes me think of Boston and gives me a home feeling." What he meant is perhaps further revealed in a later comment: "It is cold, prosaic and in some aspects dreary.... but it is the home of scholars and philosophers; and its air has the enchantment that they have lent it."

The German spas were very popular for those seeking rest and relaxation on their European tours, and the healing properties of the waters were held in the highest repute. Perhaps the most interesting picture of the leisurely life they afforded is that given in the letters of Catherine Sedgwick describing Weisbaden in 1839.

"From six to eight the water drinkers did their duty, drinking faithfully," she wrote. "Some read or lounged in a sunny corridor where a band of musicians were stationed playing gay tunes; but the approved fashion is to saunter while you sip." At one o'clock visitors sat down promptly at one or another of the resort's luxurious hotels to enjoy an elaborately served dinner, with fine roasts and Rhine wine at twenty-five cents a bottle. "The quiet and order of the table are admirable," Miss Sedgwick commented. "The servants are never in a hurry and never blunder." Promenades and concerts occupied the afternoon with the gardens of the Kur-Saal gradually coming "alive with people, hundreds sitting at their little tables ... smoking, sipping coffee, wine, and Seltzer-water, and eating ices." The evenings were given over to banqueting, *soirées musicales*, dancing, and gambling. On only one occasion did Miss Sedgwick venture into the gaming rooms, and finding them crowded with both men and women playing roulette, she wrote rather disapprovingly that it was "an odd scene for us of Puritan blood and breeding to witness."

On their visits to Holland and Belgium the tourists of this period almost always undertook one excursion that was not to command very much popular attention in later years. This was the trip to the battlefield of Waterloo which in midcentury could be made from Brussels by a daily coach service (except on Sundays) managed by an enterprising Englishman. The engaging diary of Fanny Knight, the sixteen-year-old daughter of a cotton

84

merchant from Natchez, Mississippi, touring Europe with her parents in 1854, is one among many accounts of such an excursion. Fanny found it thrilling, except that they were unmercifully plagued by self-appointed guides and beggars.

The European tour ultimately came to an end. As in the case of earlier visitors, the final conclusions of the travelers about their continental experiences often differed, but everything they wrote continued to show a deep appreciation of the European scene. Yet they were glad to be heading home. While innumerable quotations might be given expressing such patriotic sentiments, perhaps a letter from one of the boys traveling with the Reverend John Overton Choules catches the spirit of the midcentury tourist. They were returning to America after the most wonderful of tours, he wrote, but "with our hearts more warmly attached to our beloved country than when we left her shores."

VII. SOME MIDCENTURY VISITORS

AMONG the Americans visiting Europe in this period were a number who had more special pursuits in mind than sightseeing, rest and recreation, or the opportunity to mingle in European society. There were always diplomatic officials, businessmen, and students, but even apart from these hardy perennials of the European scene, other travelers sought out the Old World to combine with their continental tours what might be described as distinctive professional activities.

A rather unexpected group was one of social reformers. The men and women engaged in the feverish outburst of reform—antislavery agitation, temperance, popular education, women's rights, universal peace—which marked the 1840's and 1850's, looked abroad to see what other countries might be doing, and many of them were drawn across the Atlantic to observe in person foreign activity and foreign progress. They took part, well over a century ago, in a series of international conferences bringing together European and American leaders in all the various movements that grew out of a new awakening of the social conscience on both sides of the Atlantic.

Popular entertainers made up another and quite different category of visitors overseas. The actors and actresses of England, and to a lesser degree those of continental countries, had long since been touring the United States, but there was now an eastward as well as westward passage in the broad field of popular entertainment. The stars of the American stage dared an appearance at London theaters, and intrepid showmen were prepared to take overseas, often with great success, such typically American spectacles as minstrel shows, Indian troupes, and the early Wild West shows.

86

Nous Benjamin Franklin,

Ecuyer, Miniſtre Plénipotentiaire des
Etats-Unis de l'Amérique, près Sa
Majeſté Très-Chrétienne,

PRIONS tous ceux qui ſont à prier
de vouloir laiſſer ſurement & librement
paſſer *Mr Harmar, Colonel au Service*
des dits Etats, allant à L'Orient pour s'embarquer.

ſans *lui* donner ni permettre qu'il *lui* ſoit
donné aucun empêchement, mais au contraire
de *lui* accorder toutes ſortes d'aide & d'aſſiſ-
tance, comme nous ferions en pareil cas, pour
tous ceux qui nous ſeroient recommandés.
EN FOI DE QUOI nous *lui* avons
délivré le préſent Paſſeport, valable pour *trois*
ſemaines ſigné de notre main, contreſigné
par l'un de nos Secretaires, & au bas
duquel eſt l'empreinte de nos Armes.
DONNÉ à Paſſy, en notre Hôtel, le
17. Juin mil ſept cent quatre-vingt-
quatre. —

B. Franklin

Par ordre du Miniſtre Plénipotentiaire.

W. T. Franklin ſec

GRATIS.

Passport printed by Benjamin Franklin on his press at Passy
while he was minister to France. It is signed by him and by his
grandson, who served as his secretary. Lieutenant Colonel Josiah
Harmar had come to Paris in 1784 to deliver the ratified Treaty
of Peace after it had been passed by the Continental Congress.

The first-, second-, and fourth-class
carriages, with engine and tender, of a
train on its way to Kingstown, Ireland,
in the 1830's.

Entrance to the London and
Birmingham Railway Station, Euston
Square, London, in the 1830's.

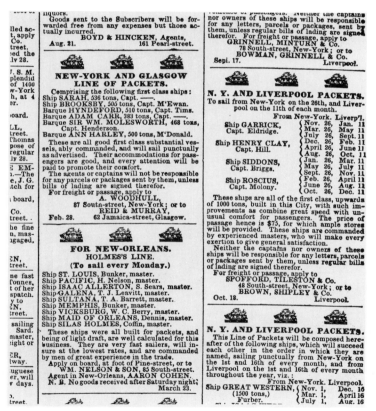

liquors.

Goods sent to the Subscribers will be forwarded free from any expenses but those actually incurred.

BOYD & HINCKEN, Agents,
Aug. 21.   161 Pearl-street.

NEW-YORK AND GLASGOW LINE OF PACKETS.

Comprising the following first class ships:
Ship SARAH, 536 tons, Capt. ——.
Ship BROOKSBY, 505 tons, Capt. M'Ewan.
Barque HYNDEFORD, 510 tons, Capt. Tims.
Barque ADAM CARR, 383 tons, Capt. ——.
Barque SIR WM. MOLESWORTH, 468 tons, Capt. Henderson.
Barque ANN HARLEY, 500 tons, M'Donald.

These are all good first class substantial vessels, ably commanded, and will sail punctually as advertised. Their accommodations for passengers are good, and every attention will be paid to promote their comfort.

The agents or captains will not be responsible for any parcels or packages sent by them, unless bills of lading are signed therefor.

For freight or passage, apply to
A. WOODHULL,
87 South-street, New-York; or to
REID & MURRAY,
Feb. 28.   62 Jamaica-street, Glasgow.

FOR NEW-ORLEANS.
HOLMES'S LINE.
(To sail every Monday.)

Ship ST. LOUIS, Bunker, master.
Ship PACIFIC, H. Nelson, master.
Ship ISAAC ALLERTON, S. Sears, master.
Ship GALENA, T. J. Leavitt, master.
Ship SULTANA, T. A. Barrett, master.
Ship MEMPHIS, Bunker, master.
Ship VICKSBURG, W. C. Berry, master.
Ship MAID OF ORLEANS, Dennis, master.
Ship SILAS HOLMES, Coffin, master.

These ships were all built for packets, and being of light draft, are well calculated for this business. They are very fast sailers, will insure at the lowest rates, and are commanded by men of great experience in the trade.

Apply on board, at foot of Pine-street, or to
WM. NELSON & SON, 85 South-street.
Agent in New-Orleans, AARON COHEN.
N. B. No goods received after Saturday night.
March 23.

nor owners of these ships will be responsible for any letters, parcels or packages, sent by them, unless regular bills of lading are signed therefor. For freight or passage, apply to
GRINNELL, MINTURN & Co.
78 South-street, New-York; or to
BOWMAN, GRINNELL & Co.
Sep. 17.   Liverpool.

N. Y. AND LIVERPOOL PACKETS.

To sail from New-York on the 26th, and Liverpool on the 11th of each month.

	From New-York.	Liverp'l.
Ship GARRICK, Capt. Eldridge.	Nov. 26,	Jan. 11
	Mar. 26,	May 11
	July 26,	Sept. 11
Ship HENRY CLAY, Capt. Hill.	Dec. 26,	Feb. 11
	April 26,	June 11
	Aug. 26,	Oct. 11
Ship SIDDONS, Capt. Briggs.	Jan. 26,	Mar. 11
	May 26,	July 11
	Sept. 26,	Nov. 11
Ship ROSCIUS, Capt. Molony.	Feb. 26,	April 11
	June 26,	Aug. 11
	Oct. 26,	Dec. 11

These ships are all of the first class, upwards of 1000 tons, built in this City, with such improvements as combine great speed with unusual comfort for passengers. The price of passage hence is $75, for which ample stores will be provided. These ships are commanded by experienced masters, who will make every exertion to give general satisfaction.

Neither the captains nor owners of these ships will be responsible for any letters, parcels or packages sent by them, unless regular bills of lading are signed therefor.

For freight or passage, apply to
SPOFFORD, TILESTON & Co.
48 South-street, New-York; or to
BROWN, SHIPLEY & Co.
Oct. 18.   Liverpool.

N. Y. AND LIVERPOOL PACKETS.

This Line of Packets will be composed hereafter of the following ships, which will succeed each other in the order in which they are named, sailing punctually from New-York on the 1st and 16th of every month, and from Liverpool on the 1st and 16th of every month throughout the year, viz.:

	From New-York.	Liverpool.
Ship GREAT WESTERN, (1500 tons,) Furber.	Nov. 1,	Dec. 16
	Mar. 1,	April 16
	July 1,	Aug. 16

Part of a page from the *Shipping and Commercial List of New-York Price Current*, New York, July 31, 1852.

The "Great Eastern" was the giant of the passenger ships of her day.
Her maiden sailing, in 1860, was from Southampton to New York.
The ship—much in advance of her time in many features—
was a failure.

The Grand Saloon of the "Great Eastern." The portières were of rich
crimson silk, the sofas were covered with Utrecht velvet, and the
buffets were of richly carved walnut, the tops being covered with fine
green marble.

Herman Melville.

Mark Twain.

Henry James.

Gertrude Stein in her studio in Paris in 1923.

F. Scott Fitzgerald with his wife and daughter in 1926.

Ernest Hemingway at a bullfight in Madrid.

Sightseeing tour leaving American Express office in Nice about 1928.

Sightseeing from a jet plane window in the 1960's.

The first European office of American Express—Paris, 1895.

The present American Embassy in London, completed in 1961.

A third group hardly constituted an innovation: it was rather a further swelling of the wave of painters and sculptors who had been going abroad for work and study ever since colonial days. A few still went to England in the eighteenth-century tradition of West and Copley, and others joined the American colony in Paris, but in the middle period of the nineteenth century, Italy was the country above all others which drew American artists. They gathered both in Rome and Florence, and their number was estimated between 1825 and 1875 to have totaled well over a hundred.

Reformers, popular entertainers, artists—however disparate their interests or diverse their offerings and borrowings—promoted new social and cultural ties between the Old World and the New. At a time when stay-at-home Americans were still vaunting their cultural independence of the Old World, and Europeans looked upon the United States as primitive and materialistic, these interchanges helped to break down American provinciality and also awoke European interest in an America that might have something to offer the world other than the cotton gin and reaping machines.

The World's Anti-Slavery Convention, held in London in the spring of 1840, was a pioneer experiment in international reform and it drew a formidable contingent from the United States. The Americans came largely from the eastern seaboard, from Boston, New York, and Philadelphia, but they broadly represented those forces in their nation's life which were attempting at this time not only to abolish slavery, but to promote all possible humanitarian reforms. There were forty-odd men and women in this delegation to the London convention, and the one thing they had in common was a spirited resolve to do whatever they could to help struggling humanity.

Among them were two couples, the men well known at the time for their zealous antislavery activity and their wives marked for even greater prominence in later years as champions of woman's suffrage. They were Henry B. Stanton, the handsome, distinguished, eloquent representative of the American Anti-Slavery Society, and Elizabeth Cady Stanton; and James Mott of the Pennsylvania Anti-Slavery Society and Lucretia Mott. Also there were James G. Birney of New York, this same year the Liberty

Party's antislavery candidate for the presidency; Wendell Phillips, the famous Boston orator and champion of all good causes; and William Lloyd Garrison, the intractable conscience of puritan New England, as much opposed to drinking, smoking, and the theater as he was to slavery, and the most fiery abolitionist of them all.

The English reformers welcomed their American counterparts warmly, but the disturbing presence of the women among them created a crisis. The convention managers would not allow them to be seated. As the dispute raged the American delegation found itself badly split, one faction regretting the question had risen and another determined to fight it through. When a final vote was taken the women lost: it was decided that they would be admitted "only behind the bar" and not allowed to speak on the convention floor. Arriving in London after this decision had been reached, Garrison was incensed. Refusing to take any part in the official proceedings of the meeting, he spent the entire session in the visitors' gallery, glowering fiercely at the pusillanimous delegates who had struck down "the sacred rights of women."

It was a storm in a tea cup, but future events suggest that the battle over seating the women delegates was more important than any action taken in regard to slavery. Meeting for the first time, Elizabeth Cady Stanton and Lucretia Mott were so closely drawn together by their mutual sense of outrage over how the women delegates were being treated, that they decided that on their return home they would summon a women's rights convention. The seed was planted for their lifelong campaign to secure female suffrage.

The convention, in the meantime, went its way and finally adopted a series of resolutions denouncing slavery as a sin wherever it was maintained, and calling particularly upon church groups to expel all slave-owners from their membership. More important than any such official action, however, were the personal associations formed between the English hosts and their American guests. There was a continuing round of teas and evening soirées at which these dedicated people reinforced their mutual determination to work together to end slavery throughout all the world. These entertainments were "generally understood to be for moral and intellectual purposes—or political as the case may be," Lucretia Mott noted in her diary, "—hence not much catering to the animal spirits."

The antislavery people in the United States were enthusiastic over what the *Liberator* called, with possible exaggeration, "the grandest assembly of human beings that ever met on the globe." John Greenleaf Whittier celebrated the occasion in verse:

> *A holy gathering! peaceful all:*
> *No threat of war, no savage call*
> * For vengeance on an erring brother!*
> *But in their stead the godlike plan*
> *To teach the brotherhood of man*
> * To love and reverence one another,*
> *As sharers of a common blood,*
> *The children of a common God!*

After the convention ended, several of the delegates went on speaking tours. Garrison, apparently recovering from his pique, traveled through Scotland and Ireland as well as England. He had been abroad seven years earlier, raising funds for manual training schools for colored boys, and was already well known in liberal circles. He was to lecture again in England in 1846, and then returning once more after the Civil War, was accorded a hero's welcome wherever he went. Lucretia Mott visited such cities as Manchester, Dublin, Glasgow, and Edinburgh, attending meetings of the Society of Friends and giving innumerable antislavery talks. Although she had been greatly upset by the convention's refusal to seat the women delegates, which she attributed not only to English usage but to "sectarian proscription" within the American delegation, she felt her visit on the whole was a great success, rejoicing in the sympathy shown in England for Negro emancipation.

Stanton gave some thirty or forty speeches in Great Britain and Ireland, and then went on to the continent where he was a delegate at two antislavery meetings in Paris. As a lively account of these travels recorded in Mrs. Stanton's diary clearly indicates, reform activity did not take up all his time. Even her sober-minded husband admitted this. "I did not attend solely to antislavery matters," he recalled years later in his *Random Reminis-*

cences, "but for six months went the beaten path of the tourist."

There were continuing contacts between the antislavery forces on either side of the Atlantic and further conventions. The Negro abolitionist Frederick Douglass, who had himself escaped from slavery, visited England in 1845, accepted on terms of complete equality by the English liberals; and six years later three other colored Americans, each a clergyman, addressed the audience at another London convention. And then in 1853, Harriet Beecher Stowe arrived on her triumphal tour. Welcomed everywhere as the author of *Uncle Tom's Cabin,* she attended a ceaseless round of meetings of Anti-Slavery Societies, Negroes' Friends Societies, Temperance Societies, and Bible Societies. Seldom has an American abroad been more generously dined (although not wined) than this zealous, energetic, little woman who had struck such a mighty blow against Negro slavery.

The very morning after her arrival in Liverpool, Mrs. Stowe found herself the guest of honor at a great breakfast party, and she was then taken to see a group of children from one of the nearby schools for the poor. "All the little rogues were quite familiar with Topsy and Eva," she wrote, "and *au fait* in the fortunes of Uncle Tom." Visiting Stratford-on-Avon, she was presented by the landlady of the White Lion with a bead purse which had been knitted by her daughter as the family read *Uncle Tom* aloud in the long winter evenings. While traveling in Switzerland, she was greeted warmly by the mistress and servant maids of an inn in the little village of St. Cergue: "all had read *Uncle Tom.*"

Among the many functions she attended in London was a Lord Mayor's dinner in her honor and an even more elaborate affair at Stafford House, the imposing mansion of the Duke of Sutherland. Upon its conclusion Lord Shaftesbury read an adulatory address to the author of *Uncle Tom's Cabin* from "the ladies of England."

The abolition of slavery was by no means, however, the only cause which served to create new bonds of association between European and American reformers. When Samuel Gridley Howe, with his irrepressible bride, Julia Ward Howe, and that other honeymooning couple, Mr. and Mrs. Horace Mann, crossed the Atlantic together in April 1843, the declared purpose of their trip was a survey of general reform activities throughout Europe. Howe, who had first won renown serving with the Greeks in their struggle for independence, had become a dedicated teacher of the blind and deaf, and Mann was already well known as an outstanding educator. The social activities that Mrs. Howe so spiritedly described in her letters home grew out of their introductions to English liberals who welcomed Howe and Mann as leading representatives of American reform.

In London the two men made the rounds of charitable institutions, "ragged schools," mental asylums, and prisons, Dickens serving as their guide on visiting Bridewell and Newgate. Going on to the continent, they visited schools in France, Germany, Switzerland, and Holland. An immediate result of the tour was a report on European educational practices which Mann submitted to the Massachusetts School Board, and a decade later it bore further fruit in an International Exposition of Educational Methods held in London.

Temperance advocates also sought out their European coworkers, numerous in England if not on the continent, and a first World's Temperance Convention was held in London in 1846. William F. Dodge, one of the "merchant princes" of his day with a consuming interest in this midcentury reform, had close association with such English temperance advocates as the influential Earl of Shaftesbury and the famous Father Mathew of Cork. Horace Greeley, another temperance man, was encouraged by what he saw being done in England on his trip in 1851, but he despaired wholly of Scotland—"I am afraid the good cause of Total Abstinence is making no headway here."

One of the most dedicated of all reformers of this period was Dorothea Dix, whose life was given over to improving the care of the insane. A quiet, gentle little woman, she had an indomitable will, and traveling abroad between 1854 and 1857 she attacked the problem of adequate asylums and nursing homes in Europe with the same impassioned zeal with which she pursued her campaign in the United States. Her tour took her to Russia and Turkey as well as western Europe. She not only, for the most part, traveled alone (stating that she found it no more difficult than in the United States), but succeeded in visiting asylums and hospitals wherever she went. "I take no refusals," was her quiet boast.

Having discovered in Scotland what she considered horrible conditions in the treatment of the insane, she was influential, in spite of considerable opposition to "the American invader," in bringing about the appointment of a Royal Commission to make further investigations; and while in Rome, after bluntly telling the Pope that the insane asylums in the Holy City were "a scandal and a disgrace," she went out herself and founded a new hospital.

The peace movement had an unusual spokesman overseas about this same time in the person of Elihu Burritt, the "Learned Blacksmith" from Massachusetts, who had taught himself all the European languages, as well as a number of others, and decided to devote his life to trying to do away with the scourge of war. He was described as a tall, slender, blue-eyed man with "an air of delicacy and refinement, and manners of great gentleness," but as in the case of Dorothea Dix, a quiet exterior masked an unswerving purpose.

Burritt organized a League of Universal Brotherhood, published a flood of pamphlets—his *Olive Leaves*—in half a dozen languages, and beginning in 1843, promoted a series of international peace congresses that were held in Brussels, Frankfurt, Paris, Edinburgh, and London. At the fourth of these meetings, held in London in 1851 with Richard Cobden the principal speaker, there were some thirty delegates from the United States. Burritt continued his pacifist campaign in Europe until the outbreak of the Crimean War, and on returning to the United States spoke out openly against the civil war in his own country.

Whatever these visits may or may not have achieved in furthering such universal causes as abolition and temperance, popular education and world peace, they were a highly interesting experience for all concerned. Americans and Europeans were brought to realize that men of goodwill on either side of the Atlantic had a great deal in common and were animated by the same ideals and the same crusading spirit.

> *Wheel about, turn about,*
> *Do jis so,*
> *An' ebery time I wheel about*
> *I jump Jim Crow.*

At the Surrey Theatre in London, in the season of 1836–37, a fantastic little man impersonating a Negro was giving a song-and-dance act that so delighted his audiences that his show ran for months. This was Thomas D. Rice, the first really successful impersonator of the Negro on the American stage, whose little shuffling dance step—"Jump Jim Crow"—had already won him fame throughout the United States and was to give a new phrase to the language.

"Jim Crow and his antics were on everybody's tongue," Henry Wikoff, a tourist visitor in London at this time wrote in *The Reminiscences of an Idler*. "... It was a phase of humanity totally unknown to this country, and to Rice will belong the glory of having introduced the plantation black to the English World."

Rice was quickly followed, in England as in the United States, by the minstrel shows to which the new vogue for black-face comedians so clearly pointed the way. They were popular abroad almost as soon as they were popular at home. On his trip in 1843, Thurlow Weed noted the presence aboard his ship, the packet "George Washington," of the "Colombian Minstrels" and asserted his confidence that they would "out-jump Jim Crow." This same year the "Virginia Minstrels" were also in London for a six weeks engagement, and were later followed by the "Christy Minstrels" and the "Ethiopian Serenaders." The latter, after giving a special performance for Queen Victoria at Arundel Castle, were such a drawing card that they had to stage morning as well as afternoon and evening shows. All classes hugely enjoyed the American novelty (Thackeray testified how moved he was by the ballads of "a minstrel with wool on his head and an ultra-Ethiopian complexion"), and the popularity of minstrel shows continued well into the 1860's.

Close upon their heels were the troupes playing *Uncle Tom's Cabin*, which was to become the world's greatest theatrical hit. P. T. Barnum was a pioneer in such ventures, taking a company to England in 1857, and others soon followed. After the Civil War, the "Tom shows" attracted even more attention. When the New York producers Jarrett and Palmer included Negroes in the casts they brought to perform both in England and on the continent, audiences everywhere were delighted with the chance to see "crowds of real American freed slaves."

93

When Barnum took his first Uncle Tom company abroad, he had in tow another very popular attraction. This was the famous General Tom Thumb. But even then it was a return engagement for this most noted of the great showman's freaks and curiosities. Tom Thumb had originally visited Europe in 1844 on a tour that was such a succession of triumphs that on his return to the United States, his sponsor proudly advertised that the beguiling midget had been "kissed by a million pair of the sweetest lips in Europe."

On his second trip in 1857, Tom Thumb again visited England and France; went on to Germany with engagements at such spas as Ems, Homburg, and Wiesbaden, and then concluded his tour in Holland. Barnum immensely enjoyed this royal progress through Europe, which was highly profitable for all concerned, and at the same time he busied himself with collecting new curiosities for his American Museum in New York. He was so cordially welcomed in England that he returned the next year to give before some one hundred appreciative audiences his famous lecture on "The Art of Money-Getting." It received the most favorable notices in the British press, including one by the sedate London *Times*.

The American invasion of the legitimate stage in England was initiated when Edwin Forrest, the great tragedian, appeared at the Drury Lane in the autumn of 1836—the same year that Rice was "jumping Jim Crow" at the Surrey. Other American actors had been in England, but Forrest was the outstanding star of the American stage in his day and the enthusiastic reception accorded him by British audiences gave his performances a significance that those earlier visits completely lacked. "We can acknowledge that in him," one London paper wrote, "the States have commenced the repayment of a heavy debt long due to the old country."

Forrest played in the great Shakespearean roles—Macbeth, Lear, Othello—which he had popularized in the United States, but he made his real hit as Spartacus, the part which Robert Montgomery Bird created for him in writing *The Gladiator*. "His magnificent person astonished those who had never seen him," wrote Wikoff, who was in the audience on the opening night of Forrest's performance. "His rich and powerful voice thrilled all who heard it. His impassioned acting quite electrified the audience. At the end he was overwhelmed with applause, and it was plain that he had secured a hold on British sympathies which he never lost."

One of the first actresses to venture abroad was Charlotte Cushman, who in the 1840's was far and away the country's leading female star. She played for a time in London with Forrest, and then stayed on in England for nearly four years with continuing success. One of her outstanding parts was that of Romeo (which she sometimes played with her sister as Juliet), and another Lady Macbeth. The English critics agreed that in her interpretation of the latter part, she acted with "topmost passion," one of them writing that it made "my blood run hot and cold."

On his trip abroad in 1844, Bayard Taylor had among his fellow passengers in the "second class" of the ship "Oxford," a company of Iowa Indians headed by their chief White Cloud. "They kept us awake half the night," Taylor recorded, "by singing and howling in the most dolorous manner, with the accompaniment of slapping their hands violently on their bare breasts."

These unhappy Indians, it turned out, were on their way abroad under the auspices of an enterprising showman, G. H. C. Melody, who planned to exhibit them in London and then take them to Paris. On their arrival (there were fourteen in the party, including five squaws and a papoose), they were met by George Catlin, the well-known Indian painter. He had come to England in 1839 with his collection of six hundred portraits (and two grizzly bears, later sold to the Regent's Park zoo), and stood ready to help and befriend any Indians coming overseas. On the promise of the Iowa that they would remain sober and follow his advice, he arranged with Melody to help out with their proposed exhibitions and then to accompany them to France.

Having set up an encampment with four wigwams at the Vauxhall Gardens, the Indians staged a series of daily shows, playing ball, dancing, and singing. With the braves arrayed in all the glory of feathered headdresses and war paint, the squaws in deer-skin costumes embroidered with beads and porcupine quills, they were a nine days' wonder. Moreover, everywhere they went on their own sightseeing tours about London, they attracted large and curious crowds. A high point of their visit was a breakfast party given by Disraeli. After serving them elaborate refreshments, he had a large dish filled with brooches, bracelets, necklaces, and other ornaments passed around from which the Indians were invited to take whatever pleased their fancy.

When the troupe went on to Paris, their exhibitions proved even more successful. King Louis Philippe received them, talking about his own experiences among the Seneca and other tribes which he had visited in his youthful days in the United States. At the close of the audience, he presented the chiefs with large gold medals and gave smaller silver ones to the other members of the party. One may well wonder what these Indians may have made of such strange experiences in lands so far away and so greatly different from their own background of forest and plain.

The year after the Iowa returned to the United States, having spent some fifteen months abroad, Catlin supervised the tour of a group of Ojibwa visiting England, France, and Belgium. In the course of their trip one of the Indians wrote of their being given an audience in Paris by the kings of France and Belgium:

> Last Saturday we saw the great chief of France, and his great chief woman; the great chief of Belgium and his great chief woman. . . . We played the Indian ballplay, shot at marks with our bows and arrows, false scalping, war dance, paddled one of our birch-bark canoes in a river among swans, wild geese and ducks. After the two great chiefs and their great women had much talk with us they thanked us, got into their carriages covered with gold, drawn by six beautiful horses, and drove to the wigwam of the great chief of France.

It was a good many years later that another band of Indians visited Europe as part of the famous Wild West Exhibition which William F. Cody—"Buffalo Bill"—took on repeated European tours in the 1880's. More than one hundred—Sioux, Cheyenne, Kiowa, Pawnee—were with the show (as well as cowboys, buffalos, steers, bronchos, elks, bears, wagons, stage coaches, and a cowboy band) when it played in London at the time of Queen Victoria's Jubilee.

"We stood right in front of Grandmother England and gave a command performance for the Queen herself," one of the Indians wrote. "She was little but fat and we liked her, because she was good to us. She said .... 'If you belonged to me, I would not let them take you around in a show like this' .... She shook hands with all of us. Her hands were very little and soft. We gave a big cheer for her, and then the shining wagons came in and she got into one of them and they all went away."

In subsequent years the Wild West Exhibition toured all Europe—not only England and France, but Italy, Austria and Germany. On one occasion the Pope received the Indians, and only with great difficulty were they restrained from breaking out into enthusiastic war whoops.

"We need art students," wrote the critic James Jackson Jarves, "who will .... go on their hands and knees .... to read the soul language of the mightiest minds of Europe."

Whether such lofty purposes were always what they had in view, scores of American painters and sculptors were drawn to Italy in the midnineteenth century, not only from such traditional centers of culture as Boston, New York, and Philadelphia, but from smaller towns and even villages reaching far into the midwest. For them Italy was the "museum of Europe," with its immense wealth of ancient sculpture and renaissance painting to be studied and copied, and this attracted them quite as much as that "dream of Arcadia" which so many travelers had discovered in the country's natural beauty, its never failing romance, and its pervasive charm.

Moreover, there was another respect in which Italy had in these years a most powerful appeal—"the celestial cheapness of the times." When Margaret Fuller was in Rome, she estimated that she could live there comfortably for six months at a cost of $400, while Nathaniel Willis somewhat earlier had noted even lower expenses for an entire year in Florence. He reported that he had rented very pleasant lodgings in a former archbishop's palace, with what he contended was the loveliest view in all Europe (it was later painted by Thomas Cole), for $3 a month! There was another $1 a month for lamps, boots and service; breakfast of coffee and toast cost six cents a day, and he could dine fashionably and well, with wine, Willis further wrote, for twenty-five cents.

The leading sculptor among those living in Rome was

97

Thomas Crawford, a marble designer from New York who first arrived in 1834 and soon became highly popular, employing an army of stone cutters in the several studios he set up in the Baths of Diocletian. He was to carve the pediment for the Capitol at Washington, together with statues of Washington and Jefferson, and his work was judged so important that the United States Government sent a ship of war to bring it to America.

William Page, another New Yorker, who had tried law and the ministry before turning to art, was probably the best of the expatriate painters in this period. Described by contemporaries as "an earnest, simple, noble artist and man," he painted with unusual originality, but unhappily the dark, rich tones that he gave to his portrait studies were destined to fade, and with age most of them became indistinguishable.

Another conspicuous member of this art colony was Harriet Hosmer, a woman sculptor whose statues and busts, exhibited throughout Europe, won her decorations from the King of Bavaria and the Empress of Russia. Miss Hosmer's personality was quite as distinctive as her sculpture. "Very willfull and too independent by half," as one of her friends admitted, she invariably dressed like a man, a black velvet cap pressed down over curls, and until the Italian police finally felt they had to put a stop to it, astounded the Romans by furiously galloping on horseback across the Campagna every afternoon.

The apartments in the Palazzo Barberini of William Wetmore Story, not only sculptor but author of *Roba di Roma*, provided something of a center for the American artists. A small, energetic, wiry little man, generous and hospitable, with a sparkling wit, he kept open house not only for painters and sculptors, but also for the long line of American writers who during these years either lived in Rome for a time or passed through the city on their Italian travels. Longfellow and Emerson met many of the artists; the historians Parkman, Prescott, and Motley were for a time of the general group; and also Julia Ward Howe (whose sister Crawford married), Margaret Fuller, and Harriet Beecher Stowe, returning after her first trip to write *Agnes of Sorrento*.

The American artists generally affected the carefully curled hair, the beards, and the velvet jackets of European fashion; visited every morning the Spanish Steps to choose their models from among the picturesquely costumed peasants and artisans, brigands and "Christian martyrs," who congregated there daily; worked throughout the afternoon in their studios or sketched among the ancient ruins; and then of an evening gathered at the Caffé Greco, in the Via Condotti. Painters and sculptors of all nationalities ("rowdy-looking chaps," commented Herman Melville when he passed through Rome in 1857), met there for endless talking, arguing, drinking.

There were also long walks on the Appian Way, horseback rides in the countryside, trips into the hills by muleback, and frequent picnics at Hadrian's Villa and on the Campagna. The peasants living nearby were sometimes startled to hear the strains of "Hail Columbia!" floating out over the evening air. On occasion, the artists and writers put on musical soirées and amateur theatricals at the Palazzo Barberini, or held seances at which the notorious Connecticut spiritualist D. D. Home (he was later expelled from Rome as a sorcerer) staged his seemingly miraculous manifestations of unseen power. More formal events were sometimes on the calendar, and one dinner on Washington's birthday was reported to have been attended by two hundred American guests.

Florence rivaled Rome throughout these years. Although Margaret Fuller, finding it "a kind of Boston," said she would not give a pin to live there, many American artists preferred it to the capital of the Papal States. With its great collections of Italian masterpieces at the Uffizi and the Pitti Palace (the American painters, admitted only seven at a time, often had to wait weeks for a chance to get in and copy them), it was a wonderful center for art study. A number of writers, including Hawthorne who started work there on the *Marble Faun*, were also drawn to Florence for its associations and because of their friendship with such English exiles as Walter Savage Landor, John Ruskin, and especially Robert and Elizabeth Browning.

The Brownings were indeed good friends of many of the Americans in both Florence and Rome. "You know Mr. and Mrs. Story," we find Mrs. Browning writing a mutual friend on one occasion. "She and I go backward and forward to tea—drinking and gossiping at one another's houses, and our husbands hold the reins." Sometimes the two families went off together to escape the torrid heat of an Italian summer at some such hill resort as Lucca. Harriet Hosmer was another close friend, dining every evening with the Brownings when she visited Florence.

Horatio Greenough, the well-known sculptor, was to live in Florence twenty-five years, becoming a familiar figure as he walked its streets of an evening with a slim greyhound on the leash, and among the many painters was Thomas Cole, one of the first recognized American landscapists. His study abroad inspired the great allegorical canvasses, deeply permeated by the romantic spirit of Italy's past, which he called "The Course of Empire."

The most famous of the American artists in Florence, however, was undoubtedly the creator of the "Greek Slave." Tall, handsome, bearded, Hiram Powers was an arresting personality, immediately attracting everyone who met him. "Mr. Powers, the sculptor," wrote Mrs. Browning, "is our chief friend and favourite. A most charming, simple, straightforward, genuine American." There were those who felt his finely chiselled busts were almost mechanically conceived, but he was nonetheless widely hailed as "the first sculptor of his age."

James Jackson Jarves was himself another Florence resident. Boston-born, he had come to Europe after living for a time in the Hawaiian Islands, and only after crossing the Atlantic developed his lifelong and consuming interest in art. Characterizing Florence as "the world's capital of Bric-a-bracdom," he was always on the search for the various artistic treasures it afforded, and most importantly, became one of the first collectors to discover Italian primitives. In 1860 he brought what had grown into a valuable and unique collection of such paintings to the United States, but was unable to arouse any interest in them. There was as yet no Metropolitan Museum in New York nor Museum of Fine Arts in Boston, and as Jarves sadly noted after exhibiting his paintings, "no will to buy them." He ultimately gave his collection to Yale University as collateral for a loan of $20,000.

Rome and Florence remained the major centers for American expatriates until Paris finally took over this role in the last quarter of the century. Yet it has to be admitted that the painters and sculptors who lived so happily in Italy did not prove to be, in the eyes of later generations, artists of very conspicuous talent. Most of them, as Van Wyck Brooks has written in The Dream of

Arcadia, were either obscure at the time and never better known, or famous in their day and since largely forgotten. Nevertheless, they set a pattern of study in Europe that would continue to draw American artists abroad; encouraged through their discovery of Italy's great masterpieces the collection of European art for America's future museums; and also gave a fresh impulse to the art schools that were slowly developing in the United States.

VIII. CHANGING PATTERNS

THE Civil War interrupted travel abroad. A considerable number of Americans remained in Europe, their ranks swelled by Southerners unable to get home, and Paris was said to be "swarming with Confederate emissaries." When John Sliddell, the most important of those envoys who like the "militia diplomats" of revolutionary days were seeking to enlist European sympathy for a rebel cause, first arrived in the French capital, he found a Confederate Woman's Aid Society in active operation. More generally, however, transatlantic journeying sharply declined under wartime conditions, and it was only after 1865 that circumstances encouraged a renewal of the annual European tours that would soon lead to the breaking of all previous records.

In the latter half of the nineteenth century, a series of developments made travel more comfortable, and at least relatively less expensive. There were faster steamships, improved means of transportation on the continent, and new tourist services smoothing the way for bewildered Americans faced with unfamiliar customs and unintelligible languages. In such circumstances, a progressive broadening as well as deepening in the stream of travel gradually took place. While the European trip still demanded more leisure and more money than the average American could afford, it began to fall within the range of middle-class families and of a larger number of people away from the Atlantic seaboard than had been the case before the Civil War. The slowly rising tide of transatlantic voyagers doubled the pre-Civil War annual total by the 1880's, and would top the 100,000 mark before the end of the century.

"How to Visit Europe."

What to expect on a venture overseas in the immediate aftermath of the Civil War was helpfully explained to prospective tourists in a feature appearing in the *New York Tribune* on June 14, 1867. It advised on steamships, suggested hotels, outlined tours, and gave shopping hints.

The Cunard Company ("solidly and rigidly managed") was first among the transatlantic steamship companies. Its chief rival was the French Line, offering the advantage of claret served at both luncheon and dinner, but it was said to handle things on shipboard rather "noisily." The Inman Line had smaller, slower, and less expensive ships, and the American Line was "the cheeriest and most patriotic." Prospective passengers were told to bring their own deck chairs and steamer rugs, together with such books and games as they might want to while away the time on what was still a two weeks' voyage; warned that they must tip the steward at least $2 (the stewardess $5 if wife or daughter were along), and strongly advised to learn at least one French phrase every day.

Arriving on the continent Americans should be on their guard, the *Tribune* declared, for they might easily be swindled, but they could nevertheless usually count on Europeans being friendly and hospitable. They were not likely to find anyone so insolent as an American hotel clerk or as piratical as an American cab driver. They need have no worries about hotels for they were becoming increasingly adapted to tourist needs. For those fearing homesickness, there was the cheering news of a Hotel Washington in Liverpool, a Hotel du New York in Florence, and in Paris both a Hotel États Unis and a Hotel de l'Oncle Tom.

Finally, the *Tribune* advised where the tourist might go to satisfy his special interests: the great centers of art were Rome and Florence; for Gothic architecture one should not miss Rouen, Antwerp, and Cologne; music meant above all Leipzig and Vienna; clothing, if inexpensive in London but if stylish, Paris; laces in Brussels and silks in Turin. It was strongly urged that the visit to Paris, "a sensual, pocket-burning city," be left to the last.

As a further sign of the times there was also appearing annually in the 1860's *Harper's Hand-Book for Travelers in Europe and the East*. Its advice on transatlantic crossings and continental tours pretty much followed that of the *Tribune* article, but it also included information on passports, letters of credit, and other practical details of foreign travel. It pointed out that especially helpful for tourists in Paris was Galignani's Reading Room, where they could have their mail forwarded and read the home newspapers. Unlike modern guides, *Harper's Handbook* had nothing on such interesting topics as climate, clothing, shopping, or tipping.

Its advertisements indicated that European resorts and hotels were becoming greatly interested in the American tourist trade. Several of the latter called attention to "baths on each floor," and one in Paris announced "a very comfortable Machine Wagon (known as a Lift)" to convey its guests to the building's upper stories. The continental railroads advised that every consideration would be given to prospective passengers from the United States, and the German spas glowingly puffed their healing waters.

For tourists generally, the famous Baedekers were now available in English, and they rapidly became the most favored of all guidebooks with their "star system" irrevocably determining just what the traveler had to be sure to see. Their accuracy was beyond question—

> *For kings and governments may err*
> *But never Mr. Baedeker.*

These guides not only described minutely every possible sight— as they have continued to do ever since—but were filled with practical advice on hotels, restaurants, means of transportation, local currencies, proper clothing, health, shopping opportunities, and tipping. With a Baedeker in hand, the tourist no longer needed to worry about what he should see or do while abroad.

Nothing could ever quite compete with it; it became almost indispensable. In a novel whose scene is laid in Europe, William Dean Howells has one of his characters (there is also an anguished complaint about the lack of ice water) comment that the old *valets de place* had quite lost out with the advent of Mr. Baedeker's maps, itineraries, tours, and starred sights.

In the ensuing years, travel conditions continued to improve, on both sea and land, until the hardships that had once given something of a sense of adventure to going abroad had been largely eliminated. At one time Thomas Bailey Aldrich, the genteel editor of the *Atlantic Monthly*, was to comment sourly that the American staying at home had on hand "a hundred conveniences which he finds wanting in the heart of European civilization." In point of fact, travel abroad had become in many ways more pleasant and comfortable than travel in America.

In the 1870's the new "greyhounds of the ocean"—twin-screw, fast-sailing, ten thousand-ton and more luxury liners, carrying several hundred first-class passengers—were year by year cutting more time off the ocean run in frantic competition for the Atlantic "blue ribbon." A passage that in the first days of steam transportation took some two weeks was halved. In the century's final decade, the new White Star Line's "Teutonic" and "Majestic" were the fastest ships afloat, with a speed averaging twenty knots on their frequent crossings, but the "Campania" and the "Lucania" of the Cunard Company soon pulled ahead of them. Then new records were set by the Hamburg-America's impressive "Kaiser Wilhelm der Grosse" and huge "Deutschland." The latter ship, a 23,000-ton, four-stacked liner, could average twenty-three knots, and in 1900 was clocked on the eastward run from Sandy Hook to Queenstown in five days, seven hours, and thirty-eight minutes.

Even more than speed, however, luxury was the great boon of all first-class passengers. Well before the end of the century, the smoking lanterns of an earlier day had completely given way to electric lighting; marbled sea-water baths were commonplace, and the ornate public rooms—still very much addicted to gilt chandeliers and scores of reflecting mirrors—included lounges, smoking rooms, music rooms and libraries. The passengers did not need to bring their own deck chairs and steamer rugs; they could now be obtained through the deck steward and reserved in advance. Gymnasiums were introduced and following the initiative of the Hamburg-America Line band concerts. Ships' newspapers were regularly published. The meals that had long since been such a special feature of the ocean voyage were more epicurean than ever.

The transatlantic steamships were "vast, turbine-wheeled, electric elevatored, separate-tabled, a la carte, parlor-suited arks," one contemporary wrote enthusiastically, while another declared that the ocean voyage had become "a perpetual picnic, minus mosquitoes and ants."

Having arrived in Europe, the American tourists found that

a wholly new travel service had become available for them. Making good his promise in the 1850's to extend his English vacation tours to the continent, Thomas Cook was prepared to offer aid and assistance on a truly magnificent scale. In 1872 Henry James referred in his *TransAtlantic Sketches* to "Mr. Cook, the great entrepreneur of travel, with his coupons and his caravans of 'personally conducted' sightseers"; ten years later James E. Scripps, a Detroit newspaperman, reported that a majority of Americans abroad appeared to be taking advantage of the Thomas Cook services. Here was perhaps the most important innovation in the field of foreign travel since the introduction of the steamship and the railroad.

Henry James was rather skeptical about a Cook's tour, feeling that such organized sightseeing might "rub off the precious primal bloom of the picturesque." However, he recognized that Americans in Europe, forever distinguished by "our much-labelled luggage, our bad French, our demand for a sitz-bath and pale ale," needed the help that Mr. Cook was perhaps best qualified to give them. Scripps was rather more enthusiastic, pointing out the great benefits of a prearranged tour which enabled a traveler not only to make transportation and hotel reservations in advance, but to pay for them through his coupons on an all-inclusive basis. The daily hotel charge for a Cook's tour, he stated in 1882, was only $2.10 a day, including bed, table d'hote, lights, attendance, and a meat breakfast.

"Suppose now that a worthy American citizen finds he has made money, and has leisure . . . . to go to Europe," a contributor to the *Chautauquan* reported in 1890. "But what about the details? Probably they buy an American guide-book—I have seen some very bad ones—and becoming bewildered with details, take refuge in that harbor of the intellectually destitute—Cook's nearest office, where a highly competent and obliging official maps out the whole thing, counts the cost, and assures them that he will see them safely through the whole adventure."

The packaged tour meant that American travelers were more than ever going to the same places, seeing the same sights, and crowding the same resorts. It meant that the old complaint of how hard it was to get away from one's fellow-countrymen was justified to an even greater extent than it had been a half century earlier. But in ameliorating the uncertainties and even risks of more independent travel, it opened up Europe for thousands of newcomers.

In meeting the needs of the increased number of tourists, the European hotels further developed many new services. They arranged for omnibuses to meet all trains, employed English-speaking concièrges to act as guides and counselors, and multiplied the bathrooms on which the Americans always insisted. Occasionally there was provided, as one traveler happily reported, "a perfectly appointed Broadway bar." In London particularly, contemporary accounts suggest a vast improvement. One visitor in 1880 stated that while there had previously been hardly a single hotel meeting American expectations, at least half a dozen were now doing so successfully. Restaurants also began to cater to patrons from the United States. The most popular in London was already Simpson's (serving a hot joint for four shillings), and there were two "American confectionaries" offering ice cream and soda.

Railway travel had of course long since completely superseded the stage coach and diligence, and reservations could be made in advance on fast, comfortable express trains. Charabancs, which were once described as "a crab-like, sideway carriage," were still popular for short excursions, and occasionally one reads of tourists taking buckboards for rides into the country. One innovation was bicycling. An increasing number of younger travelers (of both sexes, to judge by a stirring article in *Outing* entitled "We Girls Awheel Through Germany") were taking to the open road in the 1890's. It was reported that bicycling in Switzerland represented something of a problem but that the highways in France, Germany, and Italy were excellent, and the country lanes in England enchanting. Traffic did not yet offer any serious hazards. While slow-moving, horse-drawn carts, hugging the center of the road with their drivers fast alseep, were sometimes an obstacle, they could be passed with careful maneuvering. The joys of bicycling, as one happy wheelman celebrated them in verse, knew no bounds:

> *In grasses thick the young birds hide,*
> *The soaring lark salutes the morn,*

As I through Merrie England wide
Swiftly upon my wheel am borne.

One of these intrepid, enthusiastic bicyclists was a young professor from Princeton University. Woodrow Wilson made two cycling trips through England and Scotland in the 1890's. On one occasion he wrote home that nothing could be more exhilarating and entertaining, with everything conspiring "to make a great overmastering charm which itself makes the wheel run easily and with zest, as if to hurry from beauty to beauty."

Two further innovations must be noted as adding fresh dimensions to tourist travel. In 1880 the Eastman Company developed the Kodak, and a few years later picture postcards first became available. It is hard to imagine how the European traveler had ever managed without being able to take snapshots or send home postcard records of his tour—"Having a wonderful time, wish you were here"—but once such cheerful activities were possible, they became a hallmark of tourism which nothing else could rival. One wholly practical note: it was in 1891 that the American Express Company first began to issue travelers' checks.

In the matter of over-all expenses, first-class travelers in the latter half of the nineteenth century found comparatively little change from the costs of pre-Civil War days. Steamship fares were quoted anywhere from $110 to $160 in gold in the late 1860's, and thirty years later they ranged from $100 to $200. Expenses on the continent, still considering those going first-class, were estimated in the 1880's at $250 to $300 for an extensive ten weeks' tour, based on $125 for railroad travel, hotel costs at a daily rate of $2.50, and a reasonable allowance for extras. Another report in 1895 placed such costs slightly higher, or $6 a day, including transportation but without wine. Such broad estimates suggest that the total expenditures for the usual three months' trip, first-class, averaged about $750, or very little less than what they would have been in midcentury.

The economy-minded, however, could make very substantial savings by traveling on either the old, slow ships or by going second-class, and then seeking out less expensive accommodations on the continent with the possible aid of guided tours. An article in the *Chautauquan* in 1887 especially emphasized the new comforts and conveniences in second-class and the great advantages of Mr. Cook's coupon system. It advised that a three months' trip providing ample time for visits to the major cities in England and France, a boat trip down the Rhine, and a "dash into Switzerland or Italy," could be made very comfortably for $400.

This was still a relatively high figure; a European vacation was by no means cheap. Moreover, the American abroad was already being subjected to the swollen prices that European hotel and shopkeepers were convinced he could easily afford. He was paying for the privilege of being an American, as even the pre-Civil War travelers had sometimes complained, because he was everywhere "looked upon as a bird to be plucked." Nevertheless, contemporary magazine articles and the advertisements of the new travel agencies constantly emphasized the economies possible for "the light pocket book." While one writer's enthusiastic statement that more reasonable travel costs had reduced the distinction between the wealthy and the poor to a minimum was greatly exaggerated, it is clearly apparent that the less affluent were beginning to go abroad in greater numbers than had ever before been possible.

The American tourists in these years stretching from the Civil War to the close of the century found a first chronicler in Mark Twain. It was in the very year that the *Tribune* had given its helpful hints to the first postwar voyagers that as a lively young man, with a thick shock of curly reddish-brown hair, a drooping mustache, and sharp twinkling eyes, he sailed for Europe and the Holy Land aboard the two-funneled, two-masted, 1800-ton paddle-wheeler the "Quaker City." Two years later—in 1869—there appeared *Innocents Abroad*. Selling 30,000 copies within six months, the book made its author famous, marked a new approach to foreign travel, and fastened upon Americans overseas a descriptive term they would never again wholly escape.

"The days of sentimental journeyings are over," wrote Bret Harte in hailing Mark Twain's account of the experiences of the "Quaker City's" passengers. "The dear old book of travel . . . . is a thing of the past. . . . Mr. Mark Twain has used brickbats on stained-glass windows with damaging effect."

In his iconoclastic approach to Europe, Mark Twain was not as original as Bret Harte's comment suggests, but *Innocents Abroad* not only gave its readers a comforting sense of the New World's superiority to the Old, but delighted them with its humor. It was in the tradition of the western tall story, with its satire never concealed or very subtle. Mark Twain reflected all the preconceptions and prejudices of a frontier community toward a more sophisticated society, and also set forth the traditional democratic animus toward aristocracy. He was by no means unappreciative of much that he saw in Europe, but his emphasis in *Innocents Abroad* was on the other side of the coin—kingship, class privilege and church rule.

The voyage of the "Quaker City" was a tourist cruise—first of its kind—and the passenger list included the types of persons that were increasingly to adopt this easy and comfortable way of seeing Europe. They were clergymen, lawyers, doctors, retired businessmen, and widows. While Mark Twain happily found "a tolerable fair sprinkling of young folks," it was on the whole an elderly group.

With several of his smoking-room cronies, Mark Twain left the ship for a tour through England and France, dutifully taking in every sight on the prescribed itinerary. He was at once amused and at times scornful to find his fellow tourists so awed by everything they saw. Trudging through "weary miles of picture galleries" and visiting scores of churches that often seemed to him no more than dull and decaying monuments of the past, they seemed unable to speak of such dubious artistic treasures except "in the catchy ejaculations of rapture." The idea of Europe's superior civilization seemed to him a "superstition .... imposed upon the world." The pictures in the Louvre were notable in his eyes only for what they revealed of a "nauseous adulation of princely patrons."

Apart from his mocking descriptions of a cultural tradition he would not accept, Mark Twain also relates his experiences in exploring the lighter side of Paris. In typical tourist fashion he went to what had now become "the celebrated Jardin Mabille" and to a performance of the famous can-can, the new dance providing such delightfully risqué entertainment for the innocents from across the Atlantic. "I placed my hands before my face for very shame," he wrote (one is reminded of Abigail Adams and her first ballet), and then added: "but I looked through my fingers." He searched Paris for the *grisettes* of whom he had heard so much. They were a disappointment, another of Europe's romantic frauds. He declared it would be "base flattery to call them immoral."

Mark Twain's further stories about tourist reactions to the strange and unfamiliar customs of continental travel are often highly amusing, but they have a familiar ring. He and his companions found it very hard to become accustomed to such oddities as the lingering routine of the table d'hôte, the scarcity of candles in the bedrooms, and the absence of ice water. They were gradually adjusting themselves to such inconveniences, he wrote, but "we are *not* getting used to carrying our own soap."

While the mockery with which Mark Twain observed the tourists was tinged with sympathetic affection, for he was one of them, more sophisticated Americans were less tolerant of the new overseas travelers. Henry Adams was in Paris in 1867 and complained testily of the visiting hordes "who stare and gawk and smell, and crowd every street and shop." Two years later Henry James, after summarily dismissing all tourists as "vulgar, vulgar, vulgar," went on to say:

> Their ignorance,—their stingy, defiant, grudging attitude towards everything European—their perpetual reference of all things to some American standard or precedent which exists only in their own unscrupulous wind-bags— and then our unhappy poverty of voice, speech, of physiognomy—these things glare at you hideously.

Here again is an echo of past criticism, but the caustic tone of both Adams and James suggests that Americans now going abroad did indeed embrace new types. Many of them were neither as well educated nor as cultured as their predecessors in pre-Civil War days who had come largely from the more Europe-oriented eastern seaboard. Largely ignorant of Old World history and art, they might well be ill at ease and prone to gape awkwardly at so much that was completely alien to them. What their critics described as their vulgarity and unhappy poverty of speech may thus have been true enough in some cases, but perhaps also meant no more than that they had not moved in the rarefied social circles that welcomed an Adams or a James.

These travelers, in fact, were often in pursuit of culture, but their past experience had not often prepared them to appreciate the paintings, the sculpture, the architecture of Europe. They knew little more than what they had learned from guidebooks. They were typical, everyday Americans quite lost in an unfamiliar world. It is revealing, for example, to come across the forthright comment of such a loyal midwesterner as Francis C. Sessions who toured Europe in 1889. He was enthusiastic about the crowded boulevards, the cafés chantants, the illuminations of Paris, but he would not let himself be unduly impressed. "I have not seen," he wrote in *On the Wing Through Europe*, "so prosperous and thriving a city as my own city of Columbus, Ohio nor, for its size, any place so attractive in public buildings of masterly design and splendid workmanship."

That the womenfolk among these tourists were often not only more enthusiastic, but better prepared than the men to enjoy and appreciate what Europe represented, is suggested in another comment of Henry Adams:

> Bored, patient, helpless, indulgent to an extreme; mostly a modest, decent, excellent, valuable citizen, the American was to be met at every railway station in Europe carefully explaining to every listener that the happiest day of his life would be the day he should land on the pier in New York.

Other contemporary observers remarked on the restlessness and the confusion as tourists rushed from place to place at an even more hectic pace than in the period when Longfellow had derisively written of his compatriots' gobbling up so many sights in a single day. They were always in a hurry—certainly a common tourist attitude—and often seemed to be almost unaware of where they were.

"One wonders what idea they have in traveling," H. G. Dwight, a consular official in Venice, wrote toward the close of the century. "Their interest seems to be principally motion; and when they find themselves out of railway carriages, they are at a loss for employment." He was particularly annoyed when their sole interest in such an enchanting place as Venice seemed to be discovering "in a café a trick of cooling beer that has never been seen." In his rather snobbish complacency, Dwight was then even more irritated by the tourists' blatant insistence on their nationality. They favored "a lavish display of flags, commonly about the person," he complained, and often took occasion "to pin the colors in miniature to their button-hole or wear them life-size at the corsage."

Even though Henry James was scornful of tourists as tourists, he was intensely interested in his countrymen abroad—no man more so. His great concern was with the socially-elect among transatlantic visitors and their relationship with European aristocrats, the historic confrontation of New World innocence with Old World corruption. Such aspects of "the international situation" he probed with deep understanding and keen psychological insight. Looked at from a less literary view, however, the characters spread through the pages of his travel sketches and novels may also be taken as highly representative of the various types of Americans who were going abroad in the latter part of the century. They may have been wealthier and moving in higher social circles than the common run of tourists, but their attitudes had a significance which may be more broadly applied.

There is for example Christopher Newman in *The American* who as "the great western Barbarian" sweeps down upon the effete Old World in excited enthusiasm. "I want the biggest kind of entertainment a man can get," he exclaims. "People, places, art, nature, everything! I want to see the tallest mountains, and the bluest lakes, and the finest pictures, and the most celebrated men and the most beautiful women." Here surely was the spirit in which many Americans went abroad in these years, discovering and enjoying an entirely new world. They were not all the bored and helpless travelers whom Adams had seen at so many railway stations. Yet in *The Ambassadors* James also depicts this latter type of homesick traveler in Lambert Strether's friend, Mr. Way-

113

marsh. "This ain't my kind of a country," he complains petulantly. "There ain't a country I've seen over here that does seem my kind. . . . Look here—I want to go back."

There are also two distinctive types in *The Portrait of a Lady*, though expatriates rather than travelers. One is the social conservative so distraught when France sets up the Third Republic, for what, he asks, had one crossed "that odious Atlantic for but to get away from republics"; and another is the young dilettante living in France to escape the impossible circumstances of his own country's business civilization. He had "some charming rooms in Paris, decorated with a Spanish altar-lace, the envy of his female friends."

Even more familiar are those many Jamesian characters— symbols of American innocence—who are forever being "caught" in the intricate mazes of Europe's polite, cultured, and faintly corrupt society. Christopher Newman himself (though he once exploded in exasperation that the United States "could put all Europe into their breeches' pocket"), Chad Newsome in *The Ambassadors*, Isabella in *The Portrait of a Lady*, and the heroine of *Daisy Miller* are among them.

James also has a character, in one of his sketches, who is highly revealing of another common type among Americans going abroad. This is the young, excited schoolteacher who is described in "Four Meetings" as having read all the histories and guidebooks, and caught the "great American disease" beyond hope of recovery in her monstrous appetite for the picturesque and the romantic. The conversation at her first meeting with the story's narrator leads to the question of which European country he prefers:

> "There is one I love beyond any. I think you'd do the same."
>
> Her gaze rested as on a dim revelation and then she breathed "Italy?"
>
> "Italy," I answered softly too; and for a moment we communed over it.

The number of tourists during these years did not nearly approach that of the mid-twentieth century, but it was steadily rising. The transatlantic voyage had become a picnic; Mr. Cook had introduced his packaged tours, and there were Kodaks and picture post-cards. "There can be no better recreation for an American," stated a writer in *Galaxy*, than "to break away from his own restless, overworked country." The tourist agents sensed an expanding future. It was only necessary to show that costs were becoming more reasonable, one of them wrote confidently at the century's end, "that fetches them!"

IX. NEW CULTURAL TIES

A NUMBER of Americans going overseas in the closing decades
of the nineteenth century—apart from the more casual tourists
with their Baedekers and their Kodaks—were to have experiences
or make associations that once again served to strengthen the cultural ties between the Old World and the New. The writers were a
case in point. Mark Twain returned repeatedly to Europe after his
first venture as a tourist aboard the "Quaker City," meeting many
of its literary men and lecturing extensively in England. Henry
James of course continued to live there—"my choice is the Old
World, my choice, my need, my life." As in the years before the
Civil War indeed, almost every contemporary American author
of distinction crossed the Atlantic. Walt Whitman was an outstanding exception (another was Emily Dickinson), and without
ever having left his native land he was to write of overseas travel
very much as had Noah Webster nearly a century earlier:

> The argument for travelling abroad is not all on one
> side. There are pulses of irresistible ardour, with due reason
> why they may not be gainsaid. But a calm man of deep vision
> will find in this strenuous modern spectacle of America as
> great sights as anything the foreign world, or the antique, or
> the relics of the antique, can afford him.

This, however, was a minority opinion. American writers
more generally felt that they could hardly afford not to see
Europe, both for itself and to enable them better to understand
their own country.

Mark Twain's second trip cast him in a quite different role than
that of the iconoclast of *Innocents Abroad*, and it was rather as a
romantic pilgrim that we find him exclaiming that his first hour

116

on English soil was one of "delight, rapture and ecstacy." Moreover, he thoroughly enjoyed his dazzling personal triumph in London as a famous author, lionized at a series of banquets, receptions, and assemblies. "Rank, fashion and culture rejoiced in him," William Dean Howells later wrote; and Mark Twain by no means spurned the adulation of the aristocratic society that on other occasions he attacked so fiercely.

There were to be other trips, taking the cure at Marienbad and Bad Nauheim, living for a time in both Switzerland and Italy, and after almost nine years of intermittent wanderings, a last stay in London where in 1890 he staged a series of "Mark Twain Evenings" at such Bohemian clubs as the White Friars, the Vagabonds, the Savage, and the Beefsteak. Thoroughly American as Mark Twain was in every way, he strongly felt the lure of the Old World and formed close ties with his many English friends. On his final return to America, he told the ship news reporters with a flash of the old spirit of mockery that he had finished with Europe: "I am going to break both of my legs so I can't get away again."

In becoming the expatriate and exile, Henry James succumbed completely to "the subtle poison" of the sophisticated Old World to which he had been first exposed as a child. There was too much about its "lighted and decorated stage" that he enjoyed for him to be able to reconcile himself to what he considered the more barren, uncultivated society of his own country. Yet his sympathies remained basically American throughout his life ("I know what I am doing," he wrote in 1878, "and I have always my eyes on my native land"), and Americans in Europe remained his absorbing literary preoccupation.

His life abroad consisted of writing, travel, and society. As a young man living in England—handsome, something of a dandy, grave and courteous in manner—he attained a position even grander than that of Washington Irving in the 1820's. He knew many British statesmen ("behold me after dinner conversing affably with Mr. Gladstone"), and became close friends with English writers from George Eliot to Robert Louis Stevenson. He was a great club man (the Athenaeum and the Reform), a perpetual diner-out, and a popular weekend visitor at the great English country houses. As he grew older—bald, stout, and pontifical—he settled more and more securely into the grooves of an aristocratic society. There were visits to America and travel on the continent, but he made his home at Lamb House, the eighteenth-century country place he bought in Rye. Here he entertained visiting Americans, as well as his English friends, and lived on until 1916, continuing to explore the complexities of the European-American relationship which his own life in many ways so subtly epitomized.

Even before Mark Twain visited Europe or James took up his residence there, the third of the major literary figures of this period, William Dean Howells, had made the first of numerous trips abroad. Appointed consul in Venice in reward for a campaign biography of Lincoln, he lived in Italy from 1861 to 1865. What is most interesting about this first visit were Howell's typically midwestern, rather provincial reactions. "We come to Europe," he wrote a small Ohio newspaper, "for a storied past and the picturesque old. It is all vanity." He was the self-conscious patriot, at a time when the cause of democracy was at stake in his own country. He was as scornful as the Mark Twain of the "Quaker City" of the harsh rule of monarchy in the Old World. "Is it not worth the journey thither," he asked, "to learn that the Fourth of July orations are true?"

For all his critical comments, however, Howells was to enjoy his life in Venice very much. Staying with his young wife in an apartment in one of the old palaces on the Grand Canal (the rent was apparently $1 a day), and having tea every afternoon at the Caffé Florian in the piazzo of San Marco, he led a quiet, leisurely life that enabled him to devote a great deal of time to his writing. He had interesting visitors. Among others were Henry Ward Beecher, whom he describes on leaving him one day at an art gallery, as "one limp and helpless mass of enthusiasm and perspiration"; Samuel P. Langley, the future airplane inventor; Charles Hale, editor of the Boston *Advertiser*, and John Lothrop Motley.

Howells' experience in Italy, about which he was to write in *Venetian Life* and *Italian Journeys*, gave him a taste for the Old World that was to bring him back again and again. He went everywhere, and while in first writing about Venice he had been at pains to correct what he called "the sentimental errors" that were a result of the romantic posturing of earlier writers, his later travel books were deeply appreciative of the European scene. He visited London where James took him under his wing; was delighted by Paris—"after all . . . . the most fascinating city in the world"; wrote that if he were ever banished, Switzerland was where he would like to live, and spent a great deal of time in Germany, finding Berlin a "vast, spiritless place" but enjoying the spas which were attracting even more Americans than in earlier days. Howells also visited Spain, which did not draw many tourists in spite of the enthusiasm with which Irving, Ticknor, and Longfellow had once written of it. He found it a "wild, beautiful, ugly land."

His feelings toward Europe reflected the old ambivalence in the American attitude toward the Old World. "Why should we wish to find America like Europe?" he asked. "Are the ruins—and the miseries—which beset the traveler abroad so precious that he should desire to imagine them . . . in his own hemisphere?"

Some idea of the continuing European visits of writers only less well known than Mark Twain, James, and Howells is suggested by the latter's note of a dinner party in London when among the guests were John Hay, Charles Dudley Warner, Thomas Bailey Aldrich, and Bret Harte. Also living in England for a time in the late 1890's were Stephen Crane and Jack London, while Finley Peter Dunne, the creator of the inimitable "Mr. Dooley," was abroad in 1899, complaining of the tourists with that half mocking note that was always certain to please stay-at-home Americans. With the turn of the century a new group appeared. A youthful Willa Cather toured the continent in 1902, sending back letters to the *Nebraska State Journal*; Booth Tarkington supported a European holiday by describing his fellow travelers for *Everybody's*; and somewhat later Theodore Dreiser made an overseas trip about which he wrote in *A Traveler at Forty*.

The experiences of these visitors greatly differed. For Bret Harte, who first went abroad to take over a consular post at Crefeld, Germany, Europe did not provide the help or inspiration which he had hoped to find there after the success he had achieved with such stories as "The Luck of Roaring Camp" began to fade. Settling in London in 1885, he found he could not write. "I grind out the old tunes on the old organ," he wrote discouragedly, and his letters show an increasing weariness as he approached death, ill and alone. The story of Stephen Crane also had its tragic undertones. He first visited England in 1897 as the famous author of *The Red Badge of Courage*, becoming a close friend of Conrad, Ford Madox Ford, and H. G. Wells. When he later returned to live with his wife in a great dilapidated, medieval house in Surrey, he was already ill. Entertaining expansively and spending far more than he could afford, he had only a year or two to live, dying from consumption before his thirtieth birthday in 1900.

An unusual feature of several of the travel accounts of writers going abroad after the turn of the century is their shocked descriptions, whatever they may have had to say about other cities, of London's notorious slums. Living for a time in the East End, Jack London wandered about the streets in old clothes gathering material that went into *The People of the Abyss*, a stark, realistic account of the degraded life of the English poor. So completely different a writer as Willa Cather was equally depressed by this aspect of the British capital. "If the street life . . . . is in any city more gloomy, more ugly, more cruel than in London," she wrote the *Nebraska State Journal*, "I certainly don't care to see it." And Dreiser was to include in the record of his European travels a poignant chapter dealing with these same scenes which he called "Lilly: A Girl of the Streets."

For Miss Cather, however, the London slums were only a passing incident. She enjoyed the English countryside, with so many places made familiar by novelists and poets, and going on to the continent rejoiced in France as "that happy part of the world." Her lively letters also suggest that tourists might still at times find things a little difficult. The train from Paris to Avignon was "a weary journey, a journey full of heat and dust and hungry French fleas," and her hotel was "primitive enough, too; one takes a bath in a washbasin and goes to bed by candlelight." But she was generally cheerful, enthusiastic and naive, finding Europe quite engagingly different from the plains of Nebraska. Dreiser, too, was a carefree tourist who except for his chapter on London slums, seems hardly recognizable as the sternly moralistic author of *Sister Carrie* and *Jennie Gerhardt*. He sat at the captain's table on the *Mauretania*, stayed in a grand country house in England, dined at the Café de Paris, and saw Mistinguett at the Folies-Bergères.

Booth Tarkington strikes a familiar note—as had Finley Peter

Dunne—in making sport of his compatriots. He drew an amusing picture in one of his articles for *Everybody's* of the conventional tourist couple: the husband bored and homesick ("O Lord, I want to get back to a country where I can read the signs"), and his wife terribly eager ("she'll write it all out for her literary club at home"). And there is also the ancient complaint: "The place is spoiled. One can never come here without finding a lot of Americans."

> In the morning they fight duels in swaddling clothes; in the afternoon they sit in the confectionery shops and eat sugar plums; and in the evenings they drink beer and sing songs.

The quotation does not refer to Americans, but is rather the observation of a visitor from the United States on student life in the German universities. It does not tell the whole story. A salient aspect of cultural interchange between America and Europe in the latter half of the nineteenth century was the large number of American students going to Göttingen and Heidelberg, Berlin and Leipzig, Jena and Halle. The German universities were considered the best in the world. A steady stream of Americans followed where Ticknor and Longfellow had once led the way, and between 1880 and 1900 their number was estimated to be as high as two thousand.

One young man who was later to remember nostalgically such student days in the early 1870's was John W. Burgess, the well-known political scientist at Columbia University. He enrolled successively at Göttingen, Leipzig, and Berlin, following the custom of that period, and sat at the feet of such monumental scholars as Helmholtz, von Treitschke, and Theodor Mommsen. But he also recalled, in *Reminiscences of an American Scholar*, his keen enjoyment of university social life—the beer drinking, music and dancing, excursions with young women ("accompanied by their chaperons") to the countryside. The dueling was the only thing of which he disapproved. He was prepared "to make a business of study," as did most of the Americans, but it was not a monastic life.

During the vacation periods, Burgess and his friends went on walking trips in Bavaria and Austria, constantly "entranced by the beauties of the scenery." They visited Berchtesgaden, the Konigssee, and Salzburg; took a little steamer down the Danube to Vienna whose palaces, galleries, and concert halls delighted them; and then went on to Trieste and Venice. The young men of these days, unlike their more wealthy predecessors traveling by coach and carrying important letters of introduction, were setting the more popular pattern of inexpensive excursions and casual touring that has ever since characterized American student life in Europe.

While in Berlin, however, Burgess did have a number of experiences almost comparable to those of Ticknor half a century earlier. He was invited by George Bancroft, at this time the American minister to Germany and always interested in the students because of his own youthful days abroad, to Sunday evening receptions at the legation where he had the opportunity to meet both von Moltke and Bismarck. And on another occasion, he heard Wagner conducting selections from the *Neibilungen Ring* in the presence of the Emperor.

Abroad altogether three years, Burgess was to return to America tremendously impressed with Germany, and especially the scholarly atmosphere (in spite of such aberrations as the dueling) of its universities. He was one of the scholars who was to play an important role in introducing to this country German methods of graduate instruction, and more particularly a systematic approach to the study of political science. In later years he was to go back many times to lecture in both Germany and Austria, becoming the first in a long line of exchange professors appointed to promote German-American understanding.

Another quite different young man who was for a time in Germany almost twenty years later, studying at Berlin, Heidelberg, and Leipzig, was Lincoln Steffens. He was interested not only in the science and philosophy which were primarily responsible for his coming abroad, but in art and music. This future muckraker and social reformer also cheerfully succumbed to the temptations and pleasures of university life, and his *Autobiography* tells of walks in the Black Forest, rowboat rides on the Neckar River, and dancing with the peasant girls at country inns and restaurants. His work at Heidelberg would sometimes appear to have been quite overshadowed by "all the fun that was going on, in the town, on the river, in the Forest—beer drinking, dancing, swimming and boating, walking, talking and exploring the world and one another."

For all the gayer side of life in the German universities, however, the outstanding opportunities for study which they offered in science, medicine, philosophy, economics, and history were what attracted the American students. A host of young men who were later to have the most distinguished careers in education and scholarship owed an immense debt to their training abroad.

The more outstanding college presidents of the next generation were among them. Both James B. Angell and Charles W. Eliot studied in Europe. Arthur Twining Hadley attended lectures in economics at Berlin as a first step in a professional career that led to the presidency of Yale, and John Grier Hibben was a student at this same university before going to Princeton. Two other young men who went abroad together were Andrew White, later president of Cornell, and Daniel Coit Gilman, president of Johns Hopkins. The famous scholars included, among so many others, Basil Gildersleeve, the great philologist; William Graham Sumner, economist, and Herbert Baxter Adams, founder of the American Historical Association.

Taken all in all, there is perhaps no other area where the experiences of Americans abroad have had a more direct or important impact on their country's life than that embracing the students in German universities in the closing decades of the nineteenth century. They returned to encourage the establishment of graduate schools on the German model, with a more systematic program of advanced studies and provision for granting the Ph.D. degree. An energizing center for this whole new development was Johns Hopkins University, and during the 1880's and 1890's it had scarcely a faculty member who was not German-trained.

The artists were once again an interesting group living and studying abroad. "My God," exclaimed William M. Chase, when first given such an opportunity, "I'd rather go to Europe than go to Heaven." Some among them still joined the older colonies in Rome and Florence, and a few went to London, Munich (where Chase himself studied) or The Hague. These years in the late nineteenth century, however, were the period when Paris first came into its own as the city of cities for painters. Here they now con-

123

gregated as they never had before to work under the French masters and enjoy the romantic, carefree atmosphere of the Left Bank. They studied at such popular art schools as the Académie Julian, so crowded that the young novices hardly had elbow room; lived in cold, little attics which served as studio, bedroom, and kitchen; affected the flowing ties and broad-rimmed hats that were the accepted artists' costume; and gathered nightly at the Latin Quarter's restaurants, brasseries, and sidewalk cafés. This was the Paris of bohemian legend.

Whistler was an early member of this still very small Paris art colony when he first went abroad (with an allowance of $350 from his mother) in the 1850's. Gay and irresponsible, a friend of George du Maurier, he was very much a part of the life described in *Trilby*. He then went on to live in England, with which he is more closely associated, but he continued to make frequent visits to Paris and spent long summers painting in Normandy. In the 1890's he became involved in a notorious quarrel with Ruskin, who in describing "Nocturne in Black and Gold" wrote derisively of Whistler "flinging a pot of paint in the public's face." Incensed by the insult, Whistler sued Ruskin for libel, bankrupting himself in the process, and, quitting England altogether, returned to Paris. To recoup his fortunes he undertook to sell the famous "Portrait of His Mother" which the French government finally purchased for the Louvre on the advice of Clemenceau.

Living in Paris during these last years, Whistler had a house and garden on the Rue de Bac and his many American visitors generally found him at work in his atelier with the complete absorption he always brought to his painting. Since his student days he had become a drawing-room idol, and except for his gaiety and wit, there was little about him to suggest the irresponsible bohemian of the 1850's. His later contemporaries described him as something of a dandy with monocle, fawn-colored frock coat, black trousers, patent leather shoes, and ebony walking stick.

Another American artist in Paris was Mary Cassatt. The daughter of a wealthy Philadelphia family, she had been taken abroad as a child but when she wanted to live in France and take up painting, her outraged father is said to have protested angrily, "I would almost rather see you dead." This dark, slender, soft-voiced young woman had a will of her own, however, and after studying for a time in other parts of Europe in the early 1870's, she not only made Paris her home but later persuaded her family to join her there.

She was a friend and disciple of Degas, and meeting through him such other painters as Manet, Monet, and Renoir, became an impassioned convert to impressionism. It was the turning point in her life ("I hated conventional art, I began to live"), and the beginning of her career as an artist. The impressionists having invited her to exhibit with them (Degas on seeing her "Woman Bathing" refused to admit that any woman could paint so well), she rapidly achieved a high reputation throughout Europe and ultimately in the United States. Her association with the impressionists had a further significance beyond its influence on her own painting for she played an important part in introducing them to America.

Miss Cassatt did not mingle with the bohemians of the Latin Quarter. Strait-laced and very conventional in her personal life, with ample money of her own, she established herself in a studio off the Champs Elysèes and also bought a chateau some seventy miles in the country. When her family later joined her, they lived just as they would have lived in Philadelphia, with maids in white starched aprons serving afternoon tea. But while Miss Cassatt may not have known the cafés of the Left Bank, she made her salon a meeting place not only for her friends among the painters but for many other important figures in Paris, including Clemenceau, who were interested in art. She was a witty talker and a charming hostess as well as a distinguished painter.

Many other American artists later to become very well known studied in Paris. A pioneer among them, even before the Civil War, was William Morris Hunt, of Brattleboro, Vermont, who on his return to the United States exerted a strong influence in persuading his fellow painters that the French capital was where they should study. Winslow Homer was briefly there in 1867. Before going to England where in the tradition of West and Copley he was to settle permanently, John Singer Sargent lived and worked in Paris from 1874 to 1885. He started painting at the age of eighteen in the studio of Carolus-Duran, a precocious pupil from the start, and in 1884 created a sensation when he exhibited his "Madame Gautreau" (now in New York's Metropolitan Museum) at the French Salon. The lady's decolletage was so shocking that both the critics and the public fell fiercely upon the artist, and the attack was so disconcerting that it was largely responsible for Sargent's moving to London.

The successful were always a mere handful in comparison with the hundreds of art students, poor and struggling, who lingered on in Paris without obtaining any recognition whatsoever. Spending more time at the café than they did at the studio, they could not tear themselves away, and stories of their supposed dissipation drifting back to the United States began to awaken the kind of concern that had aroused Jefferson over the temptations that European society offered to American innocence. Nowhere in the world, wrote a contributor to the *Nation*, was vice so open and flagrant as in "effeminate, sickly Paris." He worriedly felt that most of the American students living there had no other purpose than to experience "la vie de Bohème."

They also had their defenders. In a somewhat later article appearing in the *Independent*, the Reverend Sylvester Beach (father of the Sylvia Beach whose bookshop, Shakespeare and Company, was to become a literary landmark in the Paris of the 1920's) was to state emphatically that these young Americans were drawn abroad "by the pure instinct of art." They were serious and conscientious rather than "scatterbrained, rollicking, unconscionable Bohemians." Beach told the *Independent's* readers that he very well knew that the temptations of Paris were "peculiarly insidious and alluring," but he assured them that in spite of this, they need not worry about their young countrymen abroad.

X. WEALTH AND SOCIETY

WRITING in the 1840's of "our world" going to Europe, the wealthy Philip Hone had singled out an unchanging aspect of foreign travel. Even though the stream of overseas visitors may have substantially broadened a half century later with the new transatlantic steamers and more convenient means of continental travel, the rich and the fashionable remained a distinctive element among traveling Americans. By the 1880's and 1890's it had become commonplace for such people to take periodic vacations abroad, tour the continent with their families, or perhaps spend the season in London, Paris, or Rome.

Among them was one group, with all the advantages of inherited wealth and a cultured background, who went abroad not in any spirit of ostentation, not from social ambition, but as the most natural thing in the world. Both branches of the Roosevelt family—Oyster Bay and Hyde Park—were representative of this conservative well-to-do class, and it is hardly surprising to find that both Theodore Roosevelt and Franklin Roosevelt were taken abroad as children, and then in turn embarked on European honeymoons. "The two innocents are now on foreign soil," we find Theodore writing his family in June 1883 shortly after his marriage, and twenty-four years later, under almost identical circumstances, Franklin is saying in a letter from France to his "dearest mama" that he and his bride Eleanor are "having the time of our lives."

On his first childhood trip, a lively enthusiastic thirteen-year old, Theodore had written a wonderful series of letters. They were all boy, and yet had the sure Rooseveltian touch. He had for example found the Vatican "magnificent—splendid," but admitted that he had most enjoyed wandering about the streets of Rome shooting at dogs with a pop gun. His comments twelve years later on his honeymoon—Paris, Switzerland, the trip down the Rhine, a tour of England—are still full of youth, vitality, and exuberance. He climbed the Matterhorn, proudly noting that he had tired out his guide; managed to keep in good trim on a rough Channel crossing ("poor baby-wife" was seasick) by vigorously walking up and down the spray-blown deck; and had "great fun" riding and hunting in England.

There was only one note in these cheerful, confident letters that seems out of character for Theodore Roosevelt. Taking time from this honeymoon tour to work on his naval history of the United States, he wrote from The Hague that he was discouraged. "I wonder if I won't find everything in life too big for my abilities," he said mournfully, but then added, "well, time will tell."

Franklin and Eleanor followed very much the same tourist route in 1905 but included Italy on their itinerary as well as France, Germany, and England. Their letters (Franklin found everything "interesting" while Eleanor was addicted to "wonderful" and "charming") give a picture of two tourists as conventional as any couple who ever crossed the Atlantic. They traveled, as they tell us, Baedekers in hand, seeing everything that was properly starred, and of an evening playing piquet or reading the Tauchnitz editions of new English novels. Franklin reports falling asleep while his bride is trying on new clothes in Paris, and Eleanor admits that she was somewhat shocked by the bathing dresses at the Lido in Venice. On returning to Paris after their Italian tour, Franklin learned that he had flunked his law examinations at Columbia and promptly broke out in hives. Still, the trip was a great success and both bride and groom reported having enjoyed it thoroughly.

If the Roosevelts had the position and assurance to be quite oblivious of any question of social status, others among the American rich approached the European tour in a quite different spirit. Especially for the *nouveaux riches*—"the steel barons, coal lords, dukes of wheat and beef"—who were seeking to storm the citadels of the old aristocracy, a trip abroad had two great advantages. In an age when conspicuous display was a hallmark of wealth, and wealth appeared to be the measure of every value, they could make a lavishly expensive European tour an outward sign of their success. It was almost comparable to ownership of a chateau at Newport, a yacht, or a string of polo ponies. And if the trip abroad could lead to some acquaintances who might provide an entrée into the more exclusive circles of European society, a further foundation would be laid for climbing the social ladder at home.

There was of course nothing new in all this. William C. Preston had in 1817 noted his countrymen's "preeminent and indecent propensity to thrust themselves upon exclusive circles." James Fenimore Cooper had scathingly criticized Americans seeking to emulate the European aristocracy as a means of winning social status. But the socially ambitious of the Gilded Age, more than Americans in any other period, sought to use foreign society as a stepping stone to entering that of their own country.

A typical example was Ward McAllister, that incredible fop of the close of the century whose one ambition was to rule the society of Newport. Having made a fortune in California—and also having married an heiress—he promptly went abroad for his social apprenticeship. If he did not actually dine with royalty on this first trip, he was at least able to approach close enough to such lofty personages that some of the glamour rubbed off. Making the most of these real or fancied associations on returning to the United States, he soon found himself successfully launched on a career that was to carry him triumphantly to the very pinnacle of fashion.

Some of the long-accepted members of American society and the more successful among these new social climbers belonged to an international set that grew increasingly flamboyant at the close of the century. It was exclusive, extravagant, and snobbish. Theirs was a Europe which provided a setting for conspicuous display and lavish entertainment centered about the more elegant seashore resorts and watering places, the international sporting events, and the gambling casinos. There was a mingling of European aristocracy and American wealth that stood quite apart from anything in the experience of the average Americans going abroad.

When the members of this set traveled, they did so in a style in which luxury easily spilled over into ostentation. They took over the special suites aboard the new liners, sometimes having their own private dining rooms and reserved deck spaces;

were accompanied by maids and valets for themselves, tutors and governesses for their children, and toured the continent under the guidance of special couriers with great mountains of baggage. Their hotels were famous: Claridge's in London, the Ritz in Paris, the Grand in Rome, and the Adlon in Berlin. Such visits, as Mrs. Cornelius Vanderbilt once commented complacently, made for "a well-rounded life."

For the ambitious there were several stages along this European route to social status. The first was meeting the right people at the right places and becoming known to the fashionable world. The newspapers and magazines could be counted upon to do their part in providing the proper publicity. In no other period of American history did the press more eagerly cover the daily life, the feverish competition, the carefully muted scandals of high society than it did in the 1890's. Copy from abroad was especially exciting. An eager public devoured every item of such absorbing news, relayed through foreign correspondents or taken from the society page of the Paris *Herald*, which pictured the glamorous activities of the international set in London and Paris, Rome, Berlin and Madrid.

The *Cosmopolitan*, one of the new ten-cent monthlies, carried frequent articles about the socially prominent women living abroad ("Transplanted American Beauties"); published photographic descriptions of the social whirl in the American colonies of Europe's major cities, and repeatedly described the comparative advantages of staying at Bad Nauheim, Carlsbad or Aix-les-Bains. The *New York Times* and the *New York Tribune*, their stories often picked up by other papers in the hinterland, faithfully covered all the society events in which Americans might participate. Upon the occasion of King Edward's death, the latter newspaper sadly lamented the probable effect on a season that had given every promise of "proving more American than ever." Happily there soon appeared to be some compensation for this unfortunate occurrence in the large number of Americans who were able to be present at the coronation of George V.

A further goal of American social ambition was presentation at court, and with the turn of the century this became more important than ever before. France no longer provided a king or emperor; the most suitable capital was London. Soon the American ministers at the Court of St. James's found that arranging for such presentations was one of their most onerous if not most important duties. The advent of Edward VII to the throne had added a new glamour to court life after the more sedate days of Queen Victoria, and on the eve of World War I, we find Ambassador Walter Hines Page rather ruefully writing about the ever-increasing number of American women—"all sorts from twenty-four karats to tinsel"—who were every year clamoring for the opportunity to curtsey before royalty.

"And presently the presentations come," Page reported in one letter home. "Lord! how sensible American women scramble for this privilege. It royally fits a few of them. . . . One rule is, I don't present any but handsome women, pretty girls: that's what you want when you are getting up a show. . . . Far too many of ours come here and marry Englishmen. I think I shall make another rule and exact a promise that after presentation they shall go home."

Page was hinting in this final comment at what was the final step, the very apex, of social success abroad—that is, the international marriage. Again this "quest for coronets" was nothing new in European-American relationships; its history was as old as that of travel abroad. The *Knickerbocker Magazine* noted in 1837 "the abject reverence for foreign titles prevalent in our fashionable society," and twenty years later a contributor to *Harper's Magazine* raised the question whether "our sweet American girls" were not over-anxious to put a little tattered feather from princely trains into their republican bonnets. It was, however, in the 1890's, that this marriage market specializing in the union of American heiresses and titled foreigners first really boomed.

Every year now saw new bonds forged between the wealth of the New World and the aristocracy of the Old. In one exciting season alone—that of 1895—a breathless press recounted the marriages of Anna Gould and Count Boni de Castellane, Consuelo Vanderbilt and the Duke of Marlborough, Mary Leiter and Lord Curzon of Kedleston, and Pauline Whitney and Sir Almeric Paget, Lord Queensborough. The greatest amount of money was probably involved in the Vanderbilt-Marlborough merger, the bride's father making a tidy settlement of $2,500,000. The rather expensive atmosphere surrounding this transaction was further suggested by the elaborateness of the wedding itself, the *New York Times* featuring the affair as the most important news of the day— "She is Now a Duchess."

These interesting alliances—which more often than not had an unhappy ending—were supplemented by others in which the brides had other claims to distinction than mere wealth. The daughter of Vice President Levi Morton married the Duc de Valençay et de Sagan, and a granddaughter of President Grant married Prince Michael Cantacuzene of Russia. The most significant of all such matches, however, had been that in 1874 of the Baltimore beauty Jennie Jerome (whose two sisters also married Englishmen) and Lord Randolph Churchill. Their son Winston Churchill was to play a rather noted part in cementing Anglo-American relations in the twentieth century.

In 1903 the magazine *McCall's* ran an article giving a full account of this marriage market which found so many young American women ("dowered with loveliness and dollars," in the phrase of Frederick Townsend Martin) uniting in holy wedlock with impoverished but titled Europeans. It listed fifty-seven recent matches, and while it did not go into precise financial details, a somewhat later investigator, the socialist historian Gustavus Myers, estimated in 1909 that as the fortuitous consequence of the foreign marriages of some five hundred American women, a total of $200,000,000 had fled the New World for the Old.

Although greatly intriguing to the general public, the social life of the wealthy American expatriates, the presentations at court, and the marriages of American heiresses with foreign noblemen, remained a cause for alarm among those who sought more vigorously to uphold republican virtue. James G. Blaine, twice Secretary of State, could hardly have felt more strongly the age-old prejudice that everything about Europe was suspect in comparison with American virtue and innocence. "Every woman who leaves the duty and decorum of her native land and prostitutes her American name to the scandals, the vices, the social immoralities and moral impurities of foreign cities," he wrote emphatically on one occasion, "not only compasses her own shame, but mars the fair name of the Republic."

Some time later Henry Watterson, the editor of the Louisville *Courier-Journal,* contributed an outspoken article to the *Cosmopolitan* vigorously assailing the *nouveaux riches* who went abroad in what he considered the vain and frivolous effort to win social status by association with European nobility. "The time may come," he concluded sarcastically, "when the rich American will find something more to his fancy than bizarre vanities and foreign loiterings; when he will stay at home . . . . no longer nursing the distemper of deriving pleasure by dipping his toes in the rather cold sunshine of a titled aristocracy, which at heart despises him."

The novelist Henry Fuller was a little more subtle in his gently ironic stories, gathered together in *From The Other Side,* which described this same snobbish approach to "the great constellation of Old-World society." He singled out particularly the "pilgrim sons" whose one wish was to discover in England the aristocratic origins that would entitle them to social recognition at home. One of his characters is amazed to discover on a transatlantic voyage a fellow passenger who seems somewhat oblivious of all this.

"Don't you want the right crest on your stationery?" he asks. "Don't you want to be decently received by your English cousins when you go to visit in your dear old home? Don't you want— Dear me, I never saw such a man in my life!"

Charles Dana Gibson, the most popular of illustrators at this time, was to wage ceaseless warfare against the American girls (and their mothers) who married for titles, and no less a social arbiter than Henry Cabot Lodge carried the attack so far as to issue a blast against the fathers of these ambitious brides. "Every pork-baron," he wrote, "will buy a European title because he comprehends that the title has a value as a trade-mark, and a trademark he understands."

> Then on Monday we drove out to the races again and lunched and spent the day with the Lord Lieutenant. Prince Francis of Teck is here and seems such a *nice* young man. . . . The Duke and Duchess de Luynes are staying with Lord Houghton and came to the races yesterday. Tomorrow the great Dublin horse show begins and we are going with Lord Houghton and then we shall return with him and all his suite and outriders to the Castle where there will be a large dinner, followed by a ball, and we shall stay there for a

night or so. The Italian Princes, the Duke d'Aosta and Count of Turin will also be staying there. What fun it all is!

This extract from a letter written in 1894 by the young Grace Wilson, who was soon to become Mrs. Cornelius Vanderbilt, tells something of the social life of those who had successfully arrived in European society. One of Miss Wilson's sisters had married Ogden Goelet, whose wealth and possession of a yacht had provided an easy entrée into the international set revolving about the Prince of Wales; another sister was to marry the Honorable Michael Herbert whose country home, Wilton House, was one of the most celebrated castles in England. With such assets in the background, this lively daughter of a wealthy Georgian who had made a fortune selling cotton blankets during the Civil War followed every year a pleasant routine of travel: Paris for shopping early in April, a Mediterranean cruise, a visit to Bad Nauheim for the "cure," London for the season opening in June, grouse shooting in Scotland, a short stay at Deauville. . . . Then after another brief shopping visit in Paris, home for a short rest at Virginia Hot Springs and the beginning of the New York winter season.

Her marriage to Cornelius Vanderbilt did not essentially alter this pattern of social life. As the imperious, determined leader of New York society, rather than a frivolous young girl dancing and flirting with her counts and barons, she still made her regular trips abroad. Every year Mrs. Vanderbilt visited wealthy and titled relatives and friends, cruised on her husband's luxurious ocean-going yacht the "North Star," went to the races at Cowes and Kiel, and generously hobnobbed with royalty. On one occasion, wearing her most spectacular jewels, she attended a performance of the opera at Naples when both King Edward and Kaiser Wilhelm were in the audience. "The *dear* king himself," she wrote her sister, "couldn't keep his eyes off our box."

About this same time Mrs. Vanderbilt received a letter from her niece, May Goelet, which suggests that a new generation was quite as socially ambitious. Miss Goelet regaled her aunt with her conquests—the Duke of Roxburghe, Lord Shaftesbury, Lord Castlereagh ("the Londonderry boy"), and a Captain Holford ("unfortunately, the dear man has no title, though a very good position"). Everything once again was terribly gay, and in this letter from Bad Homburg, Miss Goelet expressed her naive amazement that she had so many dancing partners and so many "offers." But after all she was related to Vanderbilts and Astors, heiress to a fortune in her own right. In the end she married the Duke of Roxburghe (and his Scottish castle), having in due course a son for whom King Edward and Queen Mary served as godparents.

There were many other familiar society names (including additional Vanderbilts) in this international set. Many of its members commuted regularly back and forth from Newport ("its opera glass turned forever across the sea"), and sought to add to their social distinction by capturing foreign aristocrats who might in turn visit this dazzling capital of the "Four Hundred." Some among them succumbed completely to Europe, living as expatriates in London or Paris.

James Hazen Hyde, an acknowledged society leader in New York and Newport who has been called the "greatest exquisite of the Gilded Age," moved to Paris (where he had previously been educated) under something of a cloud. The angry popular reaction to a notorious *bal masque* he once gave at Sherry's at a reported cost of $200,000 convinced him that Europe's atmosphere was more congenial than that of his own country. An equally prominent New York couple leaving the country under quite comparable circumstances were the Bradley Martins, who originally came from Troy but had won social distinction by taking a town house in London. After their return to this country they gave an even more fabulous party than that of James Hazen Hyde, with the Hotel Waldorf made over into a replica of a hall at Versailles at a reputed cost of $369,000. No more than Hyde could they face the public criticism such an extravagant affair evoked, and they retreated quickly to England.

Another expatriate who was unhappy over his countrymen's failure to appreciate him was William Waldorf Astor, the eccentric heir to a fortune of $100,000,000. Having failed in an attempt to make a career of politics because the voters of New York would have none of him, he moved to England in 1890 and nine years later became a British citizen. Making the most of his opportunities for lavish political gifts, he ultimately won the final award of a title—Viscount Astor.

Without being identified with international society as were the Vanderbilts and Astors, Andrew Carnegie spent half of every year abroad after his marriage in 1887. He had come to America from Scotland as a poor immigrant, his first job that of a bobbin boy in a textile factory; he returned as an enormously wealthy captain of industry, the friend of Gladstone and John Morley, and built for himself Skibo Castle where he regularly entertained with regal munificence. Carnegie loved England and Scotland (at one time, however, embarking on a vigorous newspaper campaign urging abolition of the monarchy), but he never lost his pride in his adopted country. Toward the close of his life he was said to have refused a British peerage because it would have meant surrender of his American citizenship.

The greatest financier of this period, John Pierpont Morgan, was an avid European traveler who toured the continent and sailed up the Nile with a splendor that rivaled that of kings. His entourage invariably included several friends, among whom would be the particularly favored lady of the moment, a battery of servants, and incredible quantities of baggage. He was on the best of terms with Edward VII and Wilhelm II, as well as European statesmen, bankers and businessmen. Two houses in England inherited from his father; year-round apartments or hotel suites in Paris and Rome, and his yacht "Corsair," generally kept in the Mediterranean, were always at his disposal for his European visits. Morgan died in 1913 while staying in Rome at his $500 a day suite at the Grand Hotel.

"Would it not be better," Bayard Taylor had asked in the course of his European travels in 1846, "for some of our rich merchants to lay out their money on statues and pictures, instead of balls and spend-thrift sons?"

Half a century later such merchants, and the whole world of wealth and society, were furiously expending a good part of their money on such imports from Europe, even though balls and spend-thrift sons were not entirely neglected. Art was highly fashionable. "It has become the mode to have taste," wrote James Jackson Jarves. "Private galleries in New York are becoming almost as common as private stables." On their European tours the *nouveaux riches* particularly were anxious to purchase everything they could—not only paintings and statues, but tapestries, furniture, rugs, pottery, silverware, every kind of *objet d'art*—to furnish the Gothic castles, elegant Renaissance palaces, Tudor mansions they were building at home.

There were also collectors whose purchasing forays reflected a more genuine quest for culture, men and women who had become interested in European paintings and sculpture for their own sake. They might still be influenced by the rivalry for social recognition that was a special hallmark of art collecting, but they often brought refinement and discrimination to the selection of what they purchased. Moreover, even when personal gratification was a primary motive, some few of the collectors of this period looked beyond their own immediate gains in the belief that through bringing some part of Europe's great heritage of art to the United States, they were culturally enriching their own country.

Among the collectors of the 1880's and 1890's, at once socially ambitious and yet discriminating in their taste, were two very wealthy, individualistic, and spectacular women: Mrs. Potter Palmer, wife of one of the richest men in Chicago, the owner of the famous Palmer House; and Mrs. John Gardner, a Boston social leader and millionairess through inheritance from her father. They were both eager and unflagging collectors; they also owed a great deal to professional advice. Mrs. Palmer was assisted by Mary Cassatt, through whom she was introduced to French impressionism, while Mrs. Gardner was helped by a youthful but already highly discerning Bernard Berenson, who first went abroad in 1887 and lived on in his villa at Florence to become the world's greatest authority on Italian painting.

Mrs. Potter Palmer, a truly regal beauty with what was reputed to be the smallest waist in Chicago, was to make her art collection one of the means which assured her position as the social arbiter of the midwest. Her husband had built for her at a cost of $700,000 a fantastically imposing "Norman-Gothic" castle, with the first Louis XVI salon in Chicago (as well as the first private elevator), a sunken bath in the shape of a swan, and a seventy-foot picture gallery. On her trips abroad Mrs. Palmer zealously sought out "the best" to furnish this tremendous mansion and to cover the walls of its gallery. She bought Corots—

which were then a "must" for every wealthy collector—and other paintings of the Barbizon school; on the advice of Mary Cassatt, she purchased the still almost unknown impressionists, paying only $5000 for four Renoirs.

In the course of her European travels Mrs. Palmer met Whistler. On one occasion in writing Joseph Pennell, the American painter described Rome as "a bit of an old ruin alongside a railway station where I saw Mrs. Potter Palmer." In 1893 President McKinley made this formidable social leader the chairman of the Board of Lady Managers for the Chicago Exposition, and she again toured Europe, meeting with royalty wherever she went, to arrange loan exhibitions from the European galleries.

After this venture Mrs. Palmer was to move on to Newport in a successful midwestern invasion of this exclusive social capital, but after her husband died in 1902 she spent an increasing amount of time abroad. When in London she occasionally played golf with her good friend Edward VII, and entertaining lavishly, once brought an entire opera company over from Paris to give a private performance of Salomé. After her death, the greater part of her collection, like the paintings owned by many other rich midwesterners, went to the Chicago Institute of Art.

In the special loan exhibition at the Chicago Fair in 1893—"Foreign Masterpieces Owned by Americans"—was one painting loaned by Mrs. Gardner. She was by then well started on that fabulous collection that was to make her Venetian palace—Fenway Court—one of the show places of Boston. Her interest in art had been first aroused while living in Paris, where she had been taken by her family as a young girl for her "finishing," and was then further developed by attendance at art classes in Boston taught by Charles Eliot Norton. What really made her collecting possible, however, was a bequest of $2,750,000 from her father who died in 1891. She could then turn to this consuming interest with unflagging zeal—and the means to purchase quite widely.

Mrs. Gardner was a self-centered, egotistic, and highly eccentric woman, who always knew what she wanted and was quite determined to get it, whether in the world of Boston society or that of international art. She had at one time shocked and horrified Boston by such youthful escapades as drinking beer at pop concerts and going to prize fights, and was never to lose her vitality, her enthusiasm, and what in spite of rather plain features was the seductive appeal of her hour-glass figure and arresting personality. She went abroad quite regularly every two years, holding court and giving elegant parties in Venice as she did in Boston, and with Berenson's constant help seeking out paintings, stained glass and other artistic treasures. Her collection was for the most part made up of Italian painters—Raphael, Correggio, Titian—but there were also some few Rembrandts, two Holbeins, a Vermeer.

An amazing woman in every way, with a host of admirers including Henry James and Henry Adams, Mrs. Gardner was to have, in the former's phrase, "a preposterously pleasant career" with her European trips, her social triumphs, and her exquisite home. Fenway Court became her monument, housing a priceless exhibition of art that perhaps justified all her social tyrannies and egotism.

In sharp contrast with the collections of Mrs. Palmer and Mrs. Gardner, was the miscellaneous hodgepodge of art objects with which William Randolph Hearst cluttered his fabulous California estate, San Simeon. Hearst was the compulsive buyer, the insatiable looter, the barbarian seeking spoils. He toured Europe to get whatever he could, and then bore it home triumphantly. The castle he had built at San Simeon boasted among its other rooms, a great medieval hall which Hearst filled with Gothic mantels, Sienese banners, Venetian stained glass, Gobelin tapestries and Italian madonnas. Some of his furnishings and art objects were almost priceless; but they were mingled with worthless trash or faked antiques. It was said that when Hearst dined at his sixteenth-century refectory table, paper napkins and ketchup bottles appropriately offset the Georgian silver candlesticks.

J. P. Morgan, whose immense wealth enabled him to disregard cost almost completely, was probably the greatest collector of this period. On his periodic trips abroad, he was constantly on the lookout. He casually spent $21,000 on one occasion for a Louis XVI gold box that caught his fancy; paid without hesitation $200,000 for a Cellini cup, and bought a Raphael altar piece—his most expensive European purchase—for $484,000. He had taste and judgment. Price was no consideration.

Morgan brought to his art collecting the same singleness of

purpose, the same bland disregard of all possible rivals, the same strong sense of possessiveness, that he brought to the collection of steel companies and railroads. Domineering and often irascible, a sometimes frightening figure with his fierce black eyes, heavy mustache and large, bulbous nose, he almost invariably had his way, winning in the world of art collecting a position comparable to that he maintained in the world of finance. He was the patrician, buying for his own personal satisfaction, and certainly without any need for conspicuous display to demonstrate his social status.

The immensely valuable collection that he built up, valued at his death at $60,000,000, was ultimately to enrich his country beyond measure. On his death nearly half of his paintings went to the Metropolitan Museum in New York, with which he had long been associated as one of its founders and directors.

XI. ON THE EVE OF ARMAGEDDON

THE YEARS from 1900 to the outbreak of World War I were "the good years." The world was peaceful and prosperous. The American people had been awakened to a new sense of their position among nations as a result of territorial expansion, and they were "looking outward" as never before. Across the Atlantic was a Europe where they could freely travel without need for either passports or visas (except for Russia and Turkey), and which welcomed visitors with warm cordiality. Everything conspired to give a new impetus to the annual exodus from the New World to the Old.

Contemporary advertisements were a constant enticement. From the Cunard Company, still boasting its unrivaled record of no passenger losses at sea, to the purveyors of Mothersill's Seasick Remedy ("Be Happy and Well While Traveling"); from the travel agency vigorously promoting Golden Rule Tours to the resort hotels in German spas advertising their elegant mud baths and mineral springs, the chorus rose and swelled. On the eve of the outbreak of European hostilities, Raymond-Whitcomb (the American Express Company had not yet entered the booming tourist industry), was offering all-inclusive "package tours" for both individuals and groups. Their spread was from $178 to $400 for a five weeks' trip to $1000 for a eight-country, all-summer luxury tour. At varied rates within this general range, Comfort Tours had a series of Three Months Excursions with "experienced escorts"; the University Travel Bureau advertised Special Tours that were "something more than accelerated sight-seeing"; the American Travel Club announced Tours of Character; and Miss Wyman's Selected Tours offered transatlantic excursions with "girls carefully chaperoned." The popular excursions—even in their prices—were already cast in a form that would become increasingly popular and extensive a half century later.

The sailing of every liner was a gay and exciting occasion in these years. Shipboard parties, with their flowers, *bon voyage* boxes, and champagne, created a festive air and the public rooms were always crowded with visitors until the stewards with their cry of "all ashore" finally cleared the decks and a flotilla of puffing tugs succeeded in moving the ship out into the harbor. Still more shipboard luxuries had been added to those which characterized the steamships of the 1890's—garden lounges, verandah cafés, swimming pools.

The four-stacked "Mauretania" and "Lusitania" (sister ships of 38,000 tons and 785 feet long) were now the proud possessors of the Atlantic blue ribbon, the former setting in 1910 a record that lasted nearly a quarter of a century when its passage from Queenstown to New York was clocked in four days, ten hours, forty-one minutes. The White Star Line lost its "perfect" ship, the supposedly unsinkable "Titanic," in her fatal collision with an iceberg in 1911, but it still had such popular vessels as the "Britannic" and the "Olympic." There were also the swift-sailing liners of the Red Star, the French Line, the North German Lloyd and Hamburg-America. It was in 1914 that the latter added to its already impressive fleet the giant "Vaterland," whose 55,000 tons and 950 foot length, providing for 5000 passengers and crew, made her the largest ship afloat. She made only two trips for her owners before war broke out, but renamed the "Leviathan" was later to play a notable role ferrying American troops to Europe.

While first-class rates had risen slightly in the past two decades, with the minimum aboard the fastest ships in these prewar days $125, a more significant sign of the times was cheaper and steadily improving accommodation in second-class. The North German Lloyd also pointed the way to what was to become increasingly important when it advertised cabin class—"comfort without luxury"—on its smaller ships sailing from Baltimore. For the enterprising college student, there was also third-class or steerage, and numbers of them, swept along by the popular interest in European travel, worked their way abroad on cattle boats.

Little change had occurred in the established patterns of continental travel since the 1890's. Some of the European hotels announced new facilities especially designed for Americans, such as private baths and telephones; the railroads ran special excursions with reduced tourist rates; but the popular itineraries, the favored places to stay, the starred sights, were very much what they had been.

In some ways overseas travel was in a transitional stage which was marked by many of the old inconveniences and at the same time foreshadowed more modern luxuries. It still had something of the leisurely atmosphere—in comparison at least with the 1960's —which had characterized the nineteenth century. Tourists who were content to travel slowly and take their time did not need to worry about reservations for railroads, hotels, or sightseeing expeditions. They enjoyed more friendly personal services—even though they might not themselves always fully appreciate them— than have their successors.

One minor feature of such travel forty-odd years ago was the great quantity of baggage the tourists were still able to bring with them. On the ocean voyage they sent their heavier pieces—the great wardrobe trunks of the period—to the ship's hold, but they filled their cabins with steamer trunks, suitcases, hat boxes, and assorted paraphernalia almost beyond the imagination of travelers in the jet age. On the continent, the railroads, omnibuses, and hotels, with readily available porters, were quite accustomed to handling such baggage, and the hotels make a great occasion of the arrival and departure of their heavily laden transatlantic guests.

The tourists themselves conformed to type. It is interesting to find an article in *The World Today* first singling out the rich, and then as might any writer in the midnineteenth century, listing clergymen, teachers, writers, artists, and students as being in the vanguard of their less easily identifiable compatriots. An equally familiar note is struck by a contributor to the *Atlantic Monthly*. He wrote that what Americans most wanted to see on their transatlantic tours was the quaint and the picturesque: "the Old World . . . . ought to look old."

Among these overseas travelers should also be noted one category—always important but particularly so in this era—which was made up of onetime immigrants returning for brief visits to the countries of their origins. They were not tourists in the conventional sense and for all their residence in the United States, even when naturalized citizens, fell into a very distinct class. They were very numerous, sometimes totaling nearly half the number of native-born citizens going abroad, and on re-visiting their old homes scattered themselves all over Europe.

> Freeing us from the compulsions and contacts of the railway, the bondage to fixed hours and the beaten track, the approach to each town through the area of desolation and ugliness created by the railway itself, it has given us back the wonder, the adventure and the novelty which enlivened the way of our posting grandparents.

So wrote Edith Wharton in 1908, describing in A *Motor-Flight Through France* one really new development in European travel. For all its hazards and inconveniences in these early days, automobile touring rapidly became both popular and fashionable among those who could afford to ship a car to Europe or to rent one there. It was generously estimated on the eve of the war that some 80,000 Americans were motoring through the Old World.

An early pioneer was Franklin Roosevelt on his honeymoon in 1905. Borrowing an automobile from his aunt, Mrs. Paul R. Forbes, then living in Paris, he courageously drove from Paris to Fontainbleau. The party set out at 9:30 in what the young Roosevelt affectionately called "the bubble" on this forty-mile trip, but as he wrote "dearest mama," things "went very badly, one busted tire and numerous stops, so we didn't get to F. till 2 p.m.!" Apparently he was not greatly impressed with the automobile's future: in this same letter he speaks of taking lessons in driving a tandem.

Actually, motoring was making a great deal more headway in Europe than in America and when Mrs. Wharton took to the open road, nothing dampened her infectious enthusiasm. In a trip that took her all over France—"the wonderful white road, flinging itself in grand coils and arrow-flights across the same spacious landscape"—she made no mention of breakdowns, tire trouble, or any other serious mishap.

An automobile in these prewar years was nevertheless hardly comparable to what it has become today, and contingencies that the tourist had to be prepared to face (without garages or filling stations) are terrifyingly suggested in an article in *Outing*, published in 1906 under the title "Taking an Automobile Abroad." It listed among the essential items with which every motorist should be equipped: a jack, a rubber pail, extra spindle bearings, other spare parts packed in grease, carbide for the generator, a tire repair kit, tubes, oil can, spark plugs, vibrator springs, contact points, extra bolts and nuts, and plenty of tools. To this rather formidable list there of course had to be added extra tires and extra gasoline.

Having given the prospective motorist fair warning, the *Outing's* contributor then became more reassuring. He wrote that on his own tour he had a little trouble crossing the Alps, having to go into reverse at one point to check his downward speed and consequently stripping his gears, but otherwise he claimed that all went well. Such mechanical troubles as he had were easily handled, and driving two thousand miles from Havre to Naples and return he had only two punctures.

The cars of these prewar days, even the Packards especially recommended for the European tour, were open touring cars and their passengers had to have dusters, goggles, lap robes, raincoats, and umbrellas in meeting the challenge of changing weather. For men a single-breasted duster with Eton collar and three patch pockets was especially recommended, together with wind cuffs, visored caps, and leggings for repair work. To protect their elaborate costumes and fashionable picture hats, women wore long linen dusters, tucked their lap robes securely about their legs, and tied down their hats with long chiffon veils knotted tightly under the chin. Luggage represented something of a problem. Suitcases, valises, and hat boxes had generally to be strapped to the running boards.

Improvements in the automobile and new tourist conveniences steadily reduced the hazards of the road during the next few years. It was no longer necessary for the motorist to be a mechanic, one commentator was writing in 1913, and if he liked to drive himself, a chauffeur had become a nuisance. Other articles pointed out that garages were being built as adjuncts to the major hotels, and gasoline could be easily obtained in most towns and villages, sometimes even at peasant homes, for anywhere from 60 cents to $1 per gallon. Milestones marked the old national routes and even signboards were creeping in. Through membership in the Touring Club de France, it had become possible to get a *triptyque,* or international permit, that obviated all trouble in crossing frontiers. With the good roads that Europe generally offered, it was confidently stated in 1914 that a continental motor tour was "as simple and practicable as any in this country."

Apart from the brave and enterprising motorists, tourists in general continued to follow the old familiar paths. There were a limited number, however, who showed an unusual interest in investigating the economic and social background of Europe, visiting factories and workshops, talking with men of affairs, labor leaders, and social workers. These travelers were the proponents of reform, graphically reflecting the spirit of the Progressive Era, whose interests somewhat paralleled those of the reformers of the midnineteenth century. They were greatly interested in what Europe might be doing to meet the new problems of an industrialized society, and went abroad to see for themselves and report their findings to their countrymen.

What they discovered added up to a quite different picture of the Old World than the traditionally orthodox view of its political and social evils—tyranny, poverty, and militarism. A contributor to the *North American Review* wrote in 1907:

> Here then is Europe, at the beginning of the twentieth century, full of life and vitality, seething with change. No! Europe is not decadent, with so much young blood coursing in her veins. She is transferring herself afresh, and her future history will be as full of thrilling pages as her past.

This was not the voice of the Jeremiahs who throughout the nineteenth century had believed that in spite of all its cultural achievements the Old World was politically doomed. American progressives were discovering that Europe had cast off its bondage to the past, developed more democratic forms of government, and embarked on experiments which suggested that the New World might well be the laggard in social progress. Scores of articles in the popular monthlies—*McClure's, Everybody's,* the *American Magazine,* the *Saturday Evening Post*—discussed "the new Germany," "the new France," "the new Italy," and even "the new Russia."

146

A first visitor very much interested in reform, even before the close of the nineteenth century, was Jane Addams. As a young woman of twenty-three she had originally gone abroad with a number of friends for "the relaxation of her nerves," but one of the things that had most impressed her was the problem of the London slums. It fired her interest as nothing else, and after further visits she was led to undertake, on the model of what was being done in London, her own work in the slums of Chicago. Toynbee Hall was the prototype of Hull House, and the latter in turn provided the inspiration for the whole settlement-house movement in the United States. Jane Addams came to know and work closely with such English leaders in social reform as John Burns, Keir Hardie, Sidney and Beatrice Webb, closely linking—as had American visitors in the midnineteenth century—the parallel social movements in the two countries.

The three best-known muckrakers of the progressive era all had European experiences. Lincoln Steffens may have spent more time during his student days in Germany enjoying life than studying economic conditions, but he was nonetheless a perceptive observer of the broad program of social reform being developed in that country. Ida Tarbell, fresh from Titusville, Pennsylvania, lived for a time in Paris, studying and also engaged in reportorial work as *"une femme travailleuse."* She loved the French capital and thought of staying there permanently, but returned to the United States and became caught up in writing for *McClure's* and then the *American Magazine.* As she later wrote in *All in the Day's Work,* it was in Paris that her social conscience was quickened by her investigations as to how the city "worked" and her glimpses of the hard life of "the gallant poor."

Ray Stannard Baker first went to Europe in 1900 with the specific purpose, as a correspondent for *McClure's,* of looking into social conditions and he was greatly impressed with what he described as "the vast and confusing activities of a newly awakened Europe." His reports ignored the conventional aspects of the foreign scene found in so many travelers' accounts in order to tell what was happening in municipal housing, agricultural reform, progressive taxation, unemployment relief, and old-age pensions. He was particularly interested in the New Germany, where he saw the man of affairs taking over the role previously played by the

147

scientist, the scholar, or the poet. He greatly admired the country's progressive, dynamic spirit, but years later in his *American Chronicle*, recalled that he had instinctively felt that its political and social system was inimical to that of the United States.

Another visitor—not a muckraker but closely associated with the progressive movement—who first toured Europe in 1909 was William Allen White, the lively, outspoken, liberal-minded editor of the Emporia *Gazette*. Accompanied by his family he made his trip primarily as a sightseeing excursion, and the novelty of such a venture for a small-town Kansan in the early 1900's is suggested by his comment that it created a local sensation, for "any Emporian's trip to Europe was a matter of townwide concern." Once abroad, White was both the eager, excited tourist thrilled "with the wonders of the Old World culture," and a penetrating observer of contemporary social life.

The family party landed in Italy, traveled through Switzerland and Germany, spent three weeks in Paris, and then went on to a longer stay in England and Ireland. With letters of introduction from President Taft identifying him as "a journalist of national reputation and a warm friend," White was able to meet many political figures in England and he also called on a number of writers. He made a pilgrimage to the Sussex home of Henry James, whom he described as "highdomed, stocky though not chubby. . . . he has lived alone so much and written so much that. . . . he creaks when he talks. But he talks well and is altogether a joy." And there was also Thomas Hardy: "He wears his clothes as an afterthought and has a scrubby wayward little mustache of blond gray that has had its own way too long to be taken in hand now. . . . He is a dear."

Over and beyond his literary visits and his indefatigable sightseeing (including London's new department store, established by the American Harry Gordon Selfridge), what most impressed White was the social ferment everywhere he went. In writing his *Autobiography* he recalled that "we found in continental Europe the people perhaps a decade ahead of Kansas and the United States in the matter of labor and agricultural legislation, and my faith was strengthened in the righteousness of the Kansas struggle by finding that it was part of the world agitation." In talks with the English labor leader John Burns, he was even more impressed with what was happening in England, and somewhat inadvertently joining a parade supporting Lloyd George's tax program, he realized more than ever that there was a worldwide unity in the progressive revolt against social injustice. "We were parts, one of another," White wrote, "in the United States and Europe."

Not all political-minded visitors were so willing to acknowledge the progress Europe was making. Two years before White's visit, William Jennings Bryan had given voice in *The Old World and Its Ways*, a travel book recording his own experiences abroad, to the ancient prejudices of midland America. In his chapter "A Word to Tourists," Bryan made it very clear that, after all, nothing about the Old World was really comparable to the New. He was but echoing the first American travelers of the eighteenth century —Elkanah Watson and Abigail Adams—when he wrote in 1907:

> After one has seen the wonders of America and the possibilities of its soil, its institutions and its people.... he can go abroad with the assurance that he will return, more widely informed, it is true, but more intensely American than before.... In all that goes to make a nation great materially, commercially, intellectually, politically and morally, our country has no peer.

The generality of travelers were no longer so chauvinistic. They recognized that European society had undergone a significant transformation in which the onetime tyranny of kings had given way to democratic advance that in many ways appeared to challenge that of the United States. The more sympathetic visitors—somewhat ironically in the light of later events—even became convinced that Europe had foresworn its militarism and its wars. Not all of them. Sidney Brooks, writing in the *North American Review*, reported on what he felt to be the "imminent contentions, the charged and sullen atmosphere.... that oppress the older world." A more general opinion, however, was that the long years of peace since the Napoleonic wars had gradually eliminated the old sources of political rivalry, and that the nations of Europe had learned to live in amity. In the optimistic spirit so characteristic of the Progressive Era, returning travelers were prepared to accept the view President Wilson expressed in March

1913 in his inaugural message: the growing cordiality among all nations foreshadowed "an age of settled peace and goodwill."

This was not to be. Within sixteen months World War I had started.

The year which witnessed this tragic outbreak of hostilities had marked a new peak in transatlantic travel. It was estimated in that fateful August 1914 that anywhere from 150,000 to 200,000 Americans were abroad. Their countrymen, so little aware of how the war was to affect the United States, were indeed in these opening days of the conflict, more concerned over what might happen to the tourists than over the course of Europe's battles.

It soon became apparent that they were for the time being hopelessly stranded. Many were without passports or other official identification papers, unable to draw upon their letters of credit or cash their travelers' checks, and with the virtually complete breakdown of transportation, they found themselves in any event unable to travel. The stories cabled home of spreading confusion, adventure and misadventure, frantic appeals for help, were given almost as much play in the newspapers as those which told of the mobilization of troops and the movement of armies. Secretary Bryan declared on August 4 that the difficulties confronting Americans abroad were greatly exaggerated, but worried relatives and friends were not so easily calmed. They insisted that the government take immediate measures to meet the emergency.

The State Department promptly instructed embassies and consulates throughout Europe to do everything possible to aid stranded Americans. But while they could issue emergency passports, they could not meet the immediate problem of money. Both Ambassador Gerard in Berlin and Ambassador Herrick in Paris urged the government to send a naval vessel to Europe with a supply of gold that would provide the necessary funds upon which Americans could draw for hotel bills and transportation.

Congress having appropriated $250,000 for immediate relief measures, President Wilson thereupon approved a plan whereby the "North Carolina," sailing for Falmouth, and the "Tennessee," going on to Bremen, would convey overseas $5,000,000 in gold allocated by American bankers to their European branches and $2,500,000 made available by the government. The operation was

placed in charge of Assistant Secretary of War Henry S. Brecken-
ridge, and soon after the two ships arrived in Europe in mid-
August, the problem of providing funds for Americans abroad had
been solved.

The chaotic conditions prevailing on the continent, however,
blocked for a time the tourists' efforts to reach the seaports where
they might get passage across the Atlantic. The railroads were
being run only for the military; all automobiles were comman-
deered. Americans flooded the major cities, clamoring for accommodations that were no longer available. Then as a few trains
gradually began to operate for civilians, the stranded travelers
crowded all available space, often abandoning their baggage and
riding in freight or cattle cars when the coaches could hold no
more.

The focal point for all Americans fleeing the continent was
London. It was the one place that offered a really hopeful chance
of finding a transatlantic passage and the frightened tourists took
over every available lodging, sleeping in hotel lobbies or wherever
they could find a place to lie down. Amid a welter of conflicting
rumors about resumed steamship sailings, chartered vessels, transport by battleship, they besieged their embassy and consulate in
mounting anxiety as to how—and when—they might get home.

Newspapers in the United States continued in the meantime
to regale the public with fantastic tourist stories, recounting with
special gusto what was happening to the prominent and wealthy.
Cornelius Vanderbilt was said to have left his hotel without
being able to pay his bill; Alfred Vanderbilt was forced to borrow
two shillings from the hall porter to get a shave; Chauncey Depew
rode a cattle car in France; and Alfred McCormick unsuccessfully
tried to buy a yacht when other means of transportation failed.
Mrs. Otto Kahn was compelled to abandon two automobiles, but
somehow managed to reach London with sixty-five trunks.

There were tales of a troupe of Negro entertainers hopelessly
stuck in a small German town, and of a Wild West Show (with
twelve American Indians) that had to leave all its animals and
baggage in Poland. Art students in Paris were totally bereft, and
no one would buy their paintings; delegates at an international
clinical congress in Vienna were stranded, and a group of Welles-
ley girls valiantly came home on an oil tanker.

An American Citizens Committee worked out such plans as it could for the financial relief and transportation of the tourists converging on London. Its chairman was Herbert Hoover. He was then living in England, where he had established headquarters for his worldwide engineering operations, and he volunteered to see what could be done through such a committee to help his fellow countrymen get home. With the guarantee of ten wealthy Americans standing behind it, the committee issued credit cards to all tourists without available funds, and then proceeded (with the aid of hundreds of volunteers) to explore every possible way to find them accommodations and to arrange transatlantic passage. During six hectic weeks it extended credit amounting to $1,500,-000, and in various other ways helped 120,000 Americans through the period of the emergency.

While the English and French steamship lines in many cases resumed their cancelled or postponed sailings, they could not entirely meet the tremendous demand. American consular agents chartered ten vessels, and many travelers were sent home on freighters, oil ships, and cattle boats. Hoover recounts in his *Memoirs* a few complaints. One woman went on a hunger strike because she was allocated quarters in the steerage, and a number of persons tried to insist on a guarantee against possible submarine attack. The tourists generally, however, were more than happy to accept any accommodations whatsoever. The crowded ships sailed the westward voyage without lights, every porthole darkened, as a precaution against possible submarine attack, but they all reached port safely. By the end of September the situation was entirely under control, with Hoover reporting that virtually all Americans who wished to do so had sailed for home.

There were to be somewhat more significant consequences to the war, but a writer in the magazine *Travel* was very explicit in his views in the summer of 1914. "One result of the foreign upheaval," he stated as the foreign travelers came home, "will be to give an immense fillip to touring in our own country."

XII. BETWEEN TWO WARS

THE Americans who poured into Europe in 1917–18, dramatically breaking all previous records, were not tourists. On their infrequent leaves and immediately after the armistice, the members of the A.E.F. may have hectically enjoyed some sightseeing and gaiety ("How ya gonna keep 'em down on the farm after they've seen Paree?"), but what they wanted above all else was to get home. While some of them were to return in later years to see the Europe they had missed while serving with the army (the American Legion held a noisy reunion that turned Paris upside down), wartime experience overseas, as a quarter of a century later, stands distinct and apart from the general record of American travel abroad.

What was then to happen during the 1920's reflected the exuberant, clamorous spirit of that colorful postwar decade. Under the happy impact of the booming days of Coolidge prosperity, several hundred thousand Americans every summer made Europe a "tumultuous playground." Culture and education were much less important motives for the overseas journey than in any other period. Escaping from the arid wastes of Prohibition and shaking off the restraints of their more responsible lives at home, thousands of Americans went abroad in a carefree, vacation spirit. Tourism took on a new guise as these throngs of visitors rushed about the continent spending their easy dollars with a prodigality that at once shocked and gratified their European hosts.

The enthusiastic estimates of the travel agencies placed the tourist total in the late 1920's as high as 500,000. This was an exaggeration. Nevertheless, in the decade's final year, careful statisticians in Washington declared that some 265,000 American citizens visited Europe and the Mediterranean, spending abroad (exclusive of transportation) the highly significant sum of $213,-000,000. This was big business, having an important effect upon the esoteric problem of the balance of international payments. "Our tourist expenditures alone in Europe since the war," Herbert Hoover glumly stated in criticizing the Allies for their failure to pay their war debts, "would enable them to take care of the entire amount."

This expansion in foreign travel was a quite natural phenomenon against the background of earlier history and the circumstances of the time. Europe was even closer than in prewar days—in actuality through faster steamship crossings, and emotionally as a consequence of the war and the experiences of the returned soldiers. Even though Wilson's bright dream of world cooperation was tragically to fade as the United States retreated once again to political isolation, the ties between the Old and the New had been strengthened. It became more than ever the ambition of Americans to see Europe for themselves.

Other developments made the transatlantic journey easier for the casual vacationer who wanted to travel for no other purpose than a good time. Even more than prosperity at home, depreciated currencies abroad brought the European trip within the reach of many thousands who could not have afforded such a venture in earlier years. Moreover, the American Express Company was now ready to help tourists fearful of the complexities of overseas adventure.

It had established an office in Paris (at 11 Rue Scribe) in 1900, but on its opening the company's president made it very clear that the American Express was in the banking and express business, not tourism. "I will not have gangs of trippers starting off in charabancs from in front of our offices the way they do from Cook's," he stated emphatically. "We will cash their Travelers' cheques and give them free advice. That's all." But tourism finally caught up with the American Express Company, and by the mid-1920's it was fully engaged in every kind of travel service, including guided tours, luxury cruises, special conventions—and charabanc trips.

There were new clients for many of these services who had come to Europe for some more special purpose but were anxious also to do as much sightseeing as possible. Businessmen associated

154

with the branch factories American industry was setting up in Europe, delegates to international expositions and trade conventions, the ever-increasing number of buyers making annual trips abroad, swelled the ranks of ordinary tourists. Scientific and cultural congresses were meeting in the major European cities, and scores of other groups—midwest farmers, advertising executives, drug manufacturers, and also women's clubs and Gold Star mothers—held sessions abroad. Many former servicemen also found occasion to bring their families to see the battlefields over which they had fought in 1918, with such tours in northern France and Belgium becoming for a time one of the most popular features of European travel.

While the visitors of the 1920's greatly enjoyed themselves, the disillusionment that followed the failure to conclude a satisfactory peace greatly influenced their general attitude toward Europe. Many were openly scornful of these foreign countries which had been "rescued" by the United States and then did not even have the decency to pay their wartime debts. Some of them were to realize through their own experiences that such prejudices were hardly justified and found themselves admiring Europe and Europeans, but the majority, having come abroad solely for fun, made little or no effort to understand why the European nations acted as they did. They were not interested in a culture and way of life which they were convinced, in phrases a century old, remained decadent and effete in comparison with the dynamic, progressive spirit of America.

One is reminded of Sinclair Lewis' *Dodsworth*. About to be dragged across the Atlantic by his scatter-brained wife, so childishly anxious to experience the refined society of cultured circles abroad, the novel's hero gets into a discussion about the proposed trip. A breezy friend is flabbergasted by the very idea:

> Europe? Rats! Dead as a doornail! Place for women and long-haired artists. . . . Only American loans that keep them from burying the corpse! All this art! More art in a good shiny spark-plug than in all the fat Venus de Mylos they ever turned out.

But when Dodsworth himself is started on his venture, he wants to make the most of it. There is much about him of "the great barbarian" sweeping down on Europe with an only half-concealed scorn, and he never feels that he could be a European—"Why should I? I'm an American and glad of it." Still, he comes to realize that there is a great deal to be learned from his experience and is convinced that apart from the familiar stereotypes—the cultural dilettante, the status seeker, the self-assertive chauvinist—there are among the tourists many others with the same serious purpose. "As I wander about Europe," Dodsworth declares, echoing Margaret Fuller eighty years earlier, "I find a whale of a lot of Americans who are going slow and quiet, and who are thinking. . . ."

However, it was the super-patriotic, boastful American rather than the thinking American who seemed to dominate the scene in the 1920's. Two very popular writers of the day reflected this attitude and perhaps intensified it. Recording his "trip acrost the old pond" in 1925, Ring Lardner (whose tour would appear to have been largely centered on night clubs, race courses, and gambling casinos) did not hesitate to declare that Europe was a very sorry spectacle in comparison with America. A year later Will Rogers, after having great fun with hoary jokes about medieval plumbing, the lack of ice water, and "acres of old masters," found very little to praise in the Old World.

"No, sir," Rogers wrote in his genial style for the *Saturday Evening Post*, "Europe has nothing to recommend it but its old age. . . . You take the Guides and the Grapes out of Europe and she is just a Sahara. It's great fun for you to see it, if somebody is paying for it, or paying you to do it. But just as a pure educational proposition or pastime, it ain't there."

Some tourists did not wait to get home before expressing their feelings. As in perhaps no previous period, they made little effort to conceal their arrogant sense of superiority, smugly disregarding or mocking such European customs as ran counter to their own ideas as to how things should be. Even more disturbing to their European hosts was the perverse delight they often took in flaunting the high buying power of their dollars in terms of the depreciated European currencies. Reports were current of Americans talking superciliously of prices in "real money" and plastering their baggage with paper francs, liras, and marks in place of the usual hotel labels.

156

The more insensitive also irritated the basically conservative Europeans by taking flamboyant advantage of their release from Prohibition and the Volstead Act. They too often made their trip abroad what Albert J. Nock, writing in the *Atlantic*, described as "a protracted debauch." The convention-goers, the fashionable international set, the more footless expatriates, and sometimes the college boys, were the worst offenders on this score. Their hosts were certainly not critical of drinking, but public drunkenness in restaurants and cafés, and on the streets, violated their sense of propriety.

Resentment of the boasting, careless extravagance, and uninhibited drinking mounted rapidly. Even though a minority of American visitors may have been actually guilty, the Europeans tended to hold them all responsible for such transgressions. But at the same time, the dollars of these spendthrift tourists were important for the European economy. The people with whom Americans came most directly in contact, from hotel and restaurant-keepers to guides and taxi drivers, were caught in the dilemma of intensely disliking the very people upon whom their livelihood largely depended. "A bunch of American tourists were hissed and stoned yesterday in Paris," read one report that Will Rogers cabled the *New York Times*, "but not until they had finished buying."

The European press made sharp attacks upon the free-spending American tourists with their callous disregard of the continent's financial difficulties. It felt they were adding insult to injury in throwing their money about so carelessly while the United States played the role of Shylock in demanding its pound of flesh in settling the war debts. Was it really necessary, one irate editorial writer asked in a French journal, to welcome "these purse-proud, gum-chewing, champagne-swizzling visitors?"

The friction and simmering hostility came to a climax during the summer of 1926. In that year, which found the franc rapidly declining in value, Paris was crowded as never before with tourists who seemed especially free with their dollars. Anti-American feeling began to assume serious proportions as angry crowds assembled in the Place de l'Opéra to demonstrate against the American Express Company buses starting off on their popular sightseeing tours. The excitement erupted on July 24 when a mob of

157

several thousand surged through police lines and forced the passengers of six buses to flee in panic. Only the arrival of additional gendarmes prevented things from getting wholly out of hand with a riot that might have had the most unfortunate consequences.

President Coolidge was stirred to action—or at least to an unusual loquacity. He promptly issued a long public statement examining the whole situation and warning American citizens of their responsibilities while they were guests of foreign countries. He was certain that the actions of the Paris mob did not represent the real feelings of Europeans toward Americans, and equally convinced that the provocations leading to the outbreak should not be laid at the door of all American tourists. But highly critical of those of his countrymen whom he described as being "a species of a bumptious nature," he called for greater understanding of people still suffering from the unhappy effects of the war. If there was any American who did not find things to his liking in Europe and could not make concessions to European sensibilities, the President emphatically declared, "his remedy is to come home."

The anti-Americanism gradually subsided; few Americans felt obliged to come home. The tide of transatlantic visitors indeed continued to rise, engulfing the popular resorts and spreading out to new and less familiar parts of the continent.

The automobile was making this more practical by freeing the traveler from his dependence on established routes and motoring expanded enormously. Americans toured the chateau country in France, went once again to Spain, vacationed along the Riviera, followed the old carriage road of the Grande Corniche to Italy, visited the northern hill towns, crossed the mountain passes into Switzerland, and motored through Germany and the Low Countries. As Edith Wharton had so enthusiastically written a decade earlier, the automobile was bringing back to an increasing number of visitors something of the novelty and sense of adventure which the favored few had once enjoyed when they traveled Europe in their private coaches. They saw more of the countries they visited; they saw more of the people outside the big cities.

In the meantime another aspect of Europe's strong attraction during the 1920's had become quite as memorable as the steadily broadening tourist invasion. A colony of expatriates—writers and artists—living in Paris was making the city something very much like the literary capital of America, and largely through the writings of Hemingway and Scott Fitzgerald, the colony attained an almost legendary fame.

These Left Bank exiles had turned their backs on America. Finding in Europe, as one of them wrote, "a keener, fuller, more satisfying intellectual life than there is at home," they were seeking the inspiration and encouragement for their writing and art that the Old World had always promised. Their attitude once again demonstrated the historic pull of a cultural sophistication which stood in sharp contrast to what was considered the heightened materialism of postwar America. Following the path of so many earlier writers and artists (it was, after all, in the 1850's that James Russell Lowell had complained of how American life "boxes us up"), this "lost generation" of the 1920's were nevertheless more self-consciously despairing of their own country than any of their predecessors.

"The most moving and pathetic fact in the social life of America today," Harold Stearns wrote dramatically in *Civilization in the United States*, "is emotional and aesthetic starvation." Only in Europe, and more particularly in Paris, with its "paintings and music, street noises, shops, flower markets, modes, fabrics, poems, ideas," as Malcolm Cowley later wrote in *Exile's Return*, did these frustrated artists and intellectuals believe they could find the freedom to fulfill their creative aspirations. Looking back upon the conventions and repressions of his own country, one of them liked to quote the sardonic comment a Frenchman had made on seeing the Statue of Liberty standing so majestically in New York's harbor: "How nice! we, too, erect monuments to the illustrious dead."

Apart from the freedom and inspiration it supposedly afforded, Paris still had as well that lighter side which had always made it so favorite a city among Americans. Its air of gaiety, its carefree pleasures had not lost their enduring appeal. Even writers, Sinclair Lewis noted somewhat derisively on one occasion, sometimes stayed on in Paris for no other reason than that they so much enjoyed it—"the wine is cheap, the girls pretty, the crêpe Suzette exalted, the place de la Concorde beautiful."

Europe in general also presented that aspect of life which

Henry James had once ascribed to nineteenth-century Italy—a "celestial cheapness." The depreciated currencies that encouraged tourist travel were no less a boon for the expatriates. They could live abroad on a scale that would have been impossible for them at home. While writers and artists in Paris might not have all the material comforts of Main Street in their lodgings on the Left Bank, their dollars went very far at restaurants and cafés. As the value of the franc continued to decline—and that of the lira and mark for those who traveled or lived in Italy and Germany—the exiles became what Cowley has called "parasites of the exchange." They sought out whatever city, whatever country, provided greater value for the funds they drew from America.

The doyenne of American writers in the French capital was Gertrude Stein ("America is my country and Paris is my home town and it is as it has come to be") who had been abroad ever since 1902. Almost as long an exile from his native land was Ezra Pound, living in England before coming to Paris, and then in time moving on again to Italy. Sherwood Anderson was a brief visitor and T. S. Eliot, already settled in London, occasionally crossed the Channel. However, it was the younger men, either staying on in Europe after their wartime experiences or returning after short visits home, who gave its distinctive flavor to the Paris colony during the 1920's. Among the writers who were primarily responsible for the American literary renaissance between the two world wars, only Faulkner was not at one time or another drawn abroad in this period.

The Hemingway of these days, a tall, virile young man, with a little toothbrush mustache, was a very familiar figure at the Left Bank cafés and bistros, but for all the hard drinking and hard playing that he so much liked to glorify, he was first of all a serious writer. The stories published in such "little magazines" as the *TransAtlantic Review, This Quarter,* and *Transition*—which were such an important expression of the period's literary activity— were the start of a career which first won popular recognition when in 1926 he published *The Sun Also Rises.* Scott Fitzgerald, so startlingly good-looking with "his fallen angel fascination," flashed in and out of Paris, lived on the Riviera, made all Europe a playground in his reckless exuberance. The better part of his life abroad in the 1920's was "1000 parties and no work," and

Tender is the Night is the self-revealing record of these years in Europe.

John Dos Passos and E. E. Cummings came back to Paris following their ambulance service experiences in 1918. The former was for a time a roving newspaper correspondent who in 1921 published his *Three Soldiers;* the latter wrote while abroad *The Enormous Room* and then for a time studied art. Archibald Mac-Leish, having given up law for poetry, shortly arrived with his family ("I date the beginning of my life from 1923") and was to remain in Europe five years, while Thornton Wilder, who was described as "rather shy and a little like a curate," lived for a time in both France and Italy. Stephen Vincent Benét had enrolled at the Sorbonne immediately after the war and then later returned to Paris to write *John Brown's Body.* Among a host of others were John Peale Bishop, Glenway Wescott, Morley Callaghan, Matthew Josephson, and Malcolm Cowley.

Never a part of this group, with few friends among the more *avant garde* writers who for their part had little respect for his writing, Sinclair Lewis was nevertheless a frequent visitor in Paris. Tall, angular, red-haired, he was usually quite alone as he strode along the boulevards, or stopped for a drink at café or bistro. While he was to salute the young experimental writers ("most of them now living in Paris") in his Nobel Prize address in 1930, he thought them "a little insane."

In later years no one roamed Europe more widely, searching, it appeared, for something he had not been able to find in America. Lewis had been rootless ever since his boyhood days at Sauk Center, his onetime wife Dorothy Thompson has suggested, but his quest for a European home was entirely futile for a man "as American as ham and eggs." He was to die in an apartment in Rome. "Only his secretary—a strange man of undistinguishable nationality," Miss Thompson wrote, ".... accompanied his poor body to the crematorium, though his death was frontpage news in every American and European newspaper."

The American painters studying in Paris were for the most part deeply involved during the 1920's in the experimental schools of cubism, surrealism, and dadaism. Those who were to become best known in the United States, however, were to revolt against the influence of "the Paris school" and, returning to their own country, became more absorbed in painting the American scene. Thomas Hart Benton, after making his way abroad from his native Missouri, first rebelled against impressionism and took up abstractionism, then rejected abstractionism, and on coming back to America made his reputation through the realistic paintings that showed little influence from his studies abroad. Grant Wood spent several years in Paris without really finding himself, but his work on a later trip to Germany provided the basis for the distinctive style found in such paintings as "American Gothic." Even John Steuart Curry had a year on the Left Bank, but it did not greatly influence his later development as an artist and his mature painting was of his native Kansas.

Three composers of this period also had very close associations with Paris and its expatriate Americans. George Antheill first performed the *Ballet Mécanique* at the Théatre des Champs Elysées; Virgil Thompson as a close friend of Gertrude Stein was to write the music for her *Four Saints in Three Acts* during his Paris days; and George Gershwin drew upon his experiences living abroad to compose *An American in Paris*.

Their writing, painting, and composing all attest to the vitality that characterized the work of many of the exiles living in Paris during the 1920's. On the periphery of this circle of writers and artists, however, were the professional bohemians, some of them disillusioned or disappointed novelists and painters, who made little pretense of real work. They were the errant and parasitic bar-flies forever hanging about cafés, ready to join any party in the Latin Quarter, dashing back and forth between Montparnasse and Montmartre in a vague alcoholic daze. Hemingway was once to draw a fine distinction between these inconsequential loafers and the serious artists. "The bums," he said, "could be seen in the cafés in the forenoons."

Stories floated home of the drinking and dissipation of these expatriates—as had the spicy tales of the "unconscionable Bohemians" of the 1890's. Magnified even beyond the accounts of life on the Left Bank found in the contemporary novels, they awoke all the old prejudices and suspicions of the depraved atmosphere of Paris. Articles in the popular magazines began to describe the European exiles generally as no more than adolescent escapists seeking inspiration in alcohol. Their only reasons for remaining abroad, wrote one indignant critic, were "dipsomania and laziness."

Yet there could be no denying the lasting worth of much of the writing and artistic creation that were the result of the experiences of these Americans living abroad. It is always startling to realize, so far as writers are concerned, how many of them over the past century and a half—Irving, Cooper, Hawthorne, James, Edith Wharton, Hemingway, Fitzgerald and others—made highly significant contributions to literature during their years in Europe. Whether the influence and inspiration of the Old World have been as important as is sometimes assumed, or whether indeed some of these writers paid a heavy price for cutting themselves off from the roots of their own culture, remains a matter of continuing controversy. But the writing done in Paris during the 1920's greatly enriched America's literary heritage.

In the late autumn of 1929 there took place that abrupt event which was to introduce a new era in American life and ultimately in the affairs of all the world: the crash of the New York stock market. Its consequences were almost immediate for overseas travel. It sounded an imperative summons to come home for many of the exiles who found themselves so unexpectedly cut off from funds in the United States, and it sharply curtailed the transatlantic voyaging of the tourists. Things had gone very wrong indeed, even before the more devastating consequences of what was to become worldwide economic depression were recognized.

The ranks of the writers and artists living in Europe had considerably dwindled even before 1929. They had come in many instances to question the superior cultural advantages of the Old World ("America is just as god-damned good as Europe," Malcolm Cowley had earlier broken out in answer to the conventional criticism of its drabness and vulgarity), and were beginning to wander home. Now their return was hurried by practical considerations. T. S. Eliot stayed in England and Ezra Pound in Italy, but they were almost the only remaining literary exiles. Such new figures as Thomas Wolfe and John Steinbeck were to make return visits to Europe in the 1930's, the former traveling especially in Germany, and Henry Miller was to become a famous expatriate. But the days when Paris seemed to be the literary capital of America were over.

As for the tourists, the reported figures show a drastic decline in numbers. The annual total was halved by 1934 to a depression low of 135,000, rose gradually to 207,000 in the next three years, and then began to decline once more. Yet these statistics, however reduced, are perhaps most significant because the totals remained as high as they did. They revealed clearly that nothing short of war itself could wholly discourage Americans from going abroad. With the steamship companies and the tourist agencies rallying all their forces, doing everything possible to reduce expenses, a flow of travel was maintained that never sank to the levels of the years before the First World War.

It was during the 1930's that the Cunard Company and the French Line added such great super-liners to their fleets as the "Queen Mary" and the "Normandie," making the ocean crossing in something less than four days. They kept up the old standards of luxury in first or even cabin class, as did many of the special cruise ships, but what was far more important was the introduction in these and other liners of tourist class. It opened new doors to overseas travel. As it became increasingly popular, with its comfortable but less luxurious accommodations, the way was prepared for still further expansion in transatlantic travel for what had been called half a century earlier the light pocketbook.

At the same time, American Express and other travel agencies were emphasizing that continental travel could still offer a relatively cheap vacation, advertising tours and excursions at sharply reduced rates. With tourist class on the steamships providing a round-trip passage at no more than $200 and railroad and bus fares also reduced, it was possible to spend a few weeks abroad in the 1930's for an over-all expenditure of less than $500.

The travelers taking advantage of these more inexpensive rates differed markedly from those of the 1920's who had thrown their dollars about so extravagantly. They were more seriously interested in sightseeing, in visiting castles and cathedrals, galleries and museums, than in making the continent a vacation playground. And while they were as hurried as ever, perhaps even more so, they were a good deal more subdued than the super-patriotic

164

tourists who had so greatly aroused the ire of their hosts in the 1920's.

Writing under the rather hackneyed title of "New Innocents Abroad," Thomas Craven was nevertheless to take these travelers to task in familiar vein. The conventional European trip, with its careless spending, precipitate haste, and lack of any real understanding, he declared caustically, had become one of the nation's most obnoxious forms of dissipation. But the tourists also had stout defenders. In an article in the *Saturday Evening Post,* Gilbert Seldes ridiculed such attacks as a silly heritage of the snobbishness of Henry Adams and Henry James. He maintained that boastfulness and vulgarity were very much the exception on the part of Americans in Europe, emphatically asserting that in their approach to the Old World they had attained a new maturity.

One phenomenal new development took place during these years between the two great world wars—airplane travel. It was only on the eve of World War II that a transatlantic passenger service was instituted, but beginning as early as 1919, cross-channel flights between London and Paris were placed on a commercial basis, and long before anything comparable had developed in the United States, air routes were spreading throughout the continent. The airplane was as important in the history of travel as the steamship, the railroad, the automobile—and even more dramatic.

The Old World's lead over the New World in commercial flying was a consequence of the heavy subsidies given to the European lines. They were able to establish 18,000 miles of air routes and were flying annually 12,000,000 passenger air miles before American commercial planes really got off the ground. As late as 1929, the latter carried only 50,000 passengers. For those overseas travelers who could afford what was still an expensive means of transportation, flying was consequently a novel and exciting feature of their continental tours which could not as yet be duplicated in their own country.

The pioneer flights across the Channel were at first on a very irregular basis and restricted to spring, summer, and fall, but American tourists were enthusiastic. "Fine enclosed planes," one of them described his means of transport in 1923, "resembling elegantly equipped limousines and supplied with lavatory accommodations." It was then but a step to extend the experiment to reach out to other European cities, and soon one could fly from Paris to Brussels, Amsterdam, Cologne (with connections for Berlin), and Madrid. The pioneer English and French lines were Imperial Airways and Messageries Aériennes, but those of the other countries setting up rival services which spanned all Europe are more familiar—K.L.M., Sabena, and Lufthansa.

The great dream of air enthusiasts was the transatlantic flight. It had been projected even before World War I, and six large planes were being readied in 1914 to compete for a $50,000 prize offered by Lord Northcliffe for the first ocean crossing. There could be little question, wrote an optimistic contributor to the magazine *Travel*, that the ocean barrier between America and Europe would be overcome "within a matter of years, perhaps months." The outbreak of war, however, postponed the realization of these bright hopes and the first experimental flights were not made until 1919. For a time, indeed, it appeared that the dirigible (recalling Philip Hone's prophecy seventy years earlier) might hold the key to successful transatlantic flying. The "Graf Zeppelin" and the "Hindenburg" carried passengers between America and Europe before any such service became practical for airplanes.

The most famous of the early transatlantic flights was that of Charles Lindbergh in 1927, and on his triumphant arrival in Paris he received what was perhaps the most enthusiastic welcome of any American ever to go abroad. When in the early morning of May 20, 1927, he took off from New York bound for Paris in his little single-engined monoplane the "Spirit of St. Louis," all the world waited breathlessly, and on his landing at Le Bourget just thirty-three and one-half hours later, there was a great sigh of universal relief. "I am Charles A. Lindbergh," the "Spirit of St. Louis's" pilot announced quietly on alighting from his plane, and the crowds at the airport almost mobbed him. It was the most dangerous part of the trip, he later recalled. On his subsequent visits to Brussels, Berlin and London—and then on his return to New York (brought back on the cruiser "Memphis")—he was again hysterically acclaimed as the hero of the age.

For all the impetus Lindbergh's flight gave to aviation, the pioneer company in transocean flying, Pan American Airways, was not ready to launch its first commercial flight between the United States and Europe until June 28, 1939. On that day the "Dixie Clipper," a forty-two ton, four-engine Boeing flying boat, carrying twenty-two passengers chosen from a waiting list of 500, took off from Port Washington, Long Island, with several thousand people, augmented by the local high school band, crowding the airport to wish the venture godspeed. Cruising at an altitude of about 8000 feet, the "Dixie Clipper" sped across the Atlantic, stopped briefly to refuel in the Azores, flew on to Lisbon where its passengers spent the night, and the next day successfully completed its flight to land at Marseilles.

Pan American's fleet of Super Clippers was soon traversing both this southern route and a parallel northern course on a regular basis, the company proudly advertising that with planes taking off twice a week, "flying the Atlantic is now routine." The fare was $675 for the round trip; accommodations provided seventy-four upholstered seats, including those in a dining salon and lounge; and the air of elegance was further sustained by dinner menus that even in 1939 included shrimp cocktail, filet mignon, and biscuit tortoni. The war was soon to interrupt this service for civilians. It was not until after 1945 that the way was clear for the spectacular postwar developments that were to revolutionize overseas travel even more than had the steamship.

"Goodby Europe."

By the close of the decade the title of this article, which Joseph Hergesheimer had contributed to the *Saturday Evening Post* in 1933, had a tragic relevancy. But even when it was first written there were harbingers of disaster, and the more perceptive travelers brought home increasingly disturbing reports. It was not yet a possible war that most worried them, though sabres were being rattled, but the rise of totalitarian governments (to say nothing of Soviet Russia) which were extinguishing democracy in both Italy and Germany and casting their long shadows over all western Europe. The tourists continued to go abroad, indeed their number somewhat increased as the United States struggled out of the depression, but they could hardly fail to be aware of the Old World's malaise.

Hergesheimer felt that Europe could no longer offer anything worth an American's crossing the Atlantic; John Peale Bishop was convinced that it had lost its primacy in the field of culture; and William Harlan Hale saw a continent seething with tensions and even Paris, spoiled by its reputation, no longer a tourist Mecca. Edmund Wilson, recalling the Old World's "solemn traditions, majestic histories," felt that it had reverted to "a pack of little quarrelsome states, maintaining artificial barriers and suffering from morbid distempers. How the map has changed since our youth!" On his visits to Germany, Thomas Wolfe was shocked by the tightening curbs on individual freedom, the suppression of the press, the outrageous anti-semitism, and the mounting war fever. "We can never learn to march like these boys," he said in a prophetic postcard to his publisher Maxwell Perkins,—"and it looks as if they were about ready to go again."

The tide of events swept on. The warlike moves of Italy and Germany—the attack on Ethiopia, the occupation of the Rhineland, intervention in Spain, pressure on Czechoslovakia—contrasted strangely with the announcements of the government travel bureaus. They were advertising "Italy—Land of Traditional Hospitality" and "Bypaths of Beauty Beckon You to Germany." But the end was at hand. At the close of September 1939 Hitler struck out at Poland, and Europe was again at war.

There was no such excitement or panic among the Americans caught overseas as there had been in 1914. The tide of travel had dropped substantially in the past two years, the season was drawing to a close, and most important, hostilities were confined that autumn to eastern Europe. Emergency committees were set up to aid those who might find themselves stranded, but Americans generally were able to make their way to Atlantic ports without difficulty, and the major steamship lines, other than those of Germany, for a time maintained regular sailings.

The pattern of 1914 was then repeated. Europe was closed to travel and three years later, in even greater numbers, American military forces again went abroad to encompass the final defeat of what had become the enemy powers.

168

XIII. THE POSTWAR SCENE

TRANSATLANTIC travel in the midtwentieth century ranged from a president flying abroad for a Summit Conference to a party of five hundred TV dealers taking a twelve-day tour sponsored by the General Electric Company; from a young draftee reporting for military duty in Germany to a wealthy socialite spending a weekend in Paris. And once again hordes of vacationing sightseers, from every walk of life, were each summer trying to see the entire continent in a few hurried weeks. Tourism had been given a wholly new impetus in these years by the unbelievable jet planes that hurtled so swiftly over the Atlantic.

The progressive democratization of foreign travel—the most significant aspect of the whole history of Americans going abroad —was of course a matter of gradual evolution. The new ships and packaged tours of the early 1900's had given it a powerful stimulus; prosperity at home and depreciated foreign currencies had an important influence in the 1920's. But being able to fly the ocean barrier speeded up such processes immensely. The jet brought a trip to Europe within the time limits of the average American's vacation, and its cost remained relatively low.

When the new steamships first opened up transatlantic travel for any considerable number of persons in the 1850's, a three month's European tour (as estimated for Little Rollo) cost an estimated $800. Something over a century later, at the beginning of the 1960's, the air lines were offering all-expense three weeks' trips on jet economy flights at approximately this same figure. Allowing for the shorter visit made feasible by faster transportation, travel abroad had surprisingly withstood the general price rise of a hundred years. A European tour had from this point of view become relatively less expensive in terms of what it had once cost than perhaps any other feature of modern living.

Little wonder that more and more people, from an ever broader segment of the population, took advantage of these new opportunities. The number annually crossing the Atlantic had by 1953 exceeded the peak total for any year in the period of Coolidge prosperity. In the next seven years it had more than doubled, and totaled some 800,000.

One category of Americans going abroad in the postwar years was entirely new and without precedent. As a consequence of the political situation which found the United States playing a major role in European recovery from the war, and then helping to bolster continental defenses against possible communist aggression, hundreds of thousands of United States citizens were in Europe on government assignment. The military forces stationed there, employees of government agencies, the dependents of both the troops and of civilian personnel (supplemented by representatives of American business firms and other temporary expatriates), made up a shifting population of nearly a million, obviously many times larger than ever before in peacetime.

In many parts of Europe there sprang up under these circumstances little American communities that differed only in their geographic background from similar communities at home. Their residents insisted on "stateside" standards of living, the maintainance of familiar habits and customs. Suburbia was transferred across the Atlantic with its schools and supermarkets, moving picture theaters and churches, ice cream parlors and country clubs. The families of the overseas troops, and those of a great many of the civilian employees, were not exiles by choice. They were prepared to accept Europe as their temporary home only so far as in their way of life they did not have to leave America.

The presence of these visitors, over and apart from the annual tourist invasion, greatly furthered that Americanization of Europe which had first occasioned alarm among some Europeans in the 1920's. Without attempting to explore fully so important a phase of cultural interaction, which has been fiercely discussed through the years, it may at least be noted that in their insistence upon things American, citizens of the United States living and traveling abroad in this period helped to introduce many new customs and products to the European world. When enterprising

170

foreign businessmen sought to satisfy the wants of the barbarians within their ranks by setting up snack bars, with hamburgers, hot dogs, milk shakes, and Coca Cola, they soon found their own countrymen enthusiastically patronizing such establishments. Filling stations (they were generally labelled Esso or Mobiloil) discovered that it was very worthwhile to advertise "American Service." In every city (though this goes back long before World War II), one could find the ubiquitous American bar attracting Europeans as well as the thirsty from the United States. It even became possible in the 1950's (in belated recognition of the hopeless appeals of so many nineteenth-century travelers) to find restaurants or cafés serving ice water!

In addition to the military and government servants, another conspicuous group among Americans temporarily living abroad were the professors and students. The grants and scholarships made available by the G.I. Bill of Rights and the Fulbright Act let loose upon European schools and universities an academic flood. Some 2000 professors were lecturing or carrying on their research activities at institutions from Edinburgh to Vienna, from Oslo to Belgrade, and in addition special centers for American studies were set up in Geneva, Bologna and Salzburg. The students were even more widely dispersed. In the years between 1949 and 1957, there were an estimated 10,000 of them in Europe on government or foundation grants, while another 1500 or more spent a year abroad under the junior year programs maintained by twenty-three American colleges. Still others—younger boys and girls—were abroad under the sponsorship of the American Field Service Committee and the Experiment in International Living.

If the origins of this academic invasion may be traced back to the little band of Bostonians who had made their way to the German universities after the Napoleonic wars, government aid and foundation grants gave it its unprecedented dimensions. During the summer and other vacation periods, moreover, the students traveled the length and breadth of Europe much as had the wandering scholars of the Middle Ages. They sometimes bicycled, sometimes hitchhiked. They stayed at the youth hostels which in every country brought together young people of all nationalities in a spirit of easy camaraderie and good fellowship.

In a quite different category were Americans who found a

reason—or an excuse—for visiting Europe in international meetings. The conventions of business and trade associations, cultural and scientific congresses, industrial fairs and exhibitions—proliferating from the foundations laid in the 1920's—drew thousands of delegates across the Atlantic every year. Rotarians, Boy Scouts, and Jehovah Witnesses staged tremendous assemblies, while smaller groups of every sort held annual meetings. Their diversity is only suggested in a report made by the Library of Congress in 1960. The list that year included an International Atom Seminar in Berlin, the International Congress of Beauty Care and Cosmetology in Amsterdam, a meeting of the Planned Parenthood Federation at The Hague. There were also an International Congress of Dental Surgeons, an International Geological Congress, a World Congress of Widows and Widowers, and at Purerend, in the Netherlands, an International Reunion of Children Born in Leap Year!

Americans were generally in the ascendancy at these international meetings. With the airplane making the transatlantic crossing so brief and expeditious, the national craze for convention-going and the age-old love of travel naturally coalesced to swell their numbers. The international conference had exerted a strong appeal ever since the antislavery conventions of the midnineteenth century. It was now more popular than ever (sometimes with the added incentive of income tax deductions) both in itself and as providing a base for further European explorations.

Both new and traditional events also augmented overseas travel. The world of society kept going back as it always had for the London season, to the more fashionable continental beaches and resorts, to the casino at Monte Carlo, to the races at Longchamps or the regatta at Cowes. International sporting matches continued to have their enthusiastic devotees. Hollywood established its transatlantic outposts, and the International Film Festival at Cannes became an annual fixture on the European calendar. The mounting postwar craze for skiing led to the discovery of resorts in Switzerland and Austria for airborne winter vacations. The Holy Year pilgrimage and the World's Fair in Brussels, the Lourdes Centenary and the Olympic Games in Rome, were very special occasions that swelled the tide of American visitors.

At the same time, immense numbers of ordinary, everyday

tourists crossed the Atlantic—as had their predecessors for a hundred and fifty years—for the most traditional reasons. They wanted to see everything they could, to discover for themselves the artistic treasures of the Old World, to enjoy a vacation away from everything that was familiar—and for that very reason somewhat dull —in their home environment.

The instinctive urge to travel and the avid curiosity of the American people generally had lost none of their strength with the passing years. The tourists of the midtwentieth century were but confirming the views Hawthorne had expressed a hundred years earlier in emphasizing the vagabond habits of his countrymen.

It had taken a little time after the German surrender in 1945 for the annual tourist invasion of Europe to get really underway. The war had left widespread devastation and had caused a complete breakdown in normal life. The want of adequate food supplies and other essential commodities, and the consequent strict rationing in effect both in Great Britain and on the continent, militated against vacation travel. The European nations, however, desperately needed dollars in their programs of economic rehabilitation. They soon began to do everything possible to encourage American tourists. They did away with the need for passport visas, extended special privileges to their guests, and in some instances (often to the embarrassment of the more sensitive visitors) modified or suspended the rationing regulations applying to their own citizens. Americans were allowed to make purchases (gasoline, for example) on a more generous basis than could the native Englishman or Frenchman.

The United States government also promoted overseas travel when in the late 1940's it embarked on the far-sighted Marshall Plan, so imaginatively designed to help the European countries help themselves. The Economic Cooperation Administration, realizing that tourist dollars spent overseas were quite as effective in helping to balance international payments as loans or grants, did everything possible to encourage such expenditures as one means of contributing to Europe's economic recovery.

The financial significance of tourism was indeed graphically demonstrated in these postwar years. The expenditures of Americans abroad rose by 1960 to an annual total of $700,000,000 and on such a scale played an important part in reducing the dollar gap that for a time so seriously impaired Europe's ability to buy from America. When the spectacular economic recovery and increased exports of the western European countries then brought about a reversal in the immediate postwar balance of payments, the United States had to reconsider its financial policy. It did not discourage Americans from going overseas, but to safeguard its own dollar reserves felt obliged to reduce drastically the value of individual European purchases which Americans could bring home duty free.

Whatever the governments on either side of the Atlantic might do to promote tourism was, however, almost negligible in comparison with the tremendous impetus given it by the growth of air travel. The commercial flights initiated by Pan American on the eve of the war could now at last be expanded to fulfill their sadly delayed promise. A host of international airlines—TWA, BOAC, SAS, KLM, Air France, Swissair, Sabena, Alitalia, and soon a revived Lufthansa—rushed in to follow where Pan American had led the way. Within a decade of the war's end, a busy day at New York's International Airport at Idlewild might see as many as fifty planes, each one carrying as many as seventy-five passengers, heading out over the Atlantic on flights that over-night carried them to Europe's major cities.

The traveling public hardly had time to adjust itself to such incredibly fast and easy means of crossing the ocean before the jets still further reduced the time of the transatlantic passage. They were first introduced for commercial flights in 1958, and quickly swept almost all other planes from the overseas air routes. In the perspective of history, an ocean journey that had taken the first Americans visiting Europe about three weeks (granted good weather conditions), could now be made in six hours.

The ocean liners continued to have their own appeal. The new ships were once again bigger and better, and more important, their traditional luxuries were progressively introduced into the onetime spartan tourist class—the ornate lounges, verandah cafés, and swimming pools. "Getting there is half the fun," the steamship companies advertised, and for such great new vessels as the

"United States," crossing the Atlantic in less than four days, it was persuasively announced that whatever class one traveled, "you feel like royalty every moment." The broader future, however, was in the air. With their own economy and tourist classes, the airplanes rapidly caught up with the ocean liners. It was in 1955 that for the first time more American travelers crossed the Atlantic by plane than by ship; in another five years, three-fourths of all those visiting Europe and the Mediterranean went by air rather than by sea.

The hundreds of thousands of Americans going to Europe every year in midcentury may be subjected to a statistical analysis that has never before been possible. The importance of their expenditures abroad led the Department of Commerce to keep a careful finger on the nervous pulse of overseas travel. Its surveys in the 1950's, largely based on questions asked in passport applications, provided a bewildering array of figures on just who was going abroad, why they were going, and what parts of Europe they intended to visit.

As in earlier years, more overseas travelers came from the East than other sections of the country, but in keeping with population shifts within the United States, California was pressing hard on New York as the leading state of origin. The number of women exceeded that of men. Including dependents joining members of the armed forces and government personnel, housewives generally made up the largest occupational category listed in passport applications. They were followed by business and professional men and then, as had so often been the case in the past, students, teachers, and retired persons. However, a far greater proportion than would have been found ever before, were classified as skilled workers and clerks-secretaries. In one typical year, as illustrative of the new types of tourists able to cross the Atlantic in considerable numbers, the Department of Commerce also listed such categories as farmers-ranchers, doctors-dentists, barbers-beauticians, tradesmen, restauranteurs, and florists.

A majority declared their purpose on going abroad to be pleasure; they were tourists following the bent of their own inclination. The next largest group (including under the circumstances prevailing in midcentury the dependents of government personnel) listed personal business, and in very much smaller numbers came commercial business, education, and health.

The first love of the American travelers was invariably France, with further evidence substantiating the age-old popularity of Paris. It was followed by Great Britain, Italy, Germany, and Switzerland. There were shifts and changes in this over-all pattern from year to year, due to such special events as the Holy Year in Rome or the World's Fair in Brussels, but the usual choice of countries conformed to the general outlines of earlier periods. The average stay abroad for the tourists was reported to be about six weeks.

Two developments are not suggested by passport statistics. An increasing number of tourists were making every effort to break away from the more conventional itineraries, and a much larger group were following them with more assiduous care than ever before.

The former were to a great extent made up of those who traveled by car, having either rented or bought an automobile in Europe, or brought their own overseas. Free to go anywhere they liked, they often sought out the byways rather than the highways of the continent, independently exploring a countryside which the more custom-bound rarely saw. Those who traveled on their own by air were also able to branch out further afield. The Scandinavian countries, Spain and Portugal, and Greece and Yugoslavia were readily accessible, and the airlines made possible stopovers almost anywhere on the entire European circuit. New vacation places, from Majorca to Crete, were continually being added to the familiar Riviera resorts or French beaches.

The more restricted travelers remained, however, in the majority, accepting the packaged tours that made foreign travel both so economical and so easy. The tourist agencies (their number rose to 3000) took care of everything—transportation reservations, hotel accommodations, chartered bus trips, special sightseeing excursions, restaurant meals, theaters, and night clubs. The services that Mr. Cook had first introduced a century earlier had been developed to the last, final, regimented detail. European travel had been placed on something like a mass production basis. It was

176

efficiently organized, nationally advertised, and astutely packaged to meet consumer demand. Whatever the customer wanted—as an individual or as a member of a group—could be arranged on a schedule that accounted for almost every minute of the pre-arranged tour.

In their glowing advertisements the agencies of European travel sounded a lyric note in the tradition of the romantic pilgrims:

> To Europe with Love! Europe! what other six letters can send the imagination soaring with such visions of romance, history and enjoyment? Where in the world can you find such enticements, such marvelous variety that a lifetime is insufficient to explore them all? Nobody can resist a romance with her!

They went far beyond their pioneer efforts in the prewar years to offer every possible kind of tour. They not only continued to promote art tours and music tours, among other old standbys, but energetically advertised garden tours, folk dancing tours, theater tours, and gourmet tours. They called upon Gene Sarazen to lead a party of golfers through Europe, employed heavy-weight Max Baer to conduct a "Tour for Men Only," and prevailed upon Louis Bromfield to escort overseas a group of "Friendly Farmers." Special study tours, including one advertised as a "Flying Seminar," were organized on every college campus throughout the land. For the most part these tours were moderately priced, announced in one case as suitable for "a Piggy Bank Budget," but occasionally ("Europe with Whipped Cream") they might run to several thousand dollars. The airlines also promoted around-Europe trips at various special rates, and introduced a new and more economical form of travel in special charter flights for as little as $290.

The steamship companies emphasized luxury cruises to the Mediterranean and the North Cape. The excursion of the "Quaker City" a century earlier had set an example (Mark Twain might not have felt entirely at home) that appealed to tens of thousands of the more affluent travelers who wanted "to luxuriate" on board ship. These cruises often meant winter as well as summer travel, and indeed the steamship and air lines both made every effort to encourage going to Europe in the off-season periods. They advertised not only special economy rates, but better accommodations, and most persuasively, fewer Americans on the continent.

Tourists still found their fellow-tourists getting in their way, once again recalling the magazine contributor in the 1840's who had advised the prospective traveler that if he wanted to enjoy Europe, he should find out where his countrymen resorted and go somewhere else. They set themselves a more frantic pace than ever, with air travel making it possible to jump from country to country in an hour or two, and all the hoary stories were revived about the harried sightseer not being quite sure where he was or what cathedral, museum, or ancient monument he was actually seeing. (One repeated tale was of the midwestern couple visiting Westminster Abbey, the husband telling his wife, "You look at the inside and I'll take the outside.") And even though hotels had become so generally modernized, the ancient complaints were still voiced as to the Europeans' inexplicable failure to arrange things on the best American standards. Still no soap in hotel bedrooms!

Something of the flavor of contemporary travel was caught in the very titles of the innumerable magazine articles dealing with an always fascinating phenomenon: "Can you Survive Your Vacation?" "Every Tour a Grand Tour," "Travel and Learn," "Mind Your Manners Abroad."

A government concerned with the political implications of foreign travel sternly warned Americans going abroad of their responsibilities. "Your regard for other ways of life and your speech and manner," a reminder on every passport application stated, "help mold the reputation of our country." On one occasion President Eisenhower added his personal appeal to all prospective travelers. "You represent us all," he said, "in bringing assurances to the people you meet that the United States is a friendly nation and one dedicated to the search for world peace."

How these midcentury "diplomats on the loose," as one magazine writer characterized them, met their responsibilities can hardly be documented. After all, there were a great many of them, and they varied, if anything, even more than had their forerunners. The "boastful American" of an earlier day was not an entirely extinct species, and even "the purse-proud, gum-chewing, champagne-swizzling visitors" who had so nearly provoked anti-American riots in the 1920's had their successors thirty years later. A Henry James might even have felt that some of his compatriots were not entirely free of the distressing vulgarity that had marked the first wave of more democratic travel after the Civil War. Tourists could not wholly slough off certain of the less happy characteristics which somehow seem to be inherent in the tribe.

The general verdict on them in contemporary articles was nonetheless favorable. Horace Sutton, the acute travel editor of the *Saturday Review*, stated emphatically that the old caricature of the free-spending, free-drinking tourist was outmoded; John Steinbeck wrote that the transatlantic sojourner was losing both his insularity and his chauvinism, and a *New York Times* survey reached the hopeful conclusion that Americans abroad were making friends for their country.

No one was to suggest that the tourists were primarily concerned with their role as envoys of goodwill. However ironic its implications in the troubled circumstances in which Europe found itself in the 1950's, the greater number of them had gone abroad to have a good time. They were on vacation. They did not travel to become involved in world problems, but rather to escape them.

The background for their journeying was the Cold War—frantic rearmament, recurrent crises, the ever constant threat of atomic holocaust. Occasionally at the beginning of a summer season, what appeared to be an imminent danger of actual hostilities caused some temporary wavering in tourist ranks. But the enthusiastic travel agents were never daunted, and their inspired advertisements invariably overcame all possible misgivings. The airlines and steamships painted such enticing pictures of Europe's attractions that ever more Americans went abroad for their vacations of "Sun and Fun."

Nevertheless, in spite of the carefree spirit of so many of the travelers, the more thoughtful, and especially those going abroad for study or other more serious purposes, were not unaware of the profoundly changed circumstances of the modern world. They were at once more certain of the status of America as a world leader (they did not need to boast of national superiority), and at the same time more willing than their predecessors to accept Europe as the original source of their culture. On the part of those who looked further afield than their immediate good time,

179

the trip abroad, that is, would appear to have brought home a deeper realization that Europe and America were mutually dependent parts of a larger Atlantic community. Certainly in comparison with the prewar years, they were conscious that their role as Americans did impose certain inescapable responsibilities.

By the 1960's, swift ocean passage by jet had its own sense of adventure, but the Atlantic was no longer the awesome obstacle that it had been for the passengers aboard the wave-tossed little sailing packets. Railroads, motor coaches, private automobiles had largely obviated the discomforts of travel by stage coach and diligence but also some of its excitement. The real Europe was less easy to discover behind the façade of Americanized hotels, arranged sights, artificially preserved antiquities, and a tourist-oriented army of shopkeepers, concièrges, taxi drivers, waiters, and guides. It was possible to see the "Stately Homes" of England with their aristocratic owners pointing out their most prized possessions, but far more difficult to win an introduction to European society. The venturesome, independent traveler forever seeking new experiences (what Elkanah Watson had described as "the novelties around me: new faces—new objects—strange customs and language") had in many cases been transformed into the passive tourist accepting whatever was offered him on his prescribed, pre-arranged, personally conducted tour. The European journey, as Daniel Boorstin wrote in "The Lost Art of Travel," had at least in some measure become "an assembly-line, store-boughten commodity."

Yet if something had been lost in the process of making European travel so readily available for great masses of people, in contrast to its onetime narrow restriction to the well-educated and the well-to-do, the price was perhaps not too heavy. What was happening was no more than what had already taken place in every field of popular recreation with increased leisure and a higher standard of living for the American people as a whole. And the trip abroad had not in its essentials changed so greatly, even though it often appeared to be symbolized by the packaged tour rather than independent adventure.

The traditional thrill of anticipation was perhaps even heightened by the swift, dramatic passage by air. The foreign scene was no less unfamiliar or less intriguing because it could be seen by chartered motor bus. Europe still displayed the same inviting charms—the lovely countryside, the fascinating cities, the monuments of an immemorial past, the treasures of art—that it had unfolded for the first transatlantic tourists. Nor was there any sign that midcentury visitors did not enjoy it as much—and perhaps gain as much from their experiences—as their predecessors.

The eager travel agencies were insisting that "the prohibitive cost of seeing Europe is largely a state of mind," and persuasively claiming that a few hundred dollars ("fly now, pay later") would enable anyone to indulge his urge to travel, satisfy his curiosity about the Old World, and enjoy a vacation overseas. "Europe is for everybody," read their glowing message. "You! Pleasure Travelers, You! Convention-Goers, You! Business Wives." With the 1960's witnessing almost a million Americans annually going abroad, such pronouncements appeared at last to be almost true.

BIBLIOGRAPHICAL NOTES

EVER SINCE that somewhat caustic contributor to the *Quarterly Review* commented in 1829 that "authorship and traveling are all the fashion," there has been a constant stream of travel books by Americans touring Europe. Such writing, supplemented by letters, diaries, journals, and reminiscences, has provided the basic source material for this book. There are some secondary sources as well, but what the travelers themselves have written has in all instances been my chief reliance. The following notes do not constitute a bibliography of American travel abroad; they list only the books and articles that have proved most useful for my particular purposes.

I. THE LURE OF EUROPE

The quotations in this first chapter are taken from Nathaniel Hawthorne, *Our Old Home* (1863); *The Diary of Philip Hone, 1821–1851*, edited by Allan Nevins (New York, 1936); Royall Tyler, *The Contrast, A Comedy*, in *Representative American Plays, 1767–1933* (New York, 1925); the *American Magazine*, May, 1785; *The Papers of Thomas Jefferson*, edited by J. P. Boyd *et al.* (Princeton, 1950—); *The Journals of Ralph Waldo Emerson*, edited by W. E. Forbes (10 vols.; Boston, 1909–14); Alexis de Tocqueville, *Democracy in America*, first published in 1835; Henry James, *Life and Letters*, edited by Alexander V. G. Allen (2 vols.; New York, 1900); *North American Review*, 1819; Phillips Brooks, *Letters of Travel* (New York, 1894).

On the general attitudes of Americans toward Europe, with many quotations from travelers, see Cushing Strout, *The American Image of the Old World* (New York, 1963).

II. EIGHTEENTH CENTURY

The more important Americans in Europe at the close of the eighteenth century have left extensive records which have been consulted in *The Writings of Benjamin Franklin*, edited by Albert H. Smyth

(10 vols.; New York, 1905–7); *The Life and Works of John Adams,* edited by C. F. Adams (10 vols.; Boston, 1850–56), and *Familiar Letters of John Adams and His Wife,* also edited by C. F. Adams (New York, 1876); *The Papers of Thomas Jefferson,* edited by J. P. Boyd *et al.* (Princeton, 1950–3); and *The Diary and Letters of Gouverneur Morris* (2 vols.; New York, 1888).

I have drawn most heavily, however, on two special sources. Elkanah Watson described his life in Europe in two books: *A Tour in Holland* (Worcester, 1790), and *Men and Times of the Revolution; or Memoirs of Elkanah Watson,* edited by Winslow C. Watson (New York, 1856). Although the latter volume did not appear until more than a half century after Watson's return to his own country, its European chapters are based on his contemporary journal. The experiences of Abigail Adams are delightfully told in *Letters of Abigail Adams* (Boston, 1848).

Four highly interesting secondary sources have conveniently brought together much of the material dealing with these Americans: Edward E. Hale, *Franklin in France* (2 vols.; Boston, 1888); Marie Kimball, *Jefferson: The Scene of Europe, 1784 to 1789* (New York, 1950); Edward Dumbauld, *Thomas Jefferson—American Tourist* (Norman, Oklahoma, 1946); and Lewis Einstein, *Divided Loyalties* (Boston, 1933), the latter dealing with American loyalists and British spies. The standard biographies, as of Franklin, Adams, and Jefferson, and also Samuel Eliot Morison, *John Paul Jones* (Boston, 1959), also proved helpful; for minor figures there were the articles in the *Dictionary of American Biography,* and for the diplomatic background, Samuel F. Bemis, *The Diplomacy of the American Revolution* (New York, 1935).

Material on the London colony of American artists is available in such autobiographical accounts as *The Autobiography of Colonel John Trumbull,* edited by Theodore Sizer (New Haven, 1953); Charles Robert Leslie, *Autobiographical Recollections* (Boston, 1860); Jared B. Flagg, *The Life and Letters of Washington Allston* (New York, 1892). There are also biographies of Benjamin West, John Singleton Copley, and Gilbert Stuart. Although largely concerned, as its title indicates, with artists in Paris, there is much interesting general material on these men in Yvon Bizardel, *American Painters in Paris* (New York, 1960).

III. A FIRST INVASION

The introductory material here has been drawn from a number of varied sources which range from contemporary travel sketches to articles in the *Dictionary of American Biography*. The principal sources for this chapter, however, are the writings of the literary and other travelers of the first half of the nineteenth century.

Washington Irving first published *The Sketch-Book* in 1819–20; *Bracebridge-Hall* came out two years later, and in 1824, *Tales of a Traveller*. Many of his letters are available in Stanley T. Williams, *The Life of Washington Irving* (2 vols.; New York, 1935). The material on Preston is drawn from *The Reminiscences of William C. Preston*, edited by Minnie Clare Yarborough (Chapel Hill, N.C., 1933). In 1909 there was published in Boston, in two solid volumes, *The Life, Letters and Journals of George Ticknor*. While Longfellow described his early travels in Europe in *Outre-Mer, A Pilgrimage Beyond the Sea* (Boston, 1834), his letters, available in *The Life of Henry Wadsworth Longfellow*, edited by Samuel Longfellow (2 vols.; Boston, 1886), are more interesting, and may be supplemented by *The Diary of Clara Crowninshield, A European Tour with Longfellow, 1835–36*, edited by Andrew Hilen (Seattle, 1956).

Emma Willard has left a fascinating account of her European trip in *Journal and Letters from France and Great Britain* (Troy, N.Y., 1833). The material for James Fenimore Cooper is especially voluminous, including certain of his novels, *The Letters and Journals of James Fenimore Cooper*, edited by James Franklin Beard (Cambridge, 1960), and most particularly, the several volumes of *Gleanings from Europe* (France, England, Italy), first published in 1837 and 1838.

Among other contemporary writings on Europe are William Cullen Bryant, *Letters of a Traveller* (New York, 1850), together with material found in the biography by Parke Goodwin (2 vols.; New York, 1883); James Russell Lowell, "Leaves from My Journal in Italy and Elsewhere" in *Fireside Travels* (Boston, 1899); *The Journals of Ralph Waldo Emerson*, edited by W. E. Forbes (10 vols.; Boston, 1909–14), and also his perspicacious *English Traits*, first published in 1856; and Nathaniel Hawthorne, *The Marble Faun* (1860), *Our Old Home* (1863), and his posthumously published *English, French and Italian Note-Books*.

A number of literary histories deal with the European experiences of such writers. Van Wyck Brooks has a chapter on "The Romantic Exiles" in *The Flowering of New England* (New York, 1936), and discusses Irving and Cooper abroad in *The World of Washington Irving* (New York, 1944). Among the books more directly related to European travel are Robert E. Spiller, *The American in England* (New York, 1926); Philip Rahv, *Discovery of Europe* (Boston, 1947) (extracts from writings over the entire period); Christopher Wegelin, *The Concept of Europe in American Fiction from Irving to Hawthorne*, Johns Hopkins dissertation, 1947; Robert Charles Le Clair, *Three American Travelers in Europe* (Philadelphia, 1945); Orie W.

Long, *Literary Pioneers: Early American Explorers of European Culture* (Cambridge, 1935); Robert B. Mowat, *Americans in England* (Boston, 1935); and Margaret Denny and William H. Gilman, *The American Writer and the European Tradition* (Minneapolis, 1950).

IV. TRANSATLANTIC PASSAGE

Apart from the travel books and diaries themselves, as noted in both the preceding and following sections, a number of studies have been made of the conditions and circumstances of the transatlantic passage. Among the most interesting are two books by Robert G. Albion: *The Rise of New York Port* (New York, 1939), and *Square Riggers on Schedule* (New York, 1938). Others include David B. Tyler, *Steam Conquers the Atlantic* (New York, 1939); W. Mack Angas, *Rivalry on the Atlantic* (New York, 1939); and August Mencken, *First-Class Passenger* (New York, 1938).

There is also some material in *Overseas Travel*, a Department of Commerce publication, Washington, 1939, specifically covering the years 1919–38 but with early statistics on transatlantic voyages. Many magazine articles also deal with this topic, one covering a wide range is John A. Gould, "Ocean Passenger Travel," *Scribner's*, April, 1891.

The quoted material in the first section of the chapter has been taken from *The Diary of Philip Hone, 1821–1851*, edited by Allan Nevins (New York, 1936), and contemporary issues of the *New York Herald*. The more general sources are those also drawn upon for travel on the continent and are among those cited for Chapters III, V, and VI.

V. THE WAYS OF CONTINENTAL TRAVEL
and
VI. THE GRAND TOUR

The descriptive material in these chapters is based on a wide and varied selection of writings, in addition to those already noted for Chapter III, and may be most conveniently noted in alphabetical order:

Jacob Abbott, *Rollo on the Atlantic* (Boston, 1853), *Rollo in Paris* (Boston, 1854), and others in this same series; Anon., *Wild Oats Sown Abroad by a Gentleman of Leisure* (Philadelphia, 1853); Henry Ward Beecher, *Star Papers* (New York, 1855); J. Ross Browne, *An American Family in Germany* (New York, 1866); John W. Burgess, *Reminiscences of an American Scholar* (New York, 1934); John Overton Choules, *Young Americans Abroad;* or a *Vacation in Europe* (Boston, 1855); John A. Clark, *Glimpses of the Old World* (2 vols.; Philadelphia, 1840); Samuel F. Cox, *A Buckeye Abroad;* or, *Wanderings in Europe, and in the Orient* (Cincinnati, 1854); A. Cleveland Coxe, *Impressions of England* (New York, 1855); Orville Dewey, *The Old World and the New* (2 vols.; New York, 1836); Maunsell B. Field, *Memories of Many Men* (New York, 1874); Margaret Fuller (Ossoli), *At Home and Abroad,* or *Things and Thoughts in America and Europe* (Boston, 1856), and also *Memoirs* (2 vols.; Boston, 1852); S. G. Goodrich, *Recollections of a Lifetime,* or *Men and Things I Have Seen* (New York, 1856); Horace Greeley, *Glances at Europe* (Boston, 1861); Edward Everett Hale, *Ninety Days' Worth of Europe* (Boston, 1861); George Stillman Hillard, *Six Months in Italy* (Boston, 1876); Julia Ward Howe, *Reminiscences* (New York, 1899), and also, for her letters, the biography by Laura E. Richards and Maude Howe Elliott (2 vols.; New York, 1916).

James Jackson Jarves, *Parisian Sights and French Principles Seen Through American Spectacles* (New York, 1852); Caroline M. Kirkland, *Holidays Abroad; Europe from the West* (2 vols.; New York, 1849); Alexander Lee Levin, "Miss Knight Abroad," *American Heritage,* XI, April, 1960; Henry Cabot Lodge, *Early Memories* (New York, 1913); Ik Marvel (Donald G. Mitchell), *Fresh Gleanings, or, a New Sheaf from the Old Field of Continental Europe* (New York, 1847); Louise Piatt, *Belle Smith Abroad* (New York, 1858); William C. Preston, *Reminiscences,* George P. Putnam, *The Tourist in Europe* (New York, 1838); William H. Seward, *An Autobiography* (New York, 1891); Catherine Maria Sedgwick, *Letters from Abroad to Kindred at Home* (New York, 1841); Benjamin Silliman, *A Visit to Europe in 1851* (2 vols.; New York, 1853); *Elizabeth Cady Stanton As Revealed in Her Letters, Diary and Reminiscences,* edited by Theodore Stanton and Harriet Beecher Blatch (2 vols.; New York, 1922); Henry B. Stanton, *Random Recollections* (New York, 1887).

Harriet Beecher Stowe, *Sunny Memories of Foreign Lands* (2 vols.; Boston, 1854), and *Life and Letters,* edited by Annie Fields (Boston, 1899); Charles Sumner, *Memoirs and Letters* (London, 1878), and also David Donald, *Charles Sumner* (New York, 1960); *Tales and Souvenirs of a Residence in Europe,* by "A Lady of Virginia" (Philadelphia, 1842); Bayard Taylor, *Views A-Foot; or Europe Seen with Knapsack and Staff* (New York, 1846), and *At Home and Abroad* (New York, 1860); Thurlow Weed, *Letters from Europe and the West Indies, 1843–62* (Albany, 1866); Henry Wikoff, *The Reminiscences of an Idler* (New York, 1880); Nathaniel Parker Willis, *Pencillings by the Way* (Auburn-Rochester, 1853); W. W. Wright, *Doré, by a Stroller in Europe* (New York, 1857).

For an interesting article on America at the Crystal Palace exhibition and other world fairs in the nineteenth century, see Merle Curti, "America at the World Fairs, 1851–1893," *American Historical Review*, LVIII, July, 1950.

VII. SOME MIDCENTURY VISITORS

For the antislavery agitation in Europe, some of the material has been taken from the previously cited writings of Elizabeth Cady Stanton, Henry Stanton, and Harriet Beecher Stowe, but it is supplemented by W. P. Garrison and Francis Jackson, *William Lloyd Garrison* (New York, 1895); Lucretia Mott, *Slavery and 'The Woman Question:' Lucretia Mott's Diary.... 1840*, edited by Frederick P. Tolles (Haverford, Pa., 1952); and a recent article, Douglas H. Maynard, "The World's Anti-Slavery Convention of 1840," *Mississippi Valley Historical Review*, XLVII, December, 1960.

On other reformers, there are the previously noted letters and reminiscences of Julia Ward Howe; Harold Schwartz, *Samuel Gridley Howe* (Cambridge, 1956); C. P. Edwards, *Horace Mann* (Boston, 1958); Helen S. Marshall, *Dorothea Dix* (Chapel Hill, N.C., 1937); and Merle Curti, *The Learned Blacksmith: The Letters and Journals of Elihu Burritt* (New York, 1937).

For the popular entertainers, major sources have included the *Reminiscences* of Henry Wikoff; Henry Birdoff, *The World's Greatest Hit* (New York, 1947), dealing with the Tom Shows; P. T. Barnum, *Struggles and Triumphs; or The Life of P. T. Barnum Written by Himself*, edited by George L. Bryan (2 vols.; New York, 1937); Montrose J. Moss, *The Fabulous Forrest* (Boston, 1929).

A contemporary record of the Indians' visits to Europe is found in George Catlin, *Catlin's Notes of Eight Years' Travel and Residence in Europe* (2 vols.; New York, 1848), while the whole story has been told in Carolyn T. Foreman, *Indians Abroad, 1493–1938* (Norman, Oklahoma, 1943). An account of Buffalo Bill's ventures is found in *William F. Cody, Story of the Wild West.... including a description of Buffalo Bill's conquests in England* (Chicago, 1888).

The American artist colony in Italy has been described in Van Wyck Brooks' *The Dream of Arcadia—American Writers and Artists in Italy, 1760–1915* (New York, 1958), but in so doing he is building on many predecessors. Its midnineteenth century phase was first recounted by William Wetmore Story in his *Roba di Roma* (London, 1862), and Henry James then carried it forward with his biography, *William Wetmore Story and His Friends* (New York, 1903). Another account is E. P. Richardson and Otto Wittman, Jr., *Travels in Arcadia, American Artists in Italy, 1830–1875* (Detroit, 1951).

Apart from the material provided by Story, there are also the writings of James Jackson Jarves, Julia Ward Howe, Nathaniel Hawthorne, and many other American writers, already noted, who visited Italy in this period; the letters of Robert and Elizabeth Barrett Browning, so closely associated with the Americans; and the biographies of such artists as Thomas Cole, Thomas Crawford, and Hiram Powers.

VIII. CHANGING PATTERNS

The material for the first section in this chapter has been taken from the *New York Tribune*, June 14, 1867, and W. Pembroke Fetridge, *Harper's Handbook for Travellers in Europe and the East* (New York, 1867), and the early English editions of the various Baedekers. For an interesting article on the latter, see W. G. Constable, "Three Stars for Baedeker," *Harper's*, April, 1953.

Further sources are Henry James, *TransAtlantic Sketches* (Boston, 1875), his novels, as noted in the text, and "Four Meetings," reprinted in *The Art of Travel by Henry James*, edited by Morton D. Zabel (New York, 1958); James E. Scripps, *Five Months Abroad* (Detroit, 1882); Henry Adams, *The Education of Henry Adams* (New York, 1931); and for the voyage of the "Quaker City," primarily *Innocents Abroad*, but also Albert Bigelow Paine, *Mark Twain* (3 vols.; New York, 1912). For a brilliant literary study of James's attitude toward Europe, see Christof Wegelin, *The Image of Europe in Henry James* (Dallas, 1958).

Other travel books of this period include Thomas Bailey Aldrich, *From Ponkapog to Pesth* (Boston, 1890); Eratus C. Benedict, *A Run Through Europe* (New York, 1871); Phillips Brooks, *Letters of Travel* (New York, 1894); Charles Farrar Browne, *Artemus Ward in London* (New York, 1867); John W. Burgess, *Reminiscences of an American Scholar* (New York, 1934); David R. Locke, *Nasby in Exile; or Six Months of Travel* (Toledo, 1882); Lee Meriwether, *A Tramp Abroad* (New York, 1887); Morris Phillips, *Abroad and at Home* (New York, 1891); Francis C. Sessions, *On the Wing Through Europe* (New York, 1889); Charles Dudley Warner, *Saunterings* (New York, 1872).

The magazine material is more than plentiful for the latter half of the nineteenth century. A few representative articles are Ralph Keeler, "The Tour of Europe for $181 in Currency," *Atlantic*, 1870; Dora M. Morrell, "A Trip Abroad for Light Pocket-Books," *Chautauquan*, 1898; Franklin Matthews, "Our Annual Travel to Europe," *Chautauquan*, 1896; J. M. Buckley, "The Traveler," *Chautauquan*,

1887; H. G. Dwight, "Americans in Europe as Seen from a Consulate," *North American Review*, 1903; Eliot Gregory, "Rolling Stones," *Century*, 1902.

The Woodrow Wilson quotation is from *Life and Letters*, edited by R. S. Baker (6 vols.; New York, 1927–37).

IX. NEW CULTURAL TIES

The statement of Walt Whitman is from his *Uncollected Poetry and Prose* as quoted in Van Wyck Brooks, *The Times of Melville and Whitman* (New York, 1947). The material on Mark Twain is from the previously cited biography by Albert Bigelow Paine; that on Henry James from previously noted sources and also *Life and Letters*, edited by Alexander V. G. Allen (2 vols.; New York, 1900); and for William Dean Howells, the various newspaper and magazine articles he first sent home from Venice, such of his books as *Venetian Life* (1866) and *Travels in Italy* (1867), and *Life and Letters of William Dean Howells*, edited by Mildred Howells (2 vols.; New York, 1928).

The experiences of other writers are found in Bret Harte, *Letters*, edited by G. B. Harte (Boston, 1926); Stephen Crane, *Letters*, edited by R. W. Stallman and Lillian Gilkes (New York, 1960); Jack London, *The People of the Abyss* (New York, 1903); *Willa Cather in Europe*, edited by George N. Kates (New York, 1956); Booth Tarkington, "Some Americans Abroad," *Everybody's*, 1907; Theodore Dreiser, *A Traveller at Forty* (New York, 1931). There is also some discussion of these writers' visits to Europe in Van Wyck Brooks, *The Confident Years* (New York, 1952).

For the students in Germany the material has been drawn primarily from John E. Burgess' previously noted *Reminiscences of an American Scholar* (New York, 1934); Lincoln Steffens, *Autobiography* (New York, 1931); and sketches of the various university presidents in the *Dictionary of American Biography*.

The artists in Paris are described in Yvon Bizardel, *American Painters in Paris* (New York, 1960); the biographies of a number of them, and various contemporary articles. Among the latter, as noted in the text, there is the interesting report of Sylvester W. Beach on "The American Student in Paris," appearing in the *Independent*, September, 1902.

X. WEALTH AND SOCIETY

International society is commented upon by many of the writers previously cited in these notes—Philip Hone, James Fenimore Cooper,

William Preston, George P. Putnam, William H. Seward, Henry Wikoff, Henry James—and further accounts of wealthy Americans abroad are drawn from very diverse sources. Francis J. Grund, *Aristocracy in America* (London, 1839; first published in the United States, New York, 1959) has extensive material; Dixon Wecter has a chapter on "The Quest for Coronets" in *The Saga of American Society* (New York, 1937); and the European milieu is occasionally noted in Cleveland Amory, *Who Killed Society?* (New York, 1960).

Among contemporary magazines, the *Cosmopolitan* ran a number of articles on rich Americans in 1903 (Henry Watterson attacked them in this same magazine), and in June 1901 *Smart Set* published an article in this genre on "The Wandering American." A contemporary book satirizing society abroad was Henry B. Fuller, *From the Other Side* (Boston, 1908).

The Theodore Roosevelt material is from his *Letters*, edited by Elting E. Morison, Vol. 1 (Cambridge, 1951), and that on Franklin Roosevelt from *F.D.R.—His Personal Letters*, edited by Elliott Roosevelt, Vol. 1 (New York, 1948).

Walter Hines Page described court presentations in Burton J. Hendrick, *The Life and Letters of Walter Hines Page* (3 vols.; New York, 1922). The material on Mrs. Vanderbilt is taken from Cornelius Vanderbilt, Jr., *Queen of the Golden Age* (New York, 1956); and that on other celebrities from Burton J. Hendrick, *The Life of Andrew Carnegie* (2 vols.; New York, 1932) (see also Carnegie's *An American Four-in-Hand in Britain* (New York, 1883); Frederick Lewis Allen, *The Great Pierpont Morgan* (New York, 1949); Edith Wharton, *A Backward Glance* (New York, 1934); and articles in the *Dictionary of American Biography*.

The whole story of art collecting in Europe has been fascinatingly told by Alice B. Saarinen in *The Proud Possessors* (New York, 1958).

XI. ON THE EVE OF ARMAGEDDON

The general material for this chapter has been taken largely from contemporary periodical sources, including a new magazine, *Travel*. One article that might be singled out particularly is J. M. Campbell, "Our Yearly Exodus to Europe," *The World Today*, January, 1907.

On motoring abroad, there were "Taking an Automobile Abroad," *Outing*, June, 1906; "Automobiling Abroad," *Outing*, May, 1908; "Motoring on European Highways," *Harper's Weekly*, January 7, 1911; "How to Plan a Motor-Trip Abroad," *Literary Digest*, June 7, 1913; "Motoring Over European Roads," *Harper's Weekly*, August 6, 1910. The personal experiences recounted are from *F.D.R.—His*

Personal Letters and Edith Wharton, *A Motor Flight Through France* (New York, 1908).

The progressives going abroad have recounted their experiences in *The Autobiography of William Allen White* (New York, 1946) and letters found in Walter Johnson, *William Allen White and His America* (New York, 1947); Lincoln Steffens, *Autobiography* (New York, 1931); Ida M. Tarbell, *All in the Day's Work* (New York, 1939); Ray Stannard Baker, *American Chronicle* (New York, 1945); William Jennings Bryan, *The Old World and Its Ways* (St. Louis, 1906).

The contemporary issues of the *New York Times* have been primarily relied upon for material on the stranded tourists, supplemented by a number of articles in *Travel* and the *Literary Digest*. Also, *The Memoirs of Herbert Hoover: Years of Adventure, 1874–1920* (New York, 1951).

XII. BETWEEN TWO WARS

Newspapers and magazines (including their advertisements), the many guidebooks, and reports from the Department of Commerce most faithfully depict the European travel scene in the 1920's. There are also a number of books—both fiction and reminiscences—centering upon the expatriates of this period; and as always, many tourists wrote extensively of their European travels.

Among the more interesting accounts of the Left Bank exiles in Paris (apart from such novels as Ernest Hemingway's *The Sun Also Rises* and F. Scott Fitzgerald's *Tender is the Night*) are Malcolm Cowley's *Exile's Return* (New York, 1934); Sylvia Beach, *Shakespeare and Company* (New York, 1959); and Samuel Putnam, *Paris Was Our Mistress* (New York, 1947). For the attitude of the expatriates, see also *Civilization in the United States*, edited by Harold Stearns (New York, 1922). Further material is also available in many autobiographical and biographical writings: Sherwood Anderson, *A Story Teller's Story* (New York, 1924); Gertrude Stein, *The Autobiography of Alice B. Toklas* (New York, 1933); Arthur Mizener, *The Far Side of Paradise* (Boston, 1951); *The Letters of F. Scott Fitzgerald*, edited by Andrew Turnbull (New York, 1963).

Among the innumerable articles on European travel in the 1920's, the following were especially interesting: Samuel Spewack, "Four Years in Europe Made Me an American," *Saturday Evening Post*, May 29, 1926; Frances Warfield, "Innocence Abroad," *Scribner's*, October, 1928; Lewis Mumford, "American Condescension and European Superiority," *Scribner's*, May, 1930; R. W. Child, "Our Foreign Imitators," *Saturday Evening Post*, March 31, 1928; Albert J. Nock, "The American Tourist in Europe," *Harper's*, May, 1927; "Getting Broadened Abroad," *Saturday Evening Post*, December 8, 1929; Hiram Motherwell, "The American Tourist Makes History," *Harper's*, December, 1929; Francis P. Miller and H. D. Hill, "Europe as a Playground," *Atlantic*, August, 1930.

Among other directly quoted sources, Sinclair Lewis published *Dodsworth* in 1929; "The Other Side," in *What of It?* by Ring Lardner, came out in 1925; the Will Rogers articles, first appearing in the *Saturday Evening Post*, were published in book form—*Letters of a Self-Made Diplomat to His President* (New York, 1926); and the accounts of the anti-American demonstrations in Paris were printed in the *New York Times*, with President Coolidge's statement appearing July 28, 1926. The new travel agency in the tourist world of the 1920's is taken up in Alden Hatch, *American Express* (New York, 1950).

Among magazine articles dealing specifically with the 1930's were Joseph Hergesheimer, "Good-By, Europe," *Saturday Evening Post*, January 7, 1933; William Harlan Hale, "Grand Tour New Style," *Atlantic*, December, 1932; Joseph Wood Krutch, "Was Europe a Success?" *Nation*, August–September, 1934; Thomas Craven, "New Innocents Abroad," *Forum*, April, 1930; Gilbert Seldes, "Tramps— Are We?—Abroad," *Saturday Evening Post*, June 11, 1932; "Europe Is America's New World," *Literary Digest*, June 6, 1936; Martha Gruening, "American Expatriates," *Nation*, June 7, 1933. There is also interesting material among other writers' accounts in *The Letters of Thomas Wolfe*, edited by Elizabeth Nowell (New York, 1956).

The more specialized accounts of developments in air travel have been taken from such histories of aviation as Henry Ladd Smith, *Airways* (New York, 1942); Norman Macmillan, *The Air-Tourist: Guide to Europe* (Washington, 1930); Matthew Josephson, *Empire in the Air* (New York, 1941); the annual volumes of the *Aircraft Yearbook*; and the contemporary press. Charles Lindbergh has told his own story in *The Spirit of St. Louis* (New York, 1953). Reports on the first transatlantic flights were taken from the *New York Times* and *Newsweek*.

XIII. THE POSTWAR SCENE

There has been no systematic attempt to cover the voluminous material on postwar travel in this concluding chapter. The statistics have been taken from such documents as the *Survey of International Travel*, 1956, and its *Supplements*, issued by the Bureau of Foreign Commerce, Department of Commerce (Washington, 1956); the annual lists of international meetings published by the Library of Congress; the *International Educational Exchange Program, 1948–1958*, issued by the Department of State, 1958; and Harlan Cleveland, Gerard J. Mangone, and John Clarke Adams, *The Overseas American* (New York, 1960).

Such magazines as *Travel* and *Holiday*, the travel section in the *Saturday Review*, the weekly travel pages in the Sunday edition of the *New York Times*, and the ecstatic literature of the travel agencies, steamship companies, and air lines tell the story of both the expansion of tourism and its current importance.

A few articles that reflect the spirit of the times are Edith Efron, "That Persistent Traveler—the American," *New York Times Magazine*, July 7, 1946; Horace Sutton, "400,000 'Diplomats' on the Loose," *Saturday Review of Literature*, January 13, 1951; John Steinbeck, "Yank in Europe," *Holiday*, January, 1956; Joseph Wechsberg, "The American Abroad," *Atlantic*, November, 1957; "U.S. Tourists: Good or Ill-Will Envoys?" *New York Times Magazine*, September 1, 1957; Horace Sutton, "Yankee Come Over; How Europe Feels About It Now," *Saturday Review of Literature*, March 16, 1957.

Year-by-year surveys of European travel may be found in the travel section of the *New York Times* and in the ASTA (America Society of Travel Agents) *Travel News*. For a recent summary, there is William D. Patterson, "The Big Picture 1961–62," reprinted from the April, May, and June issues of *Travel News*, New York, 1962.

See also the chapter on "The Lost Art of Travel," in Daniel Boorstin, *The Image, or What Happened to the American Dream* (New York, 1962).

A NOTE ON STATISTICS

THERE are no fully reliable statistics on Americans going abroad during the long period covered by this book. Beginning with 1820, however, the Department of Commerce has assembled figures of a sort which provide a basis for reasonable estimates. For the period 1820 through 1905 its statistics apply to citizens of the United States arriving from foreign countries by sea, which may be taken as approximating those visiting Europe, and while from 1906 to 1919 they are somewhat further refined, they still include some Americans returning from other than European countries.

Beginning with 1919 statistical tables were inaugurated for United States citizens departing for overseas destinations, with one category applying to Europe and the Mediterranean. These figures are the most accurate available in estimating Americans "going abroad." In recent years various other statistics have been compiled from these tables and passport applications. They provide a bewildering array of data on the number of Americans visiting specific countries, their expenditures in Europe, their purpose in travel, etc.

These figures are the basic source for the estimated totals of Americans going to Europe found throughout the text. They are most easily available in *Survey of International Travel*, Department of Commerce, 1956, and supplementary annual reports. The latter are summarized in the annual issue of the *Survey of Current Business*, also issued by the Department of Commerce.

INDEX

196

Steamships, 43–54, 105, 142, 174–75

Stearns, Harold, 159

Steffens, Lincoln, 122–23, 147

Stein, Gertrude, 160, 162

Steinbeck, John, 163

Stevenson, Robert Louis, 118

Story, William Wetmore, 84, 98–99

Stowe, Harriet Beecher, 49, 53, 55, 72, 75, 83, 90, 98

Stratford-on-Avon, 15, 72, 90

Stuart, Gilbert, 20–21

Students, abroad, 29–30, 34–36, 38, 121–23, 171

Sumner, Charles, 66, 71–72, 77

Sumner, William Graham, 123

Sutton, Horace, *quoted*, 179

Switzerland, 35, 56–57, 62, 83, 128, 172

Taft, President William Howard, 148

Taglioni, 69

Talleyrand, Charles-M. de, 35, 77

Tarbell, Ida, 147

Tarkington, Booth, 119–21

Taylor, Bayard, 64–65, 80, 95, 136

Thackeray, William Makepeace, 72, 80, 93

Thompson, Dorothy, 161

Thompson, Virgil, 162

Thorn, Colonel Herman, 77

Ticknor, George, 29, 37, 71, 119, 122; life in Europe, 34–36

"Titanic," 142

Tocqueville, Alexis de, 5, 66

"Tom shows," 93–94

Tom Thumb, General, 94

Tourists, *see* Travelers

Tours, 141–42. *See also* "Packaged tours"

Transatlantic passage, *see* Sailing packets, Steamships, Air travel

Travel agencies, 176, 181

Travelers, annual number, 1, 26–27, 44, 102, 150, 153–54, 170, 181; attitude toward Europe, 5–7, 11, 24–25, 41–42, 66–67, 85, 119, 146, 155–58; average expenses, 26–27, 64–65, 108–9, 141–42, 169, 177; contemporary descriptions, 5, 65–66, 111–14, 143, 168, 175–76; stranded in 1914, 150–52; total expenditures, 154, 173–74

Trumbull, John, 20

Tudor, William, 28

Twain, Mark, 38, 109–11, 116–18

Tyler, Royall, 2–3

Universities, *see* Students

"Valets de places," 18, 55, 104

Van Buren, President Martin, 77

Vanderbilt, Alfred, 151

Vanderbilt, Consuelo, 131–32

Vanderbilt, Cornelius, 134, 151

Vanderbilt, Mrs. Cornelius, 134

Vaughan, Benjamin, 14

Venice, 33, 38, 81, 112–13, 118, 139

Versailles, 12, 74–75

Vettura, 60

Victoria, Queen, 70, 93, 131

Wadsworth, James, 27

Wagner, Richard, 122

Warner, Charles Dudley, 119

Waterloo, 84–85

Watson, Elkanah, 19, 22, 25, 75, 180; life abroad, 11–16

Date Due

Demco 293-5